PRAISE FOR *THE LEAN SUPPLY CHAIN*

D1636324

"For many years Tesco has been regarded as a world-class retailer. In this insightful book the authors detail the way in which Tesco have utilized best-in-class practices to create a highly effective and efficient supply chain. It's timely. The authors look in detail at how Tesco have been able to build a world-class supply chain. It should appeal to a wide audience – not just those interested in retail." **Martin Christopher, Emeritus Professor of Marketing and Logistics, Cranfield School of Management**

"This book is a superlative in-depth case study of how Lean concepts, together with concepts from marketing, innovation and strategy, have combined to give Tesco an edge in grocery retailing. The supply chain and improvement chapters would be interesting and valuable to anyone in large-scale retailing. In particular the sections contrasting conventional wisdom with Tesco's counter-intuitive answers are illustrative of the effectiveness of Lean thinking outside manufacturing. Following Tesco's history from early days to international giant, and their learnings along the route – what went right and wrong – provides a classic longitudinal study showing the importance of sustained leadership and purpose. **John Bicheno, founder of the MSc Lean post-graduate degree at LERC**

"Most managers readily subscribe to the need to manage one's supply chain. Few firms make the actual leap of moving from traditional purchasing and logistics functions to developing and implementing a supply chain strategy. Barry Evans and Robert Mason provide a powerful narrative that illustrates the effort that this entails, as well as the benefits that can be reaped from taking Lean into a supply chain context." **Professor Matthias Holweg, Saïd Business School, University of Oxford**

"Much has been written about the Tesco supply chain and ingredients for its success – not least of all Lean thinking. What isn't so well recognized is that this journey began, and was very advanced, several years before the perceived introduction of Lean principles in 1995 by a home-grown talented team of people drawn from all supply chain functions. It was this team that created the bedrock for much of what is in place some 20 years later. What the Lean process did help with is creating a framework to extend this methodology to other functions outside the Tesco internal supply chain. This book shows that the principles of Lean do work – but only when they are matched with people who can make the difference. If there is one thing you will learn from this book and the Tesco experience it is that great people make a great company".

Barry Knichel, former Supply Chain Development Director, Tesco

"Any book that analyses supply chain strategies followed by leading retailers is bound to be successful. This book by Evans and Mason examines Tesco's supply chain strategies in a clear and succinct manner. It will be excellent reading for academics, students, retail managers and supply chain practitioners."

Professor Michael Bourlakis, Chair in Logistics and Supply Chain Management and Head of Supply Chain Research Centre, Cranfield University

"The book is a detailed case study on Tesco and is clearly important from a retail perspective. In the past few years there have been similar books on big branded companies such as Nokia, Starbucks, Apple, Google, etc. This book sits within this category. The bulk of the book discusses the history and evolution of Tesco and two chapters discuss the supply chain and the retail environment. The valuable contribution is within the Retail management environment and the future of retail. In summary the book's strengths are details and a good analysis of the evolution of Tesco, a good description of the strategies that Tesco has employed over the years, and an analysis of the supply chain and the models. The book will appeal to a business audience – supply chain mangers, retail managers, etc. It will also appeal to academia as it can be used on a variety of business courses."

Professor Samir Dani, Head of Logistics, Operations and Hospitality Management, University of Huddersfield

"Robert and Barry provide a well-researched and fascinating insight into the Lean philosophy that underpinned the strategies of Tesco in the era of Leahy and Clarke. Their work brings alive how the rigorous pursuit of Lean principles enabled the transition of an ordinary UK supermarket chain into a customer-centric contrarian global winner."

Steve Spall, Former Supply Chain and Distribution Development Director, Tesco UK

"Barry Evans and Robert Mason have written an essential guide not only to Tesco's development of their supply chain but also to the imaginative developments which took place within and beyond the UK's supply chains over the last five decades. As the director responsible for introducing modern supply chain management into Rowntree and Nestlé, I worked closely with Tesco management on greatly improving service both to them and to their customers, our consumers. While the UK food business remains highly competitive, all supply chain participants continue to agree to work together to benefit all through jointly tackling key supply chain issues, and also by sharing point-of-sale data immediately in order to react well to consumer purchases. The main UK manufacturers, retailers and wholesalers cooperatively developed world class Electronic Data Interchange of orders, invoices, product and location master data so that accurate data would be actioned without delay or error. Barry and Robert very well illustrate that supply chain managers cooperate so that supply chains can be truly competitive, to the great benefit of the consumer as well as of the businesses." **Professor Tom McGuffog MBE FCILT FCIPS**

"To study Tesco with such intimacy provides a fascinating insight into the logic that underpins the Tesco model and its many evolutions that have provided a sequence of change as the organization has learned new ways to compete. The authors provide a clarity and insight, over time, of how the forces of business and decisions have shaped the prosperity of this British household name. The two authors have enjoyed a remarkably privileged position and have maintained the study for many years which makes for a fantastic read and the most insightful understanding of this British mega-organization. The book is more than a book about a retailer though – it is a book on business, of challenge and dynamic markets, and how Tesco has made sense of its environment, shaped some of the market by defying tradition and convention, and how it has reacted to the turbulence of a truly global sector. There is much to learn from this account and many lessons that should inspire managers in occupations and sectors that are far beyond retailing. It is a blend of the thought-provoking and also of the practical aspects of running a modern business."
Nick Rich, Professor of Socio-Technical Systems (Operations Management), Swansea University

The Lean Supply Chain
Managing the challenge at Tesco

Barry Evans
Robert Mason

KoganPage

LONDON PHILADELPHIA NEW DELHI

Publisher's note

Every possible effort has been made to ensure that the information contained in this book is accurate at the time of going to press, and the publishers and authors cannot accept responsibility for any errors or omissions, however caused. No responsibility for loss or damage occasioned to any person acting, or refraining from action, as a result of the material in this publication can be accepted by the editor, the publisher or any of the authors.

First published in Great Britain and the United States in 2015 by Kogan Page Limited

2nd Floor, 45 Gee Street	1518 Walnut Street, Suite 1100	4737/23 Ansari Road
London EC1V 3RS	Philadelphia PA 19102	Daryaganj
United Kingdom	USA	New Delhi 110002
www.koganpage.com		India

© Barry Evans and Robert Mason 2015

ISBN   978 0 7494 7207 8
E-ISBN 978 0 7494 7208 5

British Library Cataloguing-in-Publication Data

A CIP record for this book is available from the British Library.

Library of Congress Cataloging-in-Publication Data

Evans, Barry, 1945
   The lean supply chain : managing the challenge at Tesco / Barry Evans, Robert Mason.
      pages cm
Includes bibliographical references and index.
   ISBN 978-0-7494-7207-8 — ISBN 978-0-7494-7208-5 (ebook)   1. Tesco (Firm)
2. Supermarkets – Economic aspects – Great Britain.   3. Business logistics – Great Britain –
Management.   4. Customer relations – Great Britain.   I. Mason, Robert (Business writer)
II. Title.
   HF5469.23.G74T474 2015
   381'.106541—dc23
                                                                                2014041126

Typeset by Amnet Systems
Print production managed by Jellyfish
Printed and bound by CPI Group (UK) Ltd, Croydon, CR0 4YY

CONTENTS

LIST OF TABLES

LIST OF FIGURES

FOREWORD

Daniel T Jones

The appointment of an outsider, Dave Lewis from Unilever, as the new CEO of Tesco marks the end of an era. It was an era of remarkable growth from an also-ran UK retailer to one of the largest global retail giants. This book tells the story of one of the key elements behind that growth that has not yet been told.

The transformation of Tesco's supply chain opened up many new opportunities, such as online and convenience retailing. It also continues to transform the grocery industry as retailers and suppliers across the world follow Tesco's example. The lessons from this supply chain revolution are still very relevant as Tesco and other retailers struggle to respond to changing shopping behaviours, the rise of discount retailers and Amazon and the task of managing global operations.

It all began in 1995 when Graham Booth, then Supply Chain Director of Tesco, called to ask what they might learn from the dramatic rise of Toyota, whose success we described in *The Machine That Changed the World* (Womack, Jones and Roos, 1990). Tesco had already begun centralizing distribution and introducing electronic point-of-sale tracking and were looking for the next steps. We were able to show them the big leap Toyota had made in managing their aftermarket parts distribution across the world, achieving higher availability at the point of use with only a tenth of the time and inventory in the pipeline from the factory to the repair shop. They quickly understood the significance of the switch from forecast-driven batch production and distribution to sales-driven rapid-replenishment supply chains.

This began a partnership between the Lean Enterprise Research Centre at Cardiff Business School, which I founded to spread Toyota's practices to other industries, described in *Lean Thinking* (Womack and Jones, 1996, 2003). At the time we were researching lean supply chain opportunities with a club of organizations from different sectors. Tesco joined this group with several of its suppliers. Together we carried out many experiments to work out the practical details of lean thinking in grocery retailing. As we did so we discovered new opportunities for improving customer service while reducing costs and growing sales volumes with suppliers.

This book gives an insider's perspective on this journey. Robert Mason joined our team at Cardiff with hands-on experience in managing retail stores and now researches and teaches logistics and supply chain and operations management. Barry Evans was part of Graham Booth's supply chain team at Tesco throughout this journey. Together they are uniquely qualified to distil the lessons from the Tesco supply chain story.

Toyota's lean practices challenged many widely held conventional wisdoms. Tesco's eyes were opened when a group of managers walked with us through every step along the supply chain for selected products from ingredients and packaging materials to store shelf, observing all the unnecessary waste, delays, inventories and cost. We then mapped the information flows that triggered all these activities. Reporting to the board, Graham Booth summarized the challenge of 'turning all the red traffic lights along the supply chain to green', in other words streamlining the flow of products towards the customer in line with actual demand rather than optimizing each piece of the system in isolation.

One of the early projects showed how a daily delivery from suppliers could turn warehouses carrying days or weeks of stock into cross-docking facilities, saving Tesco £400 million. Others showed how placing products in shelf-ready packaging in the factory could reduce staff time restocking shelves in stores. Further savings were made as Tesco took responsibility for picking up products from suppliers every day and coordinating logistics into their distribution centres and on to stores. Suppliers learnt how to make high-volume products in smaller batches every day in line with demand. Real-time, 24/7 replenishment ordering by stores from distribution centres and by distribution centres from suppliers eliminated much of the volatility created by systems based on forecasting demand several weeks out.

As the pieces came together and products began to flow through the supply chain Tesco realized they could quickly create a nation-wide home shopping network by picking orders in slack times in key stores rather than building expensive distribution centres. Tesco.com orders revealed gaps in their ability to fulfil orders, reinforcing the importance of achieving near-perfect availability. Because the system was based on small pack quantities rather than full pallets it became possible to replenish convenience stores at almost the same cost as for larger supermarkets. This allowed Tesco to lead the convenience revolution.

After working with other organizations I came to realize how effective Tesco's management system was in focusing activities and leveraging the gains. As Sir Terry Leahy (2012) describes in his book *Management in 10 Words*, Tesco was absolutely customer and employee focused. Managers had operational experience running warehouses and stores and spent a day a week on the front line. They were obsessed with working out the operational details of any new activity before they rolled it out across the network. And Tesco was open to challenging new ideas and willing to experiment.

Toyota's aftermarket supply chain remains the global benchmark to this day. It is no surprise that others that have followed Toyota's example, like Tesco, Zara and Amazon, have become leading players. Many other industries from medical supplies and pharmaceuticals to disaster relief still have much to learn from them. Hopefully they will get the inspiration to do so by reading this book.

THE AUTHORS

The **authors** are both based in Cardiff Business School in the United Kingdom. They have an international academic reputation and have acquired a considerable insight into Tesco and experience of the fast-moving consumer goods industry gleaned from working as managers and researching as academics during their careers.

Barry Evans worked for Tesco for over a decade in their supply chain development team implementing Lean thinking (systems thinking) into their process. Now, as an academic, his research focus is on better understanding systemic effectiveness (doing the right thing). Barry had a business background – Watneys, RHM, Royal Mail – before joining Tesco in 1995. He had roles in Tesco Distribution, then moved to Tesco Supply Chain Development as Lean Process Manager in 1999. He moved to Cardiff Business School's Lean Enterprise Research Centre (LERC) in 2005 as a researcher and retired in 2012. **Dr Robert Mason**, after a 15-year career in retail management, in the main a variety of roles with M&S, joined Cardiff Business School in 2001 as a researcher and obtained his PhD, on *Collaborative Logistics Triads in Supply Chain Management*, in 2009. He is now a Senior Lecturer in Logistics and Supply Chain Management and as well as being the Deputy Leader of the Logistics and Operations Management section is also Programme Director of its flagship MSc in Logistics and Operations Management. Robert has led and participated in a number of research programmes and has published around 100 papers on logistics and supply chain-related topics in many leading journals and conferences. His research interests centre on the optimization of supply chain system processes which includes topics such as the integration of transport and logistics into national and international supply networks, the management of inter-organizational relationships (vertical and horizontal) and the organization of enterprise to deliver customer value. He has a particular focus on the retail logistics sector.

Cardiff Business School has developed a worldwide reputation notably for its research in the logistics, supply chain management and transport fields. It is ranked second globally for publication output in the leading global journals of these fields.[1] In 2014 Cardiff Business School was ranked sixth in the UK for the quality of its research, placing it among the elite of business and management schools.[2]

Our authority to tell this story

Since the mid-1990s, researchers at Cardiff Business School have enjoyed a long-term relationship with Tesco supporting their drive to make its supply chain Lean and drive new levels of performance. In this book two academics from Cardiff Business School explain what they consider differentiates Tesco's ability to continually unlock value from their supply chain operations.

Notes

1 Carter, C R, Easton, P L, Vallenga, D B and Allen, B J (2009) Affiliation of authors in transportation and logistics academic journals: A re-evaluation, Transportation Journal, Winter, 49

2 Association of Business Schools: Ref 2014: Analysis of Business Schools' Performance [online] www.associationofbusinessschools.org/content/ref-2014-analysis-uk-business-schools-performance

PREFACE

It was clear that 2014 was a very challenging year for Tesco. The publication of this book follows a key change in the leadership of Tesco, with Dave Lewis from Unilever replacing Philip Clarke as Chief Executive in September 2014.

The most serious and dominant issue that emerged in the opening weeks of Lewis's regime as CEO was the news of the so-called 'Tesco accounting scandal' at the end of September 2014. It propelled Tesco to the front pages of the press and resulted in headlines such as 'Shaming of Tesco' and 'Britain's top grocer left reeling'. It all revolved around the counting of supplier rebates and incentives before they arrived, resulting in an estimated overstating of profits for the previous six months by around £250 million (this was later revised to £263 million, possibly spread over three years).

Although really outside the scope of this book, which focuses on how Tesco has managed its supply chain logistics and does not really venture into the world of relationships between Tesco's buyers and its supplies, the fact was that another supply chain scandal, like the horsemeat issue, had rocked Tesco to its core. The supply chain, which we claim was a core element of Tesco's competitive advantage, had again been found to be the source of a very serious problem.

An internal inquiry was launched immediately by Lewis, carried out by Deloitte and a blue-chip legal firm, Freshfields. A number of senior executives were suspended from the business to allow a full investigation to be pursued. At the end of October 2014, the Deloitte/Freshfields report was passed to the City regulator, the Financial Conduct Authority, which launched a further inquiry. The matter is also now subject to investigation from the Serious Fraud Office. Tesco conducted retraining of all 900 employees who participated in direct negotiation with suppliers. In December, the accounting watchdog, the Financial Reporting Council, formally launched its own investigation.

Some of the personnel who had been suspended subsequently left the business, although notably Matt Simister, Head of Group Food Sourcing, was reinstated in early December 2014. Jason Tarry, chief executive of Tesco's clothing line Florence and Fred, stepped in as interim Commercial Director.

Tesco's half-year results, released at the end of October, were £112 million, 92 per cent down on the year. The company also stated that it could not give an estimate for the full 2014/15 financial year, as there were too many uncertainties surrounding its future direction. Coinciding with the results was the news that Tesco's Chairman, Sir Richard Broadbent, was stepping down. In December, a trading update revealed that it did not expect full-year (to February 2015) profits to be above £1.4 billion.

Early in December too, Lewis made his first clear presentation of longer-term strategic decisions taken as CEO, with the announcement of new senior appointments. Jason Tarry was confirmed as the permanent Head of Commercial, Robin Terrell (Overseas Director) became Marketing Director, in a role intriguingly called 'Head of Customer', and Benny Higgins (Head of Tesco Bank) became Head of Strategy. Jill Easterbrook was put in charge of transforming the business, overseeing the wide-ranging review that was under way.

The initial areas of focus were confirmed too: to invest in service, with an extra 6,000 new store personnel, to improve product availability and to target better prices. In short, Tesco was clear that it wanted to begin to enhance the customer offer substantively. The Black Friday trading weekend at the end of November brought news of customers chasing bargains, and this was followed throughout December with a slightly improved trading performance.

Indeed, it is worth pausing and reflecting on the sales figures for Christmas 2014, using the Kantar WorldPanel UK data (http:// www.kantarworldpanel.com/en/Press-Releases/Christmas-sales -a-welcome-boost-for-retailers). Tesco sales for the 12 weeks to 4 January 2015 were –1.2 per cent, better than both Asda (–1.6 per cent) and Morrisons (–1.6 per cent) and only slightly behind Sainsbury's (–0.7 per cent). Given that the quarter 2 figure for UK Tesco sales had been much worse at –5.4 per cent, this represented a marked, if small, improvement. Indeed, the difference of only 0.9 per cent in sales movement against 2013 for all of the top four grocery retailers indicated how competitive the grocery marketplace was in the UK at the end of 2014, with Tesco still dominating in market share terms of 29.1 per cent for the period. The six weeks to 3 January 2015 showed even more improvement for Tesco at only –0.3 per cent, with growing sales at convenience Express stores (+4.9 per cent) and in online sales (grocery home shopping +12.9 per cent, general merchandise online +22.9 per cent and clothing online +52.4 per cent).

The market polarization still remained an issue, with discounters Aldi (+22.6 per cent) and Lidl (+15.1 per cent) and high-end Waitrose (+6.6 per cent) all continuing to do well. But, with the overall grocery market, at +0.6 per cent, showing the best growth performance since May 2014, there were some very early encouraging signs for the market as a whole as well as Tesco in particular.

The release of the Christmas trading results in early January 2015 also coincided with Lewis restating that his focus was on channelling the proceeds from a new level of financial discipline and cost control to reinvest in the core customer proposition. In more detail, three identified immediate priorities for Tesco were set out:

- regaining competitiveness in the core UK business;
- protecting and strengthening the balance sheet; and
- rebuilding trust and transparency.

Measures included new price initiatives and a clear stated aim to begin to re-establish trust in the pricing policy. This was coupled with numerous cost saving announcements, such as the closure of 43 unprofitable UK stores, a major revision of store building, the disposal of Tesco Broadband and Blinkbox to TalkTalk, the appointment of advisers to explore options for the Dunnhumby business, the initiation of consultation to close the company defined benefit pension scheme, the decision not to pay a final dividend for 2014/15 and the decision to consolidate the Tesco head office in Welwyn Garden City, with Cheshunt planned to close in 2016.

Matt Davies (ex-Chief Executive at Halfords Group plc) was confirmed as the new CEO of the UK and Ireland business from 1 June 2015.

In a further response to the concerns over relations with suppliers, to support the objective of rebuilding trust and transparency, a stated aim to regenerate relations with suppliers with new commercial income guidelines and associated year-end cash management was proposed. This was backed up with news of the launch of the Tesco Supplier Network in the middle of January (see launch video: http://www.myretailmedia.com/tube/2644).

Finally, a small development at the beginning of 2015 summed up Tesco's keenness to be seen to be more responsible and, by encouraging healthier lifestyles, to be on the side of the customer. This was the announcement of sweet-free checkouts. For more details on this announcement please see: http://www.tescoplc.com/index.asp?pageid=17&newsid=1120.

On reflection, it is early days after Lewis's appointment but some small green shoots of a turnaround in fortunes for Tesco seem to be appearing following the Christmas trading statement. These results showed that focusing on really enhancing the customer offer meant there was a continued role for the Tesco recipe of business. A return to the core values of price, service and availability certainly was instrumental in this, and these values will continue to be a strong theme throughout the Lewis tenure as CEO as he fights to lead Tesco in sustaining this improved commercial momentum.

The effective and efficient management and operation of the supply chain are key to achieving progress in all three of the objective areas of price, service and availability. This book presents a thorough appraisal of how Tesco normally attempts to do this. No doubt these methods will be relied on again and again and will be built on further in the months and years to come as Tesco strives to continue to develop its world-class reputation for supply chain logistics prowess.

Around this though are the issues of trust and transparency with regard to the way the company operates and the manner in which the supply chain is run, and these are now well recognized by Tesco as key ingredients in the mix. The supply chain may be the best organized in the world, but if trust and transparency are not there the commercial results will not materialize. With Lewis providing a new face for Tesco, allowing the company to distance itself from the horsemeat scandal, and being seen as the person who is trying to rectify the accounting scandal, perhaps there is some increased hope that Tesco may manage the challenge and use loyalty, simplicity and lean to drive growth once again.

This book is focused on how Tesco organizes and manages its supply chain – essentially the management of logistics processes (physical and information flows) that enables Tesco to serve its customers with the vast range of products and services that they value. Supply chains are at the heart of any business. They are what connect supplied products and services to end users. Despite their multifaceted structure (and sometimes inherent complexity), if they are well designed and managed they can be a major source of differentiation and competitive advantage. However, today, as supply chains are intensively competing with supply chains, they must remain up to date and relevant to ever-changing customer needs. Customers also expect the supply chains that serve them to be managed with integrity if they are to trust the supply chains' output, ie the products and services that they consume.

Grocery supermarkets essentially make nothing and thus can't be distracted through trying to compete through alternative means – by adopting a production orientation, for example. For the most part they retail essentially undifferentiated commoditized products, and thus a key focus of their competitive strategy is their ability to really sense what their customers value and to provide this value in a superior way in the eyes of their customers, predominantly through their supply chain prowess.

Despite its recent challenges, Tesco, particularly over the last 20 years or so, has led the industry, rewriting how grocery supply chains can be conceived and run to provide for all aspects of value from the customer perspective. From being an 'also-ran', as the number two player in the United Kingdom in the early 1990s, Tesco stood in 2014 at number two in terms of the global batting order of retailers. The cornerstone of this growth, we argue, has been Tesco's understanding of what customers value and providing this for them through the pursuit of mastering its supply chains. This book uncovers how this has been achieved and cites many examples of how customers' lives have been improved by the Tesco supply chain approach.

What customers really want from any product or service is what they consider to be best value – those organizations that can consistently provide superior value and gain a reputation for doing so will gain a competitive advantage and win out over their competitors. This is the traditional idea that underpins the basic marketing concept. As Theodore Levitt (1960) stated, 'Management must think of itself not as producing products, but as providing customer-creating value satisfactions. It must push this idea (and everything it means and requires) into every nook and cranny of the organization. It has to do this continuously and with the kind of flair that excites and stimulates the people in it.' Although Levitt meant his observation to be generically applicable to all organizations, leading grocery supermarkets provide a fantastic lens through which this idea can be translated into action – and consequently observed and reported upon.

In the United Kingdom, the grocery supermarket sector is highly competitive, and these competitive forces have provided a melting pot for a potentially world-beating retailer to be cast. Tesco has helped to pioneer what it takes to compete through its supply chain to continuously provide customers with superior value. And it has taken the lessons learnt in striving continuously to improve its supply chain right across its business, as processes in any organization are pervasive. Tesco thus strives to apply best-practice processes for all areas of its business, and can claim that its success, in this respect, has become a real source of competitive advantage.

However, commerce is a fast-changing beast, and it is clear that the grocery sector is as dynamic as any segment of industry in needing to adapt and change. For Tesco, this has significant implications for its supply chains and the way they are managed – the recipe that gave the best results in the past may not necessarily be the one that succeeds in the future. While this book centres on how Tesco has gained a world-class reputation for supply chain excellence, it also reflects on the challenges that Tesco now faces in ensuring that its supply chains are fit for purpose for the future as well. These challenges include the integrity issues raised by the horsemeat and accounting scandals and the consequent impact on consumer trust, the polarization in the marketplace caused by the rise of the discounters and top-end grocery retailers, the growth of convenience and online shopping, and other supply chain-connected issues. It is reasonable to assume that customers' expectations from the chains that supply them will continue to evolve for all grocery retailers. This book provides a fascinating insight into how Tesco is managing the supply chain challenge past and present.

Inevitably, there are many parts to the Tesco jigsaw that have contributed to Tesco's performance over the last 20 years or so. Here we argue that the engine room that powers Tesco – the management of its business processes, most notably its supply chain processes – is worthy of focus. The book provides insight into how Tesco has developed its approach to the 'supply chain challenge' from the strategic perspective to countless operational innovations that have been adopted.

There are lessons here for leaders of organizations large and small. Tesco strives to prove itself master of the processes involved in the supply chain operation. If you want to know more about how it strives to do this, please read on.

An introduction

Tesco has become a world-famous retailer and in 2014 was recognized as the globe's second-biggest retailer (Deloitte, 2014). Much has been written in newspapers, journals and books about the 'what' and the 'why' of Tesco. However, very few understand or even appreciate *how* all that Tesco does happens. This book concentrates on this hidden world of *how* Tesco does it, and in so doing sheds light on many salutary lessons for business today.

So what is this book about? Inevitably, there are many parts to the Tesco jigsaw that have contributed to its success. Here we address a core ingredient, for the first time pulling together a book that focuses on the engine room that has powered Tesco's growth performance for much of the last 20 or so years – its supply chain, essentially the management of logistics processes (physical and information flows) that enables Tesco to serve its customers with the vast range of products and services that they value. The supply chain for any retailer of Tesco's size – it is the UK's biggest retailer – is a huge operation, and Tesco has striven to use its prowess in this area to differentiate itself from the competition it faces. How has it done this? What are the challenges it has faced down? What ongoing supply chain issues is it trying to deal with today? What are the lessons for others? Clearly, Tesco does not get everything right in its supply chain, and many of the supply chain-based issues it is currently facing are reflected upon in this book. But Tesco has used its supply chain prowess to underpin its business model and constantly tries to prove itself master of the supply chain operation.

The book is divided into eight chapters, each of which explains a segment of the Tesco DNA in terms of how it developed a world-class supply chain operation and explores how Tesco continues to manage the supply chain challenges today. From an appreciation of the need to create a strong underlying foundation for supply chain excellence in an organization's strategy and corporate framework to detailed examples of initiatives across the supply chain, this book comprehensively paints a picture of the Tesco way. Beyond this, it explores how Tesco's approach to its supply chains has led it to becoming a smarter organization, striving to sense, think and act faster than its competitors in the cut-throat world of retail.

Anyone connected to running a business and striving to supply customers successfully with what they want day after day, month after month, year after year needs to read this story. Even the leaders of Tesco today continue to reflect on what has been achieved and what the essence of Tesco's formidable performance has been, as they are increasingly challenged to stay on top of their game.

Competing through the supply chain may seem simple to explain, but it is very hard to achieve. Moreover, it is a highly dynamic activity, as customers' expectations evolve and new supply innovations are developed, both driven in part by rapid and significant advances in technology. In addition, in recent years it appears that there is an increasingly wider demand placed on organizations that look to compete through their supply chains. They need to take fuller responsibility for what goes on in their supply chains so they are more transparent and run to the highest ethical standards. In short, the masters of chains of supply need to be trusted by their consumers and by society as a whole in this respect. For retailers that are managing wider and wider catalogues of products and are dealing with more and more complex chains of supply, while at the same time trying to optimize the value that can be gleaned from them, this is posing a new and significant set of challenges.

This chapter introduces the book and is structured around three key notions that Tesco relentlessly wrestles with to keep the business on track:

- a *clarity* of business core purpose;
- the *alignment* of the business around this core purpose; and
- the *discipline* needed to keep the business relentlessly on course.

Why the supply chain?

The successful management of the supply chain process can be the core of how to compete in business today. Invariably, however, it is not the idea that is most talked about or discussed. It is an unsung aspect of business that needs to be more openly promoted and assessed. What does competing through the supply chain mean, and why is it becoming such an important element of modern business practice?

Put very simply, any supply chain provides consumers with products and services. The activities that take place along the supply chain transform raw materials into end products through manufacturing and logistics processes so that the consumer can receive and utilize them. Thus supply chain management is a set of techniques that allows for improvements in these transformation processes so that extra value can be derived for the benefit of stakeholders. But, if the aim is to optimize the value that is supplied to end consumers, perhaps a wider understanding of the supply chain than this needs to be adopted.

Another term sometimes used to describe the supply chain is the 'value chain', first coined by Michael Porter (1985), the management strategist. 'Primary activities' included in his understanding of the 'value chain' were inbound logistics, operations, outbound logistics, marketing and sales, and services, all supported by a number of 'support activities'. Thus, a wider understanding of what could be included in the chain of supply at the downstream end, to include all aspects of marketing and service for example, as part of what customers may value, was considered by Porter as part of the mix in managing the chain of supply.

This is the view taken in this book, and it is wider than the conventional definitions of the supply chain.

Traditionally, supply chains were driven by manufacturers in many sectors and were about managing the transformation and movement of suppliers' products to sell to the marketplace. In the last 20 years or so all this has changed. Now supply chains are driven more by demand than supply in many sectors of commerce.

The grocery sector is a classic manifestation of this. Consequently, the grocery retailers have seized the opportunities to organize demand and be the customer's representative for their chains of supply. Today, the maxim is less about manufacturer competing with manufacturer. It is about supply chain competing with supply chain, with retailers orchestrating the tunes from the chains of supply that serve them.

Tesco has always been built around the basic business model of supply–buy–distribute–sell. As a result, although it is pre-eminently known as a retailer, it is also a major logistics and supply chain operator. In a spectrum of retailing it is arguably at the least creative or theatrical end, with its core business being the retailing of life's essentials – what are known as fast-moving consumer goods. In this business Tesco is a high-volume player. Thus, how it manages and organizes its logistics and its full supply chain operations has considerable significance. A small improvement in the way one supply chain process is managed, if multiplied up across its full business, can have a colossal magnified significance. So Tesco really focuses on the supply chain as a key plank of its business, perhaps more so than many businesses have historically done.

Cardiff Business School began working with Tesco on its supply chain operation back in the mid-1990s. Following on from the publication of their ground-breaking benchmarking study *The Machine That Changed the World* (Womack, Jones and Roos, 1990), two of its authors, Jim Womack and Dan Jones, had begun looking for other sectors, beyond automotive, where their ideas of what became termed 'Lean thinking' could be experimented with. The British author Dan Jones had joined Cardiff Business School, founding the Lean Enterprise Research Centre. He was eager to find out more about how organizations keen to pursue the 'Lean thinking' strategy should actually go about this objective. After all, this was the question that was continually being asked of him after over 400,000 copies of *The Machine That Changed the World* were sold in 11 languages in the first six years after its publication in 1990. What was needed was a guide of how to do Lean. To achieve this objective, many organizations from around the world that were taking the 'Lean leap' in a range of sectors were selected, with food production and distribution being a key target.

Tesco, through its Supply Chain Director at the time, Graham Booth, with the support of Barry Knichel and Peter Worsey, had linked with up with Dan Jones at Cardiff Business School and was keen to experiment with bringing in Lean thinking to Tesco. Tesco was already well known as an efficient retailer: according to Womack and Jones (1996) in their follow-up book, *Lean Thinking*, 'it appears its current inventories are only half the UK average, a quarter of the European average and an eighth the North American average'. A value stream – 'the specific activities required to design, order and provide a specific product, from concept to launch, order to delivery and raw material to the hands of the customer' (Womack and Jones, 1996) – was chosen for a can of cola and mapped. What it showed was that it took 319 days to bring the cola from bauxite mine to Tesco store. It exposed that there was a large amount of waste, in Japanese known as *muda*, specifically in terms of excessive inventories all along the supply chain. What was needed was a system-wide approach to tackling this to improve the value of the product still further for the retailer, which it could, in turn, pass on to the end consumer. 'Tesco has recently realised that to move even further in reducing inventories, stock outs, and costs on a total system basis (where more than 85 percent of the costs of a typical product like cola are outside Tesco's corporate control), it will need to improve responsiveness and ordering accuracy all the way up its value stream' (Womack and Jones, 1996).

Thus, there was an alignment between Tesco's quest to learn more about how to develop further efficiencies and wider improvements from its supply chains and Cardiff Business School researchers' ambitions to observe how the Lean paradigm could be successfully adopted by organizations outside the automotive sector and to study what impact it could have when applied beyond the factory setting to the whole supply chain system.

A basic model (Figure 1.1) is proposed to convey this approach to the way the supply chain could be managed. It conceives that the whole supply chain system has a declared purpose, with inputs and outputs. A feedback loop is integrated into the system so that it becomes intelligent and is capable of learning. The model will be referred to as the book progresses.

Finally, the supply chain is just one process that exists within the company, or between the company and others. There are thousands of other processes too, from recruitment of new staff, to welcoming

FIGURE 1.1 A basic model of a supply chain system used to support the research undertaken with Tesco by Cardiff Business School

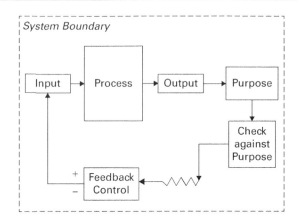

visitors, to putting a new page or video on the corporate website: processes are pervasive; they are everywhere!

So, once a generic approach to managing processes is developed for Tesco, the opportunities to repeat good practice can be applied time and time again across the whole business and in every new arena it expands into as well. This way of thinking and operating is the practice that Tesco has developed for many years. Thus, the book will attempt to lift the lid in terms of some of the content of the 'Tesco Box' (Tesco, 2007: 9), which Tesco has developed since 2001, to identify best-practice processes for all areas of the business, and apply this time and time again, after adaptation to local markets and situations.

The supply chain should, therefore, be seen as a core process, yes, but it is hoped that many of the learning points gained from looking at the Tesco supply chain in this book can be applied in any organization and in any process, in the same way that Tesco is doing.

Tesco's core purpose

For many commercial organizations their primary goal is to maximize shareholder value or, alternatively, another financially driven objective such as to make superior returns on investments. Tesco's stated goal during much of the last 20 years, what it calls its 'core purpose', is 'to create value for customers to earn their lifetime loyalty' – quite different! It is this core purpose that has acted as a strong motivating force, driving Tesco to strive to become better and better at managing the chains of supply that provide the products it retails for customers. At the outset, it is well worth spending some time briefly assessing and analysing this statement of purpose, as many of the emerging ideas from this reflection will emerge as themes throughout the book.

First, this objective is rooted in identifying a primary focus on one and only one stakeholder – the customer. All organizations clearly have many stakeholders: owners and investors, such as partners or shareholders and financial institutions, employees and their families, suppliers and strategic alliance partners, the society at large (the general public), professional associations, government and voluntary non-governmental organizations to name but a few, as well as, of course, the customer. Keeping all stakeholders happy would be an ideal. However, there are invariably trade-offs involved, which can lead to fuzziness developing around any organization's core purpose if it is not careful.

For Tesco, particularly during the whole of what we can term 'the Leahy years', from 1997 to 2011, when Terry Leahy was the CEO, the core purpose remained unchanged. It was simple and was clearly understood. It saw the key stakeholder as the end customer – the argument ensuing that, if the customer was happy, then the value thereby provided in supporting Tesco with its business would be able to be passed on to all other stakeholders.

This mentality had the advantage of simplicity at its heart. It meant that a clear aim was established that all employees and business partners could rally around. Its appropriateness as a core purpose will be debated later in the book, as in Leahy's successor Philip Clarke's reign as CEO it was changed, but it allowed Tesco's supply chain strategy, which was and is all about creating extra value for customers, to be fully integrated with the overall business core purpose, a key plank in the Tesco jigsaw. And in the early months of Tesco's new CEO Dave Lewis's regime in late 2014 perhaps we saw a return to this way of thinking, with the customer returning to the heart of the business once again.

It is also worth noting here that Tesco's stated core purpose did not contain any specific definition of what 'value' actually means. Often, it is assumed that value is synonymous with low price. Indeed, this is invariably an important aspect of what can be termed the 'value equation', but is not by any means the whole picture. What Tesco means by 'value' is a much richer interpretation of the term than this, and it envisages that supply chain improvements will not be solely about driving through efficiencies but also about providing other sources of value, as will be developed and explored through this book as a whole.

Finally, the Tesco core purpose deliberately stated that the aim was to 'earn customers' lifetime loyalty'. For customers to be committed on an enduring basis to any supplier is a challenge. To earn their loyalty in grocery retailing, where on the surface you have very little ability to differentiate your business from another in retailing commodity products, requires an altogether different level of capability. The ability to extract value from its supply chain to be passed on to customers was, and is, seen by Tesco as a key to generating the faithfulness of its customers to keep them returning to Tesco time after time, year after year.

Alignment behind purpose

As noted above, the adoption of creating value for the customer as the core purpose for Tesco allowed for the integration of the business around a single, clear and unifying goal.

Many businesses are organized around functions such as buying, merchandising, finance, production, marketing, distribution and so on. For each discipline, managers are appointed and functional goals set and incentivized by the organization, usually supported by a suite of key performance indicators. The thinking behind this strategy is that if each function performs well then the sum of the parts will mean that the performance of the organization will be optimized. This is a fallacy.

In reality customers do not care whether the production department has met its targets; they are oblivious to whether marketing can justify its brand advertising budget, and do not really take any notice of how much inventory is used to supply the goods they buy. What they mind about is the output of the supply process that cuts through all these functional departments. They will have their own value demands, which may vary over time too, but invariably these demands will revolve around price, convenience and quality.

So, by arranging all departments around a single unifying goal of serving the customer with better and better value to achieve the customer's lifetime loyalty, a business such as Tesco can align all its disparate functions around process excellence and focus on a simple, clear objective – to be consistently effective in the eyes of the customer, another important theme that will be returned to again and again throughout this book.

Corporate discipline

Supply chain effectiveness does not come about overnight. As will be explained throughout the book, every aspect of a business contributes to a successful supply chain. However, just aligning disparate functions around a core purpose is insufficient. An aspect that separates Tesco's approach to developing supply chain improvement after supply chain improvement from the approach of some of its competitors has been its capability to sustain this strategy over many years. In *Lean Thinking*, the fifth of the five principles identified by Womack and Jones (1996) when describing what 'Lean' meant was the pursuit of perfection. The idea was that once one layer was dealt with a new layer would always be presented to be overcome. What Tesco became good at was holding the last-won gain before moving rapidly as an organization to the next challenge.

A key underpinning aspect of this capability was the mantra developed under Sir Terry Leahy, when he was Chief Executive (1997– 2011), to keep things simple. His view was that, although retailers were handling vast ranges of products, dealing with millions and millions of customers, each one different with unique demands, and having to be dynamic, which an organization needs to be in coping with a constantly changing operating environment, the systems that Tesco deploys to deal with all this do not have to be over-complicated. If it was becoming hard to turn decisions into action then the volume and scale of projects needed to be scaled back to ensure it all became manageable once more, he would argue.

Later in the book, a fuller discussion on the notion of 'keeping things simple' will be developed, starting with its place in the Tesco mission statement of 'Better, simpler, cheaper' introduced in the next section of this chapter. Here, however, the idea of simplicity as a discipline tool to help Tesco's leaders keep the business on track with a consistent focus on its core purpose is argued. It provided the backbone to keep the business and supply chain strategies aligned. Leahy did not let this very clear idea of core purpose, which Tesco followed year after year, ever get muddied or confused.

Better, simpler, cheaper

The question that follows the statement of core purpose, 'to create value for customers to achieve their lifetime loyalty', is how should this be achieved? To provide direction and guidance internally to decision making, the marketing slogan 'Better, simpler, cheaper', which became synonymous with the way Tesco operates, was frequently utilized:

- better for the customer;
- simpler for the staff;
- cheaper for Tesco.

The whole slogan is underpinned by three leading academic pieces of work, each one contributing to all the parameters of the slogan:

- *The Loyalty Effect* by Frederick F Reichheld (1996);
- *Simplicity* by Edward de Bono (1998);
- *Lean Thinking* by James Womack and Daniel Jones (1996, 2003).

These pieces of academic thinking and research were synergistically intertwined with each other; for instance, keeping things simple is an important idea in Lean as well, while Lean thinking starts with the idea of identifying what is valued by the customer, and orientating the organization around achieving this would presumably be aimed at keeping the customer loyal. They also had another factor in common: each in essence was a whole business philosophy, not a bolt-on set of tools and techniques. For instance:

- Lean required standards in operations and total quality management (TQM) to be established, so that basic processes could be relied upon, before inventories could be challenged.
- Loyalty can be viewed as a business strategy that needs to be built into the entire organization and the way it thinks and behaves.
- Simplicity is a way of thinking that permeates to the heart of the culture of an organization and influences every aspect of what an organization does and what it is about (easy to state, but it takes hard, dedicated effort to achieve!).

The 'Better, simpler, cheaper' sentiment contained in this mission statement, supported by the ideas of developing customer loyalty and challenging complexity in all its forms to make things simpler and to build a Lean enterprise, became the litmus test in the Leahy era, against which all new initiatives and ideas were tested. Only if an idea hit all three requirements – better for the customer, simpler for staff and cheaper for Tesco – was it even put forward for consideration to be taken forward.

Much more will be developed around the content and implications of this mission and these principles, and the three underpinning academic works, throughout the book. However, in the fast-moving world of grocery retailing, the strength of these three principles has continued resonance for Tesco in the way it organizes itself and its supply chain operations and, we believe, is highly relevant to many other organizations as well. In recent years, Tesco may have evolved this mission and these principles slightly in an attempt to keep them fresh and up to date, as we will explore in Chapter 3. Yet, at Tesco's heart, there remains a strong ethos to serve the customer as employees would wish to be served themselves.

This sentiment is embodied through Tesco's key advertising slogan, 'Every little helps'. It was originally an internal marketing campaign and suggested that every extra little thing each employee was able to contribute would aid progress on the 'Better, simpler, cheaper' mission. It soon became the key strapline for external marketing too and is still used to help highlight, from the customer's perspective, that Tesco is trying all it can to be on the side of its customers.

Debunking conventional business thinking myths

Finally in this opening chapter, which has aimed to whet the reader's appetite for the kind of ideas and issues that will be covered in the book, one key theme of the text is introduced. It is envisaged that the text, in its applicability and relevance, will go well beyond being a biographical study of Tesco and how it manages its supply chain. As authors, we feel there are some incredibly important generic lessons that can be drawn from this analysis as well. Often counter-intuitive, although logical and inherently simple, as one would expect from an organization that prizes simplicity, the core purpose and mission statement give rise to a number of ideas, each of which will be picked up and discussed throughout the book, with a whole chapter devoted to them in Chapter 6.

Here they are merely listed, but they will be returned to in due course:

1 Get better and better at what you do.

No. Get better and better at providing for customers.

2 Efficiency wins.

No. Effectiveness wins.

3 Prove the business case before backing an initiative.

No. If It feels right for the customer it can make business sense too.

4 How to be good at business is difficult to understand but easy to do.

No. It is easy to explain but hard to do.

5 To stand out from the crowd in business you should be the cheapest or the most innovative.

No. You can compete through both innovation and price.

6 Think from production forwards.

No. Act from the customer backwards.

7 Business leadership is the art of coping with complexity.

No. Business leadership is the art of simplifying the complex.

Hopefully, these overarching themes will provoke debate.

Book structure

This introductory chapter has sown some of the seeds of what this book is all about: how Tesco has used customer loyalty, simplicity of operations and Lean thinking to drive growth through the way it organizes itself and specifically how it has applied itself to translating these principles to the way it manages its supply chain. Following this opening, each chapter will examine an aspect of the Tesco approach in more detail, with Chapter 7 considering the current challenges that Tesco is facing. The content of each chapter is as follows:

- Chapter 2 sets out the key facts about Tesco: where it stood in 2014, in terms of where it operates, which sectors it trades in, and its volumes of business. The chapter also reflects on the company's origins, setting out the discussion in four eras. A particular emphasis is given to the history of the transformation of Tesco over the last two decades or so, where it has emerged as such a dominant player in the UK market and become a truly leading global retailer.

- Chapter 3 focuses on how Tesco adopted its principles based on 'loyalty', 'Lean thinking' and 'simplicity'. Its implementation of these principles through rigorous adherence to deployment of an explicit core purpose, values, principles, strategy and management of delivery by means of its Steering Wheel (balanced scorecard) is discussed and related to how Tesco manages its supply chain.

- Chapter 4 looks at the way Tesco has refined its understanding of core purpose. This is typified by the way Tesco has given primacy to 'effectiveness first', where 'efficiency follows'. Thus the company is driven by 'sensing the customer and meeting the customer's needs'. The huge power Tesco has gained in refining data from its Clubcard loyalty card, store-based customer panels and other sources into 'gold dust' information to drive strategy formulation and prioritize and guide its implementation is debated.

- Chapter 5 is arguably the core chapter of the book, and investigates how Tesco has developed highly capable supply chains to serve its needs, to the extent that its chains of supply are now seen as amongst the best in the world.

- Chapter 6 debates Tesco's ability to think and act counter-intuitively at times to achieve continuous improvement in its systems, processes and operations. It looks at how, despite its size, Tesco has empowered all staff to take responsibility for improvement and delivery. The roles of Tesco's most recent chiefs, Ian MacLaurin (who was knighted in 1989, and created a life peer in 1996, taking the title Baron MacLaurin of Knebworth), Terry Leahy (who was knighted in 2002) and Philip Clarke, in leading this transformation by leveraging Tesco's basic business model (supply–buy–distribute–sell) will also be considered. (Tesco under its new CEO, Dave Lewis, will be considered in the Epilogue.)

- Chapter 7 brings the book up to date and considers the current challenges and themes for development that are being pursued by Tesco. The retail sector is a highly dynamic and very competitive element of modern economies. The issues that currently confront Tesco, especially in how it manages its supply chains better than its competitors in its efforts to continuously grow its business, are reviewed.

- Chapter 8 presents the conclusions that are reached, and the main lessons from the book are drawn out for the reader.

Key chapter summary points

1 Tesco has identified that a core ingredient of its performance over the last 20 years has been to do with the way it manages its supply chain.

2 Competing through the supply chain may be easy to explain, but it is very hard to achieve.

3 Grocery retailing provides a superb example to investigate how supply chain management practice can be developed in an organizational setting, as grocery retailers make nothing and often see their supply chain as an important area from which to develop a competitive advantage.

4 The supply chain can be envisaged as a simple system. The supply process takes inputs and provides outputs to try to meet a declared purpose. A feedback loop checks progress against purpose.

5 Tesco has a very clear view of what its core purpose is and consistently aims to align itself behind this purpose, with the corporate discipline to keep things on track.

6 This book will focus on how Tesco achieves this. Through this exploration we will present how many conventional thoughts on business can be challenged, with lessons for leaders of all types of business who aspire to compete through their supply chain.

Tesco past and present

Introduction

The objective of this chapter is to provide a broad summary narrative of how Tesco has developed during its 95-year history. In 2014, Tesco was recognized as the second-biggest retailer in the world (Deloitte, 2014). What have been the key landmark steps in this journey?

There are two reasons for providing a short history of Tesco at this stage of the book. First, the chapter acts as a chronological map of Tesco's evolution. Events referred to later in the book can, therefore, be placed in the correct contextual time period. Second, through the outlining of Tesco's background and evolution, an understanding of how the company's operating philosophy has been formed can begin to be derived. Tesco has learnt to believe through its experiences that one of the key ways to compete is to work to optimize all processes under its control, including the processes of the supply chain. The view that the company is there to work on behalf of its customers, and to best serve the communities in which its customers live, is embedded in Tesco's culture and derives from its history, roots and experiences.

In short, this chapter aims to explain what Tesco has achieved; later chapters will set out how it has managed this from the perspective of its approach to the management of its supply chains.

The chapter covering Tesco's past is divided into four eras:

- 1 – The early years
- 2 – Leading the development of self-service and supermarket shopping

- 3 – Continuous and multi-directional expansion
- 4 – More challenging times – refocusing the business

In each era, the main developments are outlined. A particular emphasis is placed upon the last 20 years or so (eras 3 and 4), during which time the main decisions have been taken that have helped shape much of the company we observe today.

To conclude the chapter, a summary confirms what Tesco has now become, Tesco's present, where a breakdown of the status of the company as at early 2015 is provided.

Tesco's past: 1 – the early years

Tesco is approaching its centenary. It was founded in 1919, a year after the end of the First World War, by a former member of the Royal Flying Corps, Jack Cohen. He was 21 and used his serviceman's gratuity of £30 to begin selling groceries from an east London stall. From this humble beginning, with turnover on the first day's trading just £4, he expanded the business in the ensuing years across London into a number of markets.

He also began selling wholesale to market traders. T E Stockwell was a partner in the firm of tea suppliers that produced the first own-label product sold by Jack Cohen, a pack of tea. Hence the name Tesco, derived from his and his partner's names: **T E S**[tockwell] and **Co**[hen]. In 1929 the name Tesco first appeared on a shop front, in Edgware in Middlesex.

Tesco Stores became a private limited company in 1932. Two years later Jack Cohen bought a plot of land at Angel Road in Edmonton, north London, to build a new headquarters and warehouse. It was the first modern food warehouse in the country and introduced new ideas for central stock control. At the time it opened, the warehouse supported fewer than 50 branches; by 1939 that number had doubled.

When the Second World War started, Jack Cohen introduced a Tesco rationing scheme, interestingly before the government's, to ensure that everyone had a fair share of the restricted goods available. To establish a ready source of fresh vegetables, he bought three acres of glasshouses and nine acres of grassland at Cheshunt, Hertfordshire, on which to grow cucumbers, tomatoes and fruit trees. Part of today's head office site is now on this land.

After the war, the company expanded rapidly. An important milestone over the following years included the 1947 floating of the company, known at the time as Tesco Stores (Holdings), on the stock exchange in London, at a share price of 25 pence.

Tesco's past: 2 – leading the development of self-service and supermarket shopping

After observing the new self-service concept of retailing in North America, Tesco launched its initial version of these types of stores in St Albans. Customer reaction, at first, was mixed, but the idea grew, leading to the first Tesco supermarket opening in 1958 in Maldon, Essex. Rival chains were bought up, such as 70 Williamson's stores and 200 Harrow stores in the 1950s and the Charles Phillips stores and Victor Value chain in the 1960s. Through the late 1950s and the 1960s Tesco's product range was expanded considerably. The stores grew in size to cope with the increasing range: for instance, the Leicester store was recognized as the largest store in Europe according to the 1961 *Guinness Book of Records*. A national network of supermarkets was beginning to be established.

In 1964, after lobbying by Tesco, Sainsbury's and other supermarkets, resale price maintenance (RPM) was abolished, through the new Resale Prices Act (RPA). This gave retailers freedom to set prices (except by 1979 for books and pharmaceutical goods). Before then, suppliers set the price of goods, which prevented the larger retailers, which could buy in bulk and thus had greater buying power, from undercutting the prices of smaller shops.

By 1968, Tesco was firmly established in the 'supermarket' business, opening its first superstore in Crawley, West Sussex in that year. Throughout the 1970s and 1980s the group expanded its portfolio of these superstores, especially in out-of-town sites, firmly establishing itself as the number two grocery retailer behind Sainsbury's. Petrol stations began to be added to some of the stores from 1974, indicating Tesco's willingness to introduce new types of business into the mix.

Many retailers in the 1960s and 1970s used Green Shield stamps as a means to give back to customers benefits for shopping with them. Tesco launched the concept in 1963, giving away stamps with every purchase. These stamps could be exchanged for a range of goods from a catalogue. Given that the weekly grocery shop represented a large proportion of consumer spending, the stamps became an important element of the Tesco offer.

Tesco used Green Shield stamps up until 1977, when it replaced them with a strategy focused on price, known as 'Checkout at Tesco'. This represented a huge overnight store transformation, which aimed at:

- making the Tesco offer more competitive and better value;
- improving Tesco's weak brand image; and
- bolstering Tesco's market share through building better customer loyalty.

By the time Jack Cohen, Tesco's founder, died in 1979, total sales had reached £1 billion and were still growing fast (by 1982 they were above £2 billion). He had seen his initial fledgling business develop to become one of the most famous retailing names in the UK.

The company changed its name to Tesco plc in 1983 as a new Tesco began to emerge. It revolved around the supermarket format, which became particularly focused on the growth of the large out-of-town store model, where convenient, free parking was available, and less on town-centre-based stores, with a large number of unprofitable older stores being closed. The new Tesco in the 1980s was also characterized by the development of quality own-branded goods. Customers were becoming more time-pressed, and thus products that offered quality and convenience became more sought after. Marks & Spencer was recognized as product category leader in this area and was transforming what UK customers could expect from grocery retailers. Sainsbury's had also created a credible own-brand range. By contrast, Tesco 'was the dented can merchant... coming from a long way behind' (Ryle, 2013). Many of the known suppliers were committed to the retailers they had developed partnerships with, such as Northern Foods' link with Marks & Spencer. Tesco had to persuade its supply base to invest in new product areas for it or had to encourage entrepreneurs to create new businesses to source and supply own-brand products for it. Gradually, the own-brand range grew from recipe dish meals to sandwiches, and customers began to build their trust in Tesco's ability to provide these types of products at a reliable quality.

Other initiatives through the 1980s included the computerizing of many store and distribution systems. These developments had a profound effect on ordering and replenishment processes and the customer shopping experience. In 1987 Tesco launched its 'Customer First' customer service campaign, followed in 1989 by 'Tesco Cares', a programme of customer information, ecologically sound products and practical help. Tesco was awarded a European Retail Industry Award for its development of electronic trading with its suppliers.

In summary, the 1980s had represented a very transformational period for Tesco, and for many customers their conventional image of the Tesco brand was now quite out of date with reality. In reaction to this a major marketing campaign was created. It was launched in 1989 and ran for three years, featuring the actor Dudley Moore. The campaign aimed to dispel the image of the old 'pile it high, sell it cheap' Tesco and instead show the new Tesco off, as a company that was classless, all about good quality and contemporary. This repositioning of the Tesco brand was an important building block in Tesco's journey to market itself, almost uniquely among the leading grocers, as a retailer for all sectors of society.

During this period Tesco also carried on its path of supplementing organic growth through continued takeovers. For instance, Tesco took over rival Hillards in 1987 for £220 million, and in 1994 it took over another retailer, Wm Low, for £257 million, outbidding Sainsbury's, which was also keen to develop its business in Scotland, where Wm Low was strong and Sainsbury's was under-represented.

This was a highly significant moment for Tesco. Wm Low operated 57 supermarkets, 45 of which were in Scotland, and the takeover allowed Tesco to virtually double its business in Scotland. At the time Tesco was the number two UK retailer behind Sainsbury's. Among other factors, the success it made of this takeover allowed it to power past Sainsbury's a year later, in 1995, to become the UK's number one grocer. This was a position it never gave up from that time on, leaving Sainsbury's in its wake.

In many ways this takeover illustrated a key difference between the two leading retailers. At the time analysts suggested Sainsbury's was in a better position to bid for Wm Low than Tesco – its profits per square foot of selling space were higher, and it had a bigger gap to fill in its portfolio in Scotland and the North of England than Tesco. But Tesco, under its then Chairman, Ian MacLaurin, argued that its profits per square foot were better in its larger stores than Sainsbury's, and in the end it was prepared to bid higher. It was also able to demonstrate its business strength, turning around a business declining by 6 per cent a year just before the takeover to one that was growing by over 20 per cent year on year a few months afterwards, and more profitably too, supported by Tesco's higher-margin fresh food business and own-label products.

Tesco's past: era 3 – continuous and multi-directional expansion

During the mid-1990s Tesco laid the foundations for growth in many directions, taking decision after decision that would open up huge opportunities for its future development. These changes meant that step by step Tesco metamorphosed into the organization we are more familiar with today. These initiatives can be divided into two themes:

1 Generic, organization-wide decisions that would have a long-term pervasive impact across the company. Three stand out, and thus each will be focused on in an ensuing chapter. They are:

– developing a clear structure around setting the business's mission, principles, values and strategy and refreshing each so it was clear what Tesco stood for and what it was aiming to achieve (see Chapter 3);

– becoming completely customer driven (see Chapter 4); and

– endeavouring to optimize all of its supply chain processes to support its burgeoning businesses and to provide better customer value (see Chapter 5).

2 Four bold business strategies, which set out the areas of business that Tesco would operate in. On becoming CEO in 1997, Terry Leahy set each of these domains out, along with clear associated challenges, as follows:

– 'To be the number one choice [retailer] in the UK. At the time we [Tesco] were still second behind Marks & Spencer and had only recently overtaken Sainsbury's. Most observers thought that our lead was temporary – particularly with the Walmart whale swimming our way.'

– 'To be as strong in non-food products as food. In 1997 non-food represented only 3 per cent of overall sales.'

– 'To develop a profitable retail services business (such as finance or telecommunications). In 1996, Tesco offered no such services at all.'

– 'To be as strong internationally as domestically. In 1997 Tesco only had one per cent of space overseas (and were planning to sell that the next year).'

So, from the mid-1990s onwards, Tesco was not only aiming to grow the core tree of its main UK grocery business, but aiming to use the strength of this mighty trunk activity to branch out into three clearly defined areas: *non-foods*, *retail services* and *international*.

The main stage-post campaigns and achievements in each of these four business strategy areas are now briefly discussed for era 3, the period to around 2011 when Sir Terry Leahy stepped down as CEO. Emphasis is placed on the first business strategy, to be the number one choice retailer in the UK, as this is the area where development in the management of the supply chain has had most effect.

Business strategy 1: to be the number one choice retailer in the UK

As noted above, the buy-out of Wm Low in 1994 and the subsequent overtaking of Sainsbury's to be the UK's number one grocery retailer the following year was a turning point from which Tesco never seemed to look back. However, it would be wrong to assume that the rise to this position and Tesco's virtually continuous growth in market share from then on was based predominantly on a strategy of takeovers and buyouts. Step by step through the 1990s, and on through the next decade, Tesco took meaningful decisions that enabled it to develop its core business offering organically, often wrong-footing its main competitors in the process. Selected notable campaigns and turning points, in an approximate chronological order, are summarized and briefly commented upon below.

The development of the new Value range

The date 16 September 1992 was an important date for Britain. Black Wednesday was the day when the British government was forced to withdraw the pound from the EU Exchange Rate Mechanism (ERM). At the time the UK economy was struggling, although ironically, by withdrawing from the ERM, it was then able to take control of its own destiny to a much greater extent, heralding a sustained period of growth for the UK from 1993 to 2008.

For Tesco, especially as it was trying to develop a reputation for listening to customers and being on their side, the development of the new economy range of products in 1993, known as the Value range, was a key event. As Leahy (2012) noted, it demonstrated that Tesco was 'sending a clear signal to hard pressed customers: we are on your side in tough times – you do not have to shop at the discounters'.

The One in Front campaign

All retailers were feeling the squeeze at this time and were doing all they could to cut costs to make efficiencies, so that the sales that were made could be as profitable as possible. In the stores of virtually all UK retailers this meant that staffing budgets were steadily reduced on a year-by-year basis. Unsurprisingly, this had a cumulative negative impact on staffing levels: as people left they were not replaced, and fewer temporary workers were employed to cover permanent staff holidays or times when sales uplifted from their base norm.

Where this staffing squeeze was felt the most was on the shop floor and was notably seen by the customers first-hand in terms of the length of queues at the checkout tills. By 1994, it had reached a point where there was no slack at all to support weekly trading peaks such as lunchtimes or Saturday afternoons, with the result that queues at tills became longer and longer and customers more and more irate. For the staff in stores, who invariably were working according to the motto that the customer comes first, this was very stressful: they were experiencing every day that these strategies represented merely words over substance.

Tesco was not immune from this, but audaciously launched a new campaign in 1994 entitled One in Front. Quite simply, seemingly to its competitors overnight, Tesco announced that if customers had more than one person in front of them at the checkout then another till would be opened without question. In a flash it removed the frustration of queuing for supermarket shopping at Tesco.

This was a major investment and risk – if Tesco could not match its words with deeds then the promise would look hollow and trust would be lost. The fact Tesco pulled it off was a telling statement to its employees and its customers that again it was listening to customers, sensing their needs and on their side.

This campaign posed a real question to competitors whose checkpoint service lagged far behind in comparison, and which would have to spend a great deal of money in staffing resources to make a similar promise. It also showed that Tesco was developing a capability to deliver what it said it was going to do, something that many other retailers would have been struggling to compete with at the time.

The launch of Tesco's Clubcard

Probably the most far-reaching development, which also had a huge bearing on Tesco pushing to become the UK's number one grocer and then pulling away, was the launch of the Tesco Clubcard early in 1995. This not only provided Tesco's customers with real incentives to be loyal to Tesco, but also gave Tesco data about its customers, which presented a new opportunity to really begin to understand them. Famously, Tesco's Chairman at the time, Ian MacLaurin, was quoted as saying just after Clubcard's launch that he had learnt more about his customers in the first three months than he had in the previous 30 years. The Tesco Clubcard will be discussed in Chapter 4.

Extended store opening hours and Sunday trading

The Shops Act 1950 restricted stores' opening hours, preventing them opening on a Sunday outside Scotland, where stores had legally traded on a Sunday for some time. An attempt in 1986 to liberalize Sunday trading had failed to get through Parliament, but a compromise alternative, backed by large retailers such as Tesco, was passed, allowing retailers from 28 August 1994 the opportunity to trade for six hours on Sundays anytime between 10 am and 6 pm. Interestingly, some of the large retailers, such as Marks & Spencer and Waitrose, fought against Sunday opening at the time, but Tesco was clear that many customers wanted to shop on a Sunday from its experience in Scotland and campaigned strongly for the change in legislation.

Tesco went further in the following years, noting that the patterns of life for many customers had changed and were continuing to evolve. In short, society was becoming more heterogeneous, and for some customer segments, for instance those who worked outside the common 9–5 weekday pattern or who worked on shifts, there might be a desire to be able to shop at different times of the day or night. First Tesco extended its opening hours, and then in 1996 it opened its first 24-hour store.

Again, Tesco was demonstrating that it was listening to the customer and showing that it would be the pioneer of change, to better serve particular needs of its prospective customer population, in a ground-breaking manner. This innovation was typical of a new way of thinking that was beginning to manifest itself in the actions that Tesco was taking.

It was not too costly to deliver either, as most of the larger Tesco stores that moved to 24-hour opening were open anyway through the night for stock replenishment. With a minor readjustment to how this was managed, to minimize customer disruption, Tesco was able to show the customers again that it was on their side.

The first of the Tesco Extras

The UK shopping formats Tesco operated under continued to develop. With the ranges expanding, there was a growing need for a new format of store that would allow the non-food offer space to grow without compromising on the food-selling area. A new format of hypermarket, bigger than a superstore, was thus developed, with the first Tesco Extra opening in 1997 at Pitsea in Basildon, Essex. At the start of 2014 there were 238 Tesco Extras in the UK.

The launch of the Tesco Finest range

A policy to make Tesco relevant to a broader range of customer had begun with the launch of its own-brand Value range in 1993, as noted above. This was mirrored with the development of the up-market Finest brand in 1998. In 2014 these two brands are among the biggest brands in the UK, each turning over more than a £1 billion a year.

The move to Finest was crucial in making Tesco a retail outlet that could appeal to the full socio-economic spectrum of customers. For years, Tesco in its brand image had been synonymous with the saying of its founder, Jack Cohen, of 'Pile it high and sell it cheap.' What Tesco managed to pull off throughout the 1990s, and has continued to develop through to today, was the ability not to be labelled any more as a niche retailer in terms of the market segment it aimed itself at. It was able to appeal to a much fuller spectrum of the UK population, positioning that was unique among grocery retailers.

The pioneering development of home shopping

The strategy to become a more attractive destination for more upmarket customers proved to be highly successful. It was also instrumental in laying a foundation for Tesco's ability to enter the home shopping market.

In the mid-1990s the potential for the use of the internet for shopping began to be recognized. Personal use of computers with internet connectivity was very low, but the concept's potential to change how we might shop in the future was attracting considerable attention. However, the conventional view was that grocery shopping was not an activity that could be easily moved to e-shopping formats. The view was that the volume of business needed to support a picking and delivery operation from a dedicated warehouse for home shopping via internet orders made the business unworkable as a profitable enterprise. In spite of this view, plenty of start-ups tried this business model, notably in the United States, but each was destined to fail, notably Webvan and Peapod.

Tesco, seeing that this was what customers wanted, however, went against the conventional wisdom, and made it work with an innovative and completely different business model. Tesco's solution involved picking and delivering from stores, not dedicated warehouses at all. The team that had led the Clubcard launch were again largely involved with the launch of Tesco.com, and Tesco, with its growing knowledge of its customers developed through the Clubcard, and the fact that it had engaged many of early internet adopters through its launch of the Finest range, trialled and then successfully launched grocery home shopping in 100 stores in August 1999 and went on to achieve over 90 per cent coverage of the UK within 12 months. By 2003 this had reached 96 per cent. Tesco was the only truly nationwide online food retailer,[1] and 70 per cent of the Irish population could also receive an online Tesco.com food delivery by this time.

The first major UK grocery retailer to prioritize convenience stores

Another example of Tesco furthering its reputation for spotting market opportunities and acting upon them before the competition came from the move to provide more convenient, smaller stores in towns and cities and in local neighbourhoods.

Big sites had been acquired at the edge of towns, and this had been seen as the battleground for supermarket retailing throughout the 1980s and 1990s. However, Tesco began to see that there was also a growing market within conurbations for people who wanted to shop in smaller batches, but more frequently. The first Tesco Metro was opened in 1994, with many more stores branded as this type of outlet over the ensuing years. But it was the move to launch a serious business in smaller neighbourhood stores in the next decade that really wrong-footed competitors and led to a sea-change in terms of UK grocery shopping.

The Tesco Express format was defined in 1999 as 'petrol station forecourt shops selling a range of everyday products' (Tesco, 1999). From a base of 17 Expresses in 1999, the format began to be expanded upon after the joint venture with Esso was announced in

February 2000, through which a plan to create a further 150 Tesco Express stores was put forward. By 2002 Tesco had 109 Express stores and through this expansion was learning how the Tesco supply chain could best serve the smaller-format stores effectively and efficiently, so that they could trade successfully and profitably. A step change in strategic focus in the area of neighbourhood retailing for Tesco was about to be proposed.

In 2000, the Competition Commission drew a clear distinction between mainstream grocery retailing and the convenience store sector. Tesco had a much lower share of the latter 'top-up' market, so not only did it represent an area where Tesco could grow but also it was a segment where, if any takeover activity was initiated by Tesco, it was less likely to attract questioning in terms of it being anti-competitive. Tesco also, in its mission to deliver customer value, was becoming increasingly aware that time and energy savings were being increasingly sought by consumers. This represented a major shift in consumer consumption patterns, indicating consumers would really welcome the enhanced convenience that could be offered by stores offering the quality associated with Tesco, over a selected, tailored range, more locally convenient for them.

As usual, Tesco moved quickly. It acquired T&S Stores in October 2002. It brought in 1,202 outlets, which ranged from quite small newsagents to larger convenience stores. Tesco successfully converted around a third of these premises to the Tesco Express format, and retained the T&S operating company to serve the smaller stores under the One Stop brand. To be able to absorb so many stores so quickly was an impressive feat and led Tesco to further acquisitions in the area. In March 2004 it acquired Administore, which operated 45 stores trading under the Harts, Cullens and Europa brands, and in 2005 it bought 21 BP/Safeway stores.

On a like-for-like basis, the Tesco Express chain became Tesco's fastest-growing format of store, with the chain of Expresses having grown to over 1,000 stores by 2009.

Further UK supermarket growth through acquisition

From its inception, one of Tesco's strategies, as has already been noted, had been to acquire businesses and take them over. However, in the

UK over the last decade or so, this option has been less available to the company, as the market share it has developed and extended could be argued to have a potential impact on the competitive operation of the total UK grocery market if more businesses were bought up. Nevertheless, after Morrisons brought Safeway, Tesco was allowed in 2004 to buy 10 of the 52 Safeway stores that Morrisons was obliged to sell by the competition authorities as part of its acquisition. And, as has been discussed above, Tesco has used acquisition as part of its convenience store development strategy. The fact that it has been allowed to do this is an interesting topic on which to reflect, as it sheds light on how the UK government's regulation of competition in the grocery sector has evolved over the last 10 to 15 years or so.

In the UK, the Office of Fair Trading (OFT) and the Competition Commission are the two bodies that have the main responsibility for enforcing competition law. Over the last two decades, competition in the UK grocery market has been reviewed by two major inquiries.

The first, in October 2000, was run by the Competition Commission and led to a Code of Practice to better regulate the relationship supermarkets have with their suppliers.

However, there was ongoing disquiet that suppliers were still being exploited and that smaller shops were being put out of business by the big retailers. As mentioned in the discussion above on Tesco's move to prioritize convenience stores, one of the key debates has surrounded the Competition Commission's distinction in the 2000 report between what it called 'one-stop' and 'top-up' shops. It effectively defined the large superstores, where the weekly grocery shop took place, and the more local, smaller neighbourhood grocery stores as two separate markets. This permitted large grocery retailers, like Tesco, to acquire store chains in the 'top-up' convenience market following the report's publication, which they duly did.

However, critics have argued that little consideration was given in the 2000 report to the market concentration that would occur when the growth in 'top-up' convenience stores was combined with the market share of the 'one-stop' business the market leaders held. This led to the OFT referring the industry to the Competition Commission again, in May 2006. The inquiry was completed in April 2008 and concluded that in many respects the grocery retailers in the UK were 'delivering a good deal for consumers'. But it stated that steps needed to be taken to 'improve competition in local markets' and 'address relationships between retailers and their suppliers'. Actions it recommended included a strengthened and revised Code of Practice and the appointment of an enforcing independent ombudsman. Eventually, after the general election of 2010, the new Coalition Government determined that it would locate the ombudsman within the OFT. After the publication of a draft bill and a further inquiry, a bill to establish an adjudicator was published in May 2012.

In July 2013, more detail was provided with the publishing by the UK government of *Groceries Code Adjudicator*. It applies to retailers with turnover of more than £1 billion a year and will be run on a levy basis of £800,000 a year split between the largest retailers. Complaints, backed by corroborated evidence that there has been a breach of the Groceries Code, will be investigated. If the Adjudicator decides there has been a breach, a range of penalties is available, including a fine of up to 1 per cent of UK turnover of the retailers involved. The Adjudicator has had the authority to apply penalties since April 2014, using any evidence collected from 25 June 2013.

It would appear that most of the large grocery retailers are taking this very seriously, as they recognize that their public reputation for integrity in working with their suppliers is very important in the overall picture of wider esteem that many of their customers hold for them. We will see how the system works, however, as there is some concern that suppliers will be reluctant to come forward to raise a complaint.

This final discussion has spilt over to some of the current issues facing Tesco. In summary, during this third era (from the mid-1990s to 2011), Tesco managed to grow its core UK grocery business considerably. This impressive performance was partly achieved through Tesco's ability to take a number of quite pioneering steps at the time, each linked by a common focus to try to provide better value for customers. The cumulative effect was quite extraordinary. Tesco's market share for groceries grew year by year throughout this period in a quite unprecedented manner. By listening to its UK grocery customers and then quickly and decisively acting across the whole UK business, Tesco was able to steal a significant march on all its competitors. By the end of 2010 Tesco's market share in the UK had risen considerably to 30.7 per cent.

However, the ability to sense what the customer values and come up with solutions that can address their needs is one thing. Being able to match these promises, to deliver the supply chain solutions week after week, year after year, is equally if not more important. How Tesco has gone about this is what this book will try to explain in the ensuing chapters.

Business strategy 2: develop the non-food business to match the food business

Tesco had been predominantly recognized as a grocery retailer up until the mid-1990s, although it had introduced Home'n'Wear departments in its larger stores from the 1960s. Leahy, when he became CEO in 1997, set out the goal of substantively changing this, calling for a non-food offer to be developed, which Tesco duly went about building.

Non-food businesses have the attractiveness of a higher profit margin associated with them than foods. Tesco felt that many segments in this division of retail could be developed competitively, so it began to expand its non-food businesses significantly. Table 2.1 gives a fuller list of typical non-food product categories. Interestingly, all these goods are excluded from the Groceries Code mentioned above by the Competition Commission.

Increased space was devoted to these offers in the growing number of Tesco Extras, and more space was created too in the core supermarkets, which sought to carry an ever enhanced range of non-food products. Successes included the launch of clothing brands such as Cherokee and Florence and Fred, which grew quickly, and the introduction of in-store pharmacies, opticians and photo labs. The Homeplus format of stores was launched in October 2005 at Denton in Manchester. These were stores of around 30,000 square feet that stocked a wide range of non-foods, as was catalogued in the Extra stores, but without the food offering.[2]

Tesco experimented in numerous areas, from house building and estate agents to legal services. Each time it entered into a new area, entrenched business models were challenged and new pioneering

TABLE 2.1 Categories of non-food departments commonly covered by today's grocery retailers

Petrol	Toys
Clothing	Plants and flowers
DIY products	Perfumes
Pharmaceuticals	Cosmetics
Newspapers and magazines	Electrical appliances
Books	Kitchen hardware
Greetings cards	Gardening equipment
CDs, DVDs, videos and audio tapes	Tobacco and tobacco products
Bikes, and bike and car accessories	Luggage and travel goods

methods of conducting business were tried out, sometimes with success, sometimes not.

Beyond the physical stores Tesco also sought to expand its offering online through a fully dedicated subsidiary company, formed in 2000: Tesco.com. Unrestricted by the boundary walls of the store format the new dotcom business offered a wide and ever-expanding range of non-food lines. For example, as early as 2000, the book store had 1.2 million titles, and in home entertainment a further 300,000 CDs, DVDs and videos were catalogued too.[3] Through the early part of the ensuing decade Tesco.com led the way as the 'world's biggest online supermarket', growing each year in terms of sales by around 30 per cent. By 2003, the range included electrical items, from mobile phones to plasma televisions and washing machines, with stationery and office ranges being added in ensuing years.

Following these successes a comprehensive online and catalogue offering was launched in September 2006, branded as Tesco Direct. It was supported by the ability for customers to collect their orders in-store at one of 200 Tesco Direct in-store service desks if they did not want the order delivered to their home. Convenient solutions for customers were again driving pioneering initiatives rolled out across the UK business. Sales in Tesco Direct grew quickly, even as the UK economy suffered after the banking crisis of 2007/08, growing by over 50 per cent in 2008/09 and 28 per cent in 2009/10 as the investments began to be paid off and the business headed 'towards profitability'.[4]

In summary, all the way through the 2000s, Tesco's non-food business continued to grow and develop, online and in-store.

Business strategy 3: to build a profitable retail services division

Retail services were the other key area where Leahy felt Tesco had massive potential to develop products and grow. Other retailers, such as market leader at the time Marks & Spencer, had shown how finance products could be grafted on to the range of products provided by retailers. M&S had used its Chargecard to develop a number of financial services such as insurance and credit services.

In 1997 Tesco created Tesco Personal Finance as a joint venture with the Royal Bank of Scotland (RBS). Following the first product launch, a Visa credit card, other products were soon developed, including loans, insurance and the Instant Access Savings Account (Tesco Bank[5]). Within just a few years (by August 2003) Tesco Personal Finance had built up 4 million customer accounts. Product ranges continued to be developed, including Tesco Compare, launched in 2007. In 2008 Tesco bought out RBS's 50 per cent share and a year later created Tesco Bank.

With the creation of Tesco Bank in 2009, a new stand-alone strategy had to be developed and followed through, supported by a programme to move products from RBS systems to Tesco's over the ensuing years. Offices in Edinburgh, Glasgow and Newcastle were also opened in 2009 and 2010 to house the registered office and the service centres.

Tesco Telecoms was also launched, offering brands such as Tesco Mobile and Tesco Talk.

These changes meant that, step by step, Tesco in the UK metamorphosed into the organization we are familiar with today.

But the UK represents only around 3 per cent of global GDP. However strong Tesco was to become in the UK, it needed to supplement this with overseas growth and needed a clear strategy to achieve this.

Business strategy 4: international expansion

Tesco first expanded overseas in France, owning a French retailer, Catteau, from 1992 to 1997. Although this was to prove an unsuccessful venture, it did provoke some useful lessons, which Tesco were good at learning from. A fresh international strategy was developed. The French experience suggested that moving into developed markets where it could not quickly become a lead player was fraught with problems. Far better to identify emerging markets where there was an opportunity to more easily become the lead player or at worst number two.

With the changes during the early 1990s in eastern Europe following the fall of the Iron Curtain in 1989 new opportunities were arising and being identified by Tesco. Its first venture into this region was in Hungary in 1994 after it acquired S-Market, an existing retailer operating in the north-west of the country. Next it entered the Polish market in 1995, followed by the Czech Republic and Slovakia, both in 1996. By and large each of these moves have proven to be highly successful, with Tesco being able to establish itself as lead player in most of these markets.

International expansion was further spread in the late 1990s and into the next decade through the entry into the Asian market, first in Thailand, under the Tesco Lotus brand, in 1998, and then in South Korea in 1999, where in partnership with Samsung it began operating under the Homeplus brand. Homeplus is now Tesco's largest international business, with revenue in 2012/13 of over £5 billion from 550 stores employing 26,000 people and serving 6 million customers a week[6]. Tesco opened its first store in Malaysia in 2002 and Japan in 2003. In Taiwan, the business it had developed since 2000 was swapped with Carrefour stores in the Czech Republic and Slovakia in an exchange deal plus £39.1 million paid by Tesco.[7]

The company subsequently also bought a 50 per cent stake in a Chinese retailer, the Hymall chain, in 2004 (increasing this to 90 per cent by the end of that year), and in India announced plans in 2008 to develop a wholesale cash-and-carry business in Mumbai in conjunction with assistance from the Tata Group. This is a franchise agreement with Trent Ltd, a part of the Tata Group. Operating under the name Star Bazaar, Tesco provides 80 per cent of the stock sold in stores supported by a modern distribution centre in Mumbai. The 2013 announcement by the Indian government to allow foreign investment in multi-brand retail allows for the joint venture with Trent to be developed, and as of 2014 this is being reviewed.

Closer to home Tesco developed a market-leading position in the Republic of Ireland as well. It had traded in Ireland in the 1980s but had sold its operations there in 1986. In 1997 it re-entered this market, after purchasing Power Supermarkets Ltd, and has become well established as a leading player in Ireland. This business, then owned by Associated British Foods, was sold to Tesco for £630 million and transferred 75 stores in the Republic of Ireland and 34 stores in Northern Ireland.

Outside Ireland, eastern Europe and the Far East, Tesco also entered Turkey in 2003, where it now trades under the name Tesco Kipa. And in 2007 Tesco entered the US market with the Fresh & Easy concept, a venture that attracted a great deal of media attention, as it meant that Tesco was entering the backyard of the world's number one retailer, Walmart. Walmart had entered the UK market in 1999 after taking over Asda, and at the time many commentators felt that this would have far-reaching consequences for retailing in the UK. It was considered that many retailers would be forced to look at new ways to compete or they would lose market share. From the time of the takeover, however, Tesco was able to increase market share substantially, not lose share, while Asda, in broad terms, was really only able to maintain its position, jostling for the number two spot with Sainsbury's. So, while Tesco seemingly had successfully competed with Walmart in Tesco's home territory, the question that was raised was how it would get on when it chose to compete in Walmart's homeland.

In reality, the timing of this move coincided with the global financial crisis, and despite substantial investment Tesco announced in 2013 that it was pulling out of the Fresh & Easy format it had developed in the United States.

Era 3 concludes

During this third era Tesco as a company had fundamentally changed. It had taken the good parts of its culture from its past, for example its entrepreneurial zeal, and repackaged this into a new zest for business across a range of diversified areas. From its core UK grocery business, to its expanding businesses in non-food, retail services and international, Tesco had delivered a rapidly growing company across many fronts simultaneously. It was now respected as one of the UK's most successful companies and had shown an ability to ride out the difficult economic times that many companies had faced since the financial crisis of 2007 and the banking collapse of 2008.

In 2007 a fifth strategic objective was added: 'to put community at the heart of what we do'. This strategy included many areas, including an ambitious agenda to promote green consumption and to play a positive role in tackling climate change, more tailored efforts to encourage customers to buy local and regionally sourced products, and support for smaller suppliers to gain easier access to Tesco to build new possibilities for local sourcing.

In June 2010 Sir Terry Leahy announced his retirement as CEO of Tesco. David Reid, Tesco's Chairman, in the 2011 annual review summarized what had been achieved as follows: 'Terry is undoubtedly one of the leading businessmen of his generation. Under his leadership we have more than quadrupled our sales and profits, expanded into 13 countries outside the UK and entered new markets such as online retailing and financial services.' Tesco prepared itself for a new era, with a new person at the helm.

Tesco's past: era 4 – more challenging times – refocusing the business

When Sir Terry Leahy stepped down after 14 years as CEO he was replaced by Philip Clarke, who became the new Group Chief Executive in March 2011. In reflecting on the size of business that Tesco had become he created a number of CEO positions;[8] these included Tim Mason as Deputy CEO and Chief Marketing Officer and CEO of Fresh & Easy, Richard Brasher as CEO of the newly created UK and Republic of Ireland business, and David Potts as the first CEO of Asia, while Laurie McIlwee took responsibility for group strategy as well as his role of Chief Financial Officer. Andrew Higginson and Lucy Neville-Rolfe continued in their roles as CEO of Retail Services and Executive Director (Corporate and Legal Affairs) respectively.

During the period from 2011 to when Clarke stepped down as CEO in mid-2014, the company has taken a slightly different approach from that of the Leahy era. This was for a variety of reasons, but fundamentally trading across many parts of its business had become tougher. This forced the company to look hard at how it was positioned in each of the markets in which it traded.

In summary, this period could be described as a time when the focus was on pruning the Tesco tree, cutting out areas of business that were not proving to be as successful as the company hoped, and overhauling all the other areas of trade to ensure they were fit for purpose and able to compete in today's and tomorrow's marketplaces, where the customers' demands are constantly evolving. It was also been a time when a few new shoots of activity were nurtured, especially in the technology-empowered digital world.

The key steps taken from March 2011 until the middle of 2014 are outlined below.

Ending the space race

The growth in the internet and in multi-channel retailing in recent years is leading to a fundamental review of how retailers serve their customers with different types of products. Internet retailing for commodity goods (products that are essentially the same irrespective of which retailer the customer buys them from) centres on price in a more accentuated way than before. This is because customers can more easily compare prices for goods between retailers than they could when physically having to move from shop to shop to compare prices. While customers are increasingly learning to access these channels to seek out great deals, retailers have to review how they best serve the customer. In addition, with the emergence of Tesco Express stores and more convenience stores from Tesco's competitors too, customers had less reason to visit the larger Tesco superstores as often as they had in the past.

For Tesco, these were key factors behind one of the first steps that Clarke announced on becoming Chief Executive to end the so-called 'space race' (ie opening more and more large-format stores) and to concentrate its efforts on developing smaller convenience stores, refurbishing existing supermarkets, and online investment.

Customers' trust and confidence in Tesco

Right from the start of Clarke's tenure as Tesco leader he emphasized that trust was key if Tesco was going to be successful in 'Winning Customers in a World of Change'. This was the title of his speech at the World Retail Congress on 19 September 2012, where he argued that technology was playing a substantial role in redefining how customers were shopping. Smartphones, he said, 'have given birth to the always-on, networked shopper, empowered like never before to find and share value – or the reverse – whenever or wherever they are'. He added: 'Individuals using the technology are powerful; individuals using technology together are all-powerful.'

He foresaw that Clubcard would enable a 'mass personalized' approach where vouchers tailored exactly to what each customer buys are provided, not vouchers that those in the same customer segment might appreciate. He went on to argue that 'trusted brands are those which embrace mass personalisation' and that 'the need to build a strong, trusted brand is greater than ever'.

Shortly after this speech, in January 2013 news broke that raised the question of what grocery supply chains the consumer would trust. The Irish Food Safety Authority had called Tesco to tell it that batches from three frozen beefburger lines had tested positive for horsemeat. Although not ostensibly an issue of food safety it was nevertheless very newsworthy, and called into question the confidence customers could have in the products retailers such as Tesco offer. Clearly, the issue of consumer trust, which Clarke had recognized was so critical to the way its customers valued the Tesco brand, was being severely tested.

Tesco's response was very honest, transparent and immediate. All products identified as having horsemeat were withdrawn, as well as all products sold by the same producer. As many communication channels as possible were used (newspaper, TV, etc) to highlight the issue and to communicate clearly what Tesco was intending to do about the situation.

Then in February 2013, after Tesco had withdrawn its Everyday Value Spaghetti Bolognese from display the week after Findus products from the same factory were reported to be at risk of containing horsemeat, Tesco confirmed its product too had contained horsemeat. And, after more than 500 products had been DNA-tested and found to be clear of horsemeat contamination, a further Tesco product tested positive for between 2 and 5 per cent horsemeat, frozen Tesco Simply Roast Meatloaf.

The supply chain, which had done so much to empower Tesco in being able to deliver sustainable growth, had been shown up as having severe cracks, which threatened the reputation of the whole brand. This is an issue that will be discussed later in the chapters that focus on Tesco's supply chain management (Chapter 5) and the challenges Tesco faces (Chapter 7), but suffice to say at this stage that this series of events during the first half of 2013 had the potential to have a very damaging long-term effect on the company's reputation and consequently performance.

A number of far-ranging steps were taken by Tesco to regain control over the products it retailed, especially those with the Tesco name on them,[9] and begin to rebuild any lost trust. Three steps were outlined by Philip Clarke in February 2013:

1 The Tesco team would go right up each supply chain to ensure that all the suppliers Tesco used were performing in the way the customer would expect. This included the need for strong traceability of all raw materials too.

2 Tesco would launch a new digital website so that all the steps that Tesco was taking to ensure its supply chains were in order were clearly set out. In the end this would make the hidden world of the Tesco supply chain much more transparent so customers could see the farmers, the factory workers and so on in action and be able to witness, almost first-hand, the care and attention that people handling Tesco products put into their tasks of preparing Tesco products.

3 If Tesco ever had to remove a product from sale because there was a question of the trust the customer could place in it, a substitute would be offered at no extra cost to the customer.

The implication of these steps was that even more emphasis would be placed on developing longer-term relationships with suppliers, so that trust between Tesco and its supplying base could be better developed. The recognition that a trusting link with suppliers was at the heart of creating the trusting link Tesco sought with its customers was made crystal clear by Clarke.

It should be emphasized at this stage that Tesco was not the only retailer involved. Horsemeat was a problem all over the eurozone and, in the UK, Lidl and Iceland also stocked the frozen burger that in January 2013 brought the scandal to public attention. So other stores and many manufacturers became involved with horsemeat-contaminated products identified in goods they either sold or manufactured. But the impact on Tesco's reputation had been undeniable. An Ipsos Mori poll in December 2013[10] found that Tesco and Iceland had endured a bigger fall in their reputations than other supermarkets: asking people if they felt more or less favourable towards the six major supermarkets, the poll found that 20 per cent of adults perceived Tesco less favourably, with Iceland being the next most affected retailer, with 14 per cent having a less favourable opinion.

UK focus

The core of Tesco is its UK business. In 2012/13 over 65 per cent of the company's sales and profits were generated in this market.[11] When Clarke had become the CEO in 2011 he had inserted his long-time colleague Richard Brasher as CEO of this area of the business in the newly created UK (and Republic of Ireland) trading region. This was different to the way Leahy had done it. He had managed the UK business as a key operation he was responsible for as well as fulfilling the chief executive brief.

However, as the UK business was so important to the group, and as it was also under pressure in terms of its performance, there was perhaps an inevitable tension that arose between Brasher and Clarke, despite Brasher's long history of working with Clarke across the Tesco business. This resulted in Brasher leaving in March 2012.[12] Clarke then took on full control of the UK business, which was beginning to lose momentum and market share.

Clarke instigated what he called 'Building a Better Tesco: The UK Plan.[13] Tesco admitted that 'we have not been at our best and we are making changes' ('Building a Better Tesco: The UK Plan'). The plan was ambitious and far-reaching, being structured under six all-embracing headings:

- 'Colleagues and service';
- 'Stores and formats';
- 'Price and value';
- 'Range and quality';
- 'Brand and marketing';
- 'Clicks and bricks'.

The scheme was backed by a huge financial reinvestment centred squarely upon the UK business. Many asserted that it was looking tired compared to the competition, as Tesco had arguably put too much into investing overseas and elsewhere across the business. Tony Hoggett (Managing Director, Tesco UK Superstores) highlighted in 2013 that customers were feeding back the feeling that Tesco's UK superstores were 'a little bit functional and a little bit efficient and lacked the warmth and friendliness they were looking for... and they wanted to see a few more staff around on the sales floor'.[14]

So a key focus of the plan centred on fundamentally rethinking these large superstores. A substantial campaign to refresh the look and content of these formats was extensively experimented with. Ultimately, the prototype was unveiled in the summer of 2013 as a new vision of what Tesco would offer.

The new design for Tesco's UK superstores included a stronger emphasis on the presentation and the priority given to fresh food, even putting bakery and the coffee shop at the entrance to the store. An improved look and feel to the stores was also created by, for instance, using timber cladding, which is a much more natural material, clearer and more appealing in-store signage, better lighting and the incorporation of the restaurant chain Giraffe and of course the aforementioned coffee shop, Harris + Hoole, the chain Tesco had acquired a year earlier. Clarke envisaged that these large stores would 'have to become a more attractive destination for customers; they have to be able to give people excitement and something new'.[15] Supporting this was a large investment in recruitment, training and equipment to try to engender a more helpful and friendlier shopping experience.

Another area that is worthy of note here, in the UK Plan, is the overhaul and relaunching of the Value (2012) and Finest (2013) ranges.

The makeover of the Finest range was launched in October 2013. Tesco's premium brand, which had been launched 15 years earlier in 1998, represented a strong opportunity to underline Tesco's credentials at the quality end of the market spectrum. Finest was already a very successful range, taking over £1 billion annually,[16] and the revamp was backed by a sponsorship in the UK of ITV's drama *Downton Abbey*, and represented a thorough overhaul and extension of this branded flagship range. In all, 400 new products were created across virtually all product groups, again backed by a fresh new packaging look, which attempted to emphasize the care and passion that Tesco had put into these lines as well as each product's key point of differentiation.[17]

Before this a relaunch of the Value range was one of the first achievements of the Clarke reign. Tesco had been the first supermarket to launch a value range, 20 years earlier, and this rebranding of the Everyday Value range in April 2012 was seen as timely. Most of the other supermarkets were also in the process of rebranding their equivalent ranges, and the success of the discount chains, such as Aldi and Lidl, in growing their market share was evidence that Tesco needed to ensure the range reflected as much as possible the values that this segment of customers was looking for. A spokesperson stated: 'we have listened closely to what our customers want and Everyday Value will provide products that taste better, look better and are healthier – still at the same price'.[18] The packaging was also changed, with the established blue and white stripe being replaced.

Ultimately, beyond this, a crucial area of the value equation that many customers were clearly increasingly focusing on needed to be reappraised: the price customers paid for the goods they bought. The discount chains, notably Lidl, Aldi, Iceland and recently even

Poundland, B&M and Farmfoods, had all established a foothold in the UK, and all gained market share in 2013. Consumers, including many in employment who had not seen meaningful pay rises in a number of years, were shopping around for the best bargains and, in short, placing more emphasis on lowering the amount they paid out on their weekly grocery shop. Tesco could not afford to be seen to be too far out of kilter in this regard, and thus the pressure was on to show that Tesco was able to compete on price.

As a consequence, in late February 2014 a fresh campaign of lower and more stable prices, under the strapline 'Down and staying down', was announced,[19] and in early March Clarke announced that the profit margin of 5.2 per cent would no longer be held to, as Tesco would become better at providing lower and more stable prices for groceries. This represented a major strategy shift and, while it did not mean the end of promotions, it did indicate a move away from a promotional emphasis towards more stable, lower prices. The price of four litres of milk, for example, was reduced from £1.39 to £1.00, and accompanying this was a clear note that farmers would not be paid any less for their product, an important point in Tesco's attempts to rebuild consumer and supplier confidence that it would treat the supply base fairly. We will return to Tesco's attempts to compete with the discount end of the competitive market in Chapter 7, which looks at the challenges faced in managing Tesco and its supply chain.

Focusing on technology

As noted above, Clarke, a former IT Director at Tesco, had identified that the digital world was having a pervasive impact on a business such as Tesco, influencing the way its customers behaved and shopped and the way Tesco operates and supplies its products. A hallmark of his tenure as CEO of Tesco was the emphasis given to investing in technology and to understanding what changes in technology meant and will mean to the company. Much of these developments will be referred to in later chapters, as they directly influence what customers value and how this value is best catered for throughout the activities of the chain of supply.

In summary, retail supply chains were moving to become multi-channel, whereby customers could search for, select, buy and receive delivery of goods and services across a variety of processes. The challenge was to manage this multi-channel environment seamlessly in the eyes of the customer, what has become known as the 'omni-channel solution'. Retailers such as Tesco have a distinct advantage compared to their virtual rivals that do not own any physical stores, as they can integrate these stores into the online shopping experience. For instance, Tesco's Click & Collect service has become very popular with customers, saving them time, energy and money, ie providing them with enhanced value, Tesco's ultimate mission. Click & Collect allows customers to place orders online and then travel to a nearby store or other designated collection point and pick up their order. In 2014 this was offered at no additional charge to the customer. (This is a simple description of a very comprehensive offer, which will be discussed further in Chapter 7, looking at Tesco's current situation.)

But Clarke took Tesco further on this path in an attempt to redefine and enlarge what Tesco stood for and was about. He envisaged that internet retail could drive the evolution of the retailer's strategy and should be very much part of its new objective of building a multi-channel business. Two developments are worth mentioning here.

First, Tesco since 2011 had taken significant steps to becoming a digital entertainment brand. In April 2011, Tesco bought an 80 per cent share in Blinkbox,[20] which offered users more than 9,000 films to stream via the internet. It subsequently acquired stakes in music download in We7,[21] a music download and streaming business, and Mobcast,[22] an e-book platform with 130,000 titles that can be read on digitally connected devices.

With Tesco now seeking to integrate its multi-channel strategy with digital entertainment under one leader, Michael Cornish,[23] the co-founder of Blinkbox, Tesco were positioned to evolve substantively in this area in the future. A new digital campus was being developed in London, in Shoreditch, where mobile apps would be developed, and in Farringdon, where the Blinkbox brand would be based.

Second, Tesco in 2013 launched its new android tablet, Hudl. Hudl was sold in four colour choices and came with Google Apps pre-loaded on it. As well as allowing users to conduct all the activities they normally would on a tablet, the Hudl had a 'T' symbol in the bottom left corner that allowed users to quickly gain access to all Tesco's services: Tesco Bank, Tesco.com, Tesco Direct, Blinkbox and so on. Clubcard customers could also enjoy free TV and films too. Priced at £119 (with £100 worth of vouchers available in the box), it represented a competitive package, which sold well after launch.

Online growth continues – building multi-channel capabilities

The sixth area of focus of the UK Plan mentioned above was 'Clicks and bricks'. This went beyond the focus on new technology already described. Since 2011, the trend of an increasing proportion of business being conducted online has continued apace. Tesco supported this by taking numerous initiatives during recent years as part of its efforts to develop a full multi-channel offering, which was increasingly demanded by customers. These steps, sometimes large, sometimes small, incrementally sewed together the physical and virtual retail processes customers could use, so that they can combine the processes optimally to suit their situational requirements. In the UK these developments included:

- launching and quickly extending Click & Collect for groceries, which in 2014 was available in over 200 locations in the UK;
- launching and quickly expanding a free Click & Collect for clothing, available in over 900 stores;
- adding free Click & Collect to the Tesco Direct service so that goods ordered online could be delivered to the store free of charge at over 1,700 stores;
- prompt supply chain service for Click & Collect Direct and Click & Collect Clothing: orders made before 3 pm could be collected in store after 4 pm the next day (with Saturday orders available after 4 pm on Mondays), which compared to a standard delivery to the home (two to five days) costing £3.00 or an Express delivery (next day) to the home, costing £5.95, and orders over £50 delivered to the home were free;
- setting up a free return channel through stores for clothing and Direct goods purchased online;

- offering free UK returns by post for clothing bought online;
- the introduction of one-hour delivery slots for Tesco groceries and Tesco Direct deliveries to the home.

Clarke,[24] in an appraisal of what he termed 'our multichannel Christmas', argued that 'multichannel is about refining all these elements and making them work together to create an all-round shopping experience which feels like it was built just for you.' He stated that 'online sales were approaching 8%, £450m in the six weeks of Christmas alone', and grew by 11 per cent. This gives a feeling for the scale of business being conducted at the end of 2013 through online ordering at Tesco. Clothing was where online sales were up most markedly, increasing by 70 per cent, he stated, with general merchandise up 25 per cent.

Interestingly, given how much emphasis had been placed on offering store-based Click & Collect services to work seamlessly with online ordering, over 70 per cent of online clothing and general orders during the Christmas 2013 period were picked up from a Click & Collect in-store desk.

International decisions

As detailed in the earlier discussion, in the previous era, from the mid-1990s to 2011, Tesco had expanded its retail operations into a number of countries, with a focus on Eastern Europe and Asia. Notably added to these developments was the initiative to enter the United States under the Fresh & Easy store brand. Each market was been thoroughly reviewed, resulting in some significant strategic centred on how Tesco wanted to trade in each market in which it operated, and even whether it wanted to continue to operate at all in some of these countries. The principal decisions taken since 2011 are summarized below.

United States

After announcing in February 2006 that it was going to enter the US market, Tesco did so in 2007 and developed the store brand Fresh & Easy. It invested heavily to grow a business from scratch, in total spending over £1 billion of capital. This was focused on creating a network of stores in three states (California, Nevada and Arizona) and a distribution centre. The timing of this new venture coincided with an unprecedentedly challenging trading climate, as the financial crisis and banking collapse hit from 2007/08 onwards, affecting California particularly badly. The state was especially exposed to sub-prime mortgages, which many have seen as the root cause of the global economic downturn that ensued. By the end of 2012, 200 stores had been opened, but Tesco was not able to make them operate profitably.

Clarke faced up to the situation. Either more money would have to be invested in the business to cover the losses and try to turn it around or Tesco would have to pull out of its US subsidiary. Following the resignation of the President and CEO of Fresh & Easy, Tim Mason, in December 2012, in the end, in April 2013, Tesco announced it was pulling out of the US market.

In September 2013 Tesco announced that it would be able to sell 150 of the 200 stores as an ongoing business, with 50 of the stores closing completely. On 27 November Yucaipa Companies became the new owner of Fresh & Easy as the sale was completed.

Japan

Another international market where the decision was taken to stop trading was Japan. After almost 10 years, Tesco announced in 2012 that it was paying local supermarket operator Aeon £40 million to take on the chain of stores in Japan from Tesco.[25] The company had announced in August 2011 that it felt 'a sufficiently scalable business' could not be built in the country. Japan was a fairly small operation, with a market share of only 0.1 per cent, so Tesco had never really attained any volume of business in the country.

China

Tesco began trading in the world's biggest grocery market, China, in 2004. Since then Tesco has developed a chain of 131 stores, mostly hypermarkets, although with some Express format outlets as well, in the eastern seaboard areas of the country. There is also now a grocery home delivery service in Shanghai.

In August 2013, Tesco announced that it was in talks with China Resources Enterprise (CRE) about merging the two companies' hypermarkets and supermarkets in China. Tesco's 131 stores would combine with CRE's almost 3,000 outlets, which trade under the Vanguard brand. This would create what the two parties argue would be the leading multi-format retailer in China.

CRE is state-run and would control 80 per cent, while Tesco would have 20 per cent. CRE suggested that the venture would bring together 'their deep understanding of local customers, established nationwide infrastructure and proven track record as a partner with Tesco's global retail expertise, international sourcing scale and supply chain capabilities'.[26]

India

As noted above, following the Indian government's move to allow foreign investment in multi-brand retail, Tesco in early 2014 were looking at plans to further develop the joint venture it entered into in 2008 with the Tata subsidiary Trent, which trades under the Star Bazaar store brand.

Malaysia

By early 2014 Tesco had grown to operate 47 hypermarket stores in Malaysia, supported by two modern distribution centres. Of Tesco's 4,000 own-brand products, 90 per cent were produced in Malaysia. Sime Darby, a large Malaysian conglomerate, partnered with Tesco in this country. Food and non-food lines could also be accessed online, with deliveries made to the home, as in the UK.

South Korea

Tesco South Korea in early 2014 was currently the largest international Tesco business. As well as the 520 Homeplus stores, the online business is particularly important, reflecting the advanced demand for online retail in the country.

Innovative developments in recent years have included the virtual store, where customers can review displays of products such as milk and fruit at the bus stop or train station and order the lines on their smartphones by scanning the QR codes for delivery to their home. Tesco by 2014 had 22 of these around the country (to see more, access the video illustration of this: 'Tesco Homeplus Virtual Subway Store in South Korea', YouTube). Three distribution centres support the store network.

Thailand

Tesco by early 2014 had 1,433 stores in Thailand, making it the second-largest international business in trading terms. Tesco operates hypermarkets and many Express stores.

In 2013, the dotcom business was launched in Thailand. A mobile app has been developed so customers can access Tesco Lotus products from their mobiles too.

Turkey

With 191 stores across Turkey in 20 cities, Tesco has traded in the country since the acquisition of Kipa in 2003. Larger supermarkets and Express stores ensure the retail formats are increasingly customized to local demands.

Central Europe

Tesco continues to trade resiliently in many Eastern European countries. Features that are now common in the UK are being rolled out to each national market in turn. These developments include store ongoing openings across Tesco's established retail formats, notably including more Extra and Express stores, a wider selection of food and non-food products, Clubcard, online ordering, home delivery options and so on.

Local sourcing is a feature that has been championed in many of the countries since Tesco entered their national markets.

There are some trading differences to Tesco in the UK, such as the stand-alone Florence and Fred clothing stores in the Czech Republic, but on the whole the Central European countries' offer is one that is following the UK lead set by Tesco when it is deemed each market is ready for it.

Ireland

The Irish economy has been hit particularly hard during the aftermath of the financial crisis and banking collapses in 2007 and 2008. Following on from this, the crisis surrounding the euro was felt especially by the peripheral countries of Europe, including Ireland. While there are encouraging signs emerging in the macro economy, especially in and around Dublin, the trading climate is still very competitive. Tesco in mid-2014 was still the market leader in Ireland, but was losing market share, especially to discounters Aldi and Lidl, which were quickly gaining larger shares of the market themselves, admittedly from a much lower base.

The Tesco offer in Ireland follows in a very comparable manner the way Tesco operates in the UK. Tesco trades through the Extra, superstore, Metro and Express formats, and Tesco clothing is fully available and links with the full UK website (delivery costs €3.95 or is free on orders over €50). Tesco Clubcard, Tesco Bank and Tesco Mobile are all run in a similar manner.

There are differences though. For example, Tesco's price promise in 2014 was against Aldi or Lidl, whereas in the UK it was against Asda, Sainsbury's and Morrisons, and there are no links to Tesco Direct and Blinkbox from the Tesco Ireland website.

Tesco in 2014 had 142 stores across Ireland and as in other parts of the Tesco business continued to provide a great deal to support local suppliers.

Conclusion of era 4

Tesco has found trading conditions to be much tougher in recent years, which is not something it has encountered for a long time. The discussion above of era 4 has provided a summary of activities and of the most notable events that have impacted on the Tesco business from 2011 to mid-2014.

By mid-2014 it was clear that Tesco was beginning to face up to many of its challenges. It appeared to be sensing and listening to the customer once more and was determinedly taking a fresh and innovative course, especially in its UK business, where it was two years into a £1 billion turnaround plan with the UK accounting for around two-thirds of its revenues and profits. But the knocks to Tesco's reputation following the horsemeat scandal, the problems in the United States, Japan and to some extent China, and the cooling of its performance in the UK had meant that Tesco was not perceived and respected as strongly as it was in the past. As it responded to these pressures and to the ever changing retail world, the question of whether Tesco would rediscover its magic touch was one that many retail market analysts were pondering at this time.

Tesco – the present day

So where has Tesco reached today? Part of the answer to this has been alluded to earlier in this chapter. Under Philip Clarke's leadership a slightly different Tesco emerged, but many of the hallmark traits that underpinned Tesco's performance from the mid-1990s until recent times are still evident.

As this book was being written, Clarke announced that he was stepping down as CEO to be replaced by Dave Lewis from Unilever. This was a significant development as for the first time Tesco would be led by a CEO who had not been brought through the Tesco ranks.

Justin King, the boss of Sainsbury's, one of Tesco's main competitors in the UK, stepped down as CEO in July 2014 after 10 years in charge. Overall, he was credited with making Sainsbury's strong again during his reign, but Sainsbury's market capitalization in mid-2014 was £6 billion. Compare that with Tesco's, which as one point in 2014 stood at £26 billion. Through this comparison alone, the scale difference that has emerged between retailers that only 20 years before had been a very similar size of business becomes fully apparent.

However, as we have noted, there is no doubt that trading has become tougher for Tesco in recent years. We will reflect on this and look at some of the challenges Tesco faces going forward in Chapter 7.

To conclude this chapter, here is a range of key facts (Tesco Annual Review 2013a) that describe the nature and scale of the Tesco business when it became the second-biggest retailer in the world at the beginning of 2014. Tesco:

- handles 75 million shopping trips a week;
- employs over 500,000 people;
- runs over 6,500 stores;
- delivers food to a half-million homes a year;
- has 40 million customers using loyalty schemes like Clubcard;
- works with suppliers from over 70 countries;
- manages the logistics of delivering more than 3 billion cases of food to stores a year.

Conclusions

This chapter has aimed to set the scene for the book, to provide a potted insight into what Tesco has achieved over the last 95 years since its inception in 1919 to mid-2014 (an addendum in the epilogue charts the most noticeable events over the closing mouths of 2014 during the early period of the Lewis CEO tenure). The chapter has described the 'what' of the Tesco journey. Subsequent chapters will explore 'why' and 'how' Tesco achieved this growth.

Key chapter summary points

1　The company was founded in 1919, a year after the end of the First World War, by a former member of the Royal Flying Corps, Jack Cohen.

2　In 1947, Tesco Stores (Holdings) was floated on the London Stock Exchange.

3　Over its 95-year history Tesco has evolved continually, increasing sales and profits almost every year through takeovers and organic growth.

4　During this time Tesco effectively has had only four leaders: Jack Cohen, Ian MacLaurin, Terry Leahy and Philip Clarke.

5　Tesco's history can be divided into four eras, each reflecting a distinct chapter in Tesco's evolution into the company we are familiar with today.

Notes

1　Tesco Annual Review 2003
2　Tesco Annual Review 2006
3　Tesco Annual Review 2000
4　Tesco Annual Review 2010
5　http://corporate.tescobank.com/20/about-us/history/
6　Tesco confirms sale and leaseback deal in South Korea, Tesco news release, 3 January 2014

7 Mark Tran, Tesco to pull put of Taiwan, *Guardian*, 30 September 2005

8 Tesco Annual Review 2011

9 tinyurl.com/a4vzz46

10 Horsemeat in the Food Supply Chain: One Year On

11 Tesco in the UK, www.tescoplc.com/index.asp?pageid=280, accessed 30 January 2014

12 Nathalie Thomas, Tesco's UK chief executive Richard Brasher falls at the final hurdle, *Daily Telegraph*, 15 March 2012

13 Tescoplc Video Library, accessed 30 January 2014

14 Tescoplc Video Library, accessed 30 January 2014

15 Tesco unveils new superstore after profits drop, *BBC News Business*, 8 August 2013

16 Andrea Felsted, Tesco relaunches its premium range, *Financial Times*, 7 October 2013

17 Tesco Finest: Relaunch interview with Leonie Foster, Brand Marketing Director Tesco, YouTube

18 Jon Whiteaker, Tesco Value rebranded as 'Everyday Value', *Retail Gazette*, 4 April 2012

19 S Vizard, Tesco looks to end 'frivolous' promotions with £200m price investment, *Marketing Week*, 25 February 2014

20 Tesco Buys into Blinkbox, *Marketing Week*, 20 April 2011

21 Tesco Buys into Music Service We7, *Marketing Week*, 14 June 2012

22 Tesco Apes Sainsbury's with eBook Move, *Marketing Week*, 4 September 2012

23 Tesco Appoints Michael Cornish Group Digital Officer ahead of Hiring Spree, *Marketing*, 10 June 2013

24 Our Multichannel Christmas: Philip Clarke Talking Shop, https://www.tescoplc.com/talkingshop/index.asp?blogid=177, 9 January 2014

25 Zoe Wood, Tesco Offloads Japanese Operation, *Guardian*, 18 June 2012

26 Tesco in talks with China resources enterprise, *BBC News*, 9 August 2013

Tesco and strategy
Managing the what, why and how

Although there have been some changes over recent years, particularly during Philip Clarke's tenure as the CEO of Tesco, many of the hallmarks of the Tesco strategy formed during the Leahy era, which delivered an almost unprecedented run of sales, profit and market share growth for Tesco, still remain. Chapter 2 discussed *what* Tesco has achieved. This chapter discusses the way Tesco laid the foundations for this success, in its strategy formulation.

In Chapter 2 we also outlined the three organization-wide decisions that Leahy took in his early days as CEO of Tesco from 1997 that would have a profound long-term impact on the company. Each will be examined over the next three chapters:

- developing a clear structure around setting the business's mission, principles, values and strategy and refreshing each so it was clear what Tesco stood for and what it was aiming to achieve (Chapter 3);

- becoming completely customer driven: *why* Tesco exists (Chapter 4); and

- endeavouring to better optimize all of its processes, notably its supply chain, to support its burgeoning businesses and to provide better customer value: *how* Tesco does business (Chapter 5).

Introduction

This chapter focuses on the way Tesco formulated its strategy at the outset of the era, which saw it climb from being UK's number two retailer behind Sainsbury's to the second-biggest retailer in the world in 2014 behind Walmart (Deloitte, 2014). It looks at how the leaders of Tesco, from the early to the mid-1990s, looked truthfully at what Tesco had become, how Tesco was now perceived by its customers, and what was needed to face up to the facts. The lessons learnt from this period of introspection were indeed profound, and from the mid-1990s onwards Tesco, motivated by a new vision and a fresh strategy, was able to propel itself continually forward, eventually to become the size of company we see today, with a turnover in excess of £72 billion a year.

The chapter aims to examine two things. First, it sets out to present and appraise the strategic approach that Tesco developed at the outset of this period of remarkable growth. Second, it looks at how Tesco's strategy has evolved to meet the needs of today's marketplace, comparing the Tesco strategy under Philip Clarke with the one that existed for much of the Leahy era.

Tesco's strategic approach

In the years leading up to the mid-1990s, Leahy (2012) recalls, 'confidence in Tesco's strategy gave way to doubt'. Faced with the new discounters Aldi (in 1989) and Lidl (in 1994) arriving in the UK from Germany, Sainsbury's ongoing strong performance in the south of England, and Asda beginning to build low-price targeted stores in the north of England, he noted that 'morale was flagging and a sense of crisis was beginning to set in'. This is the point when Leahy was asked to take on the role of Marketing Director. He felt that 'finding the truth' about what its customers thought of Tesco 'was absolutely essential: it was the only way we would get out of the rut of being a middle-ranking supermarket' (Leahy, 2012), he passionately argued.

So began the core idea of the new strategy, which Leahy was to go on to repeat many times during his time as CEO at Tesco, of 'putting the customer at the core of everything we did'. This may seem trite and common sense – it was not for example that Tesco was not trying to do this, in part, in preceding years. But, from this time on, what Tesco set out to do with zest, better than anyone else for a sustained period, was to really listen to customers, to sense what they were feeling and needing, and importantly to act on this insight across the whole business, time after time. Leahy's core idea was not just about words or sentiment, but went deep into the Tesco culture, driving its orientation, thinking and actions.

Thus, for Tesco, in the mid-1990s, a transformational strategy was formulated and fine-tuned over the following years. Many aspects of it are still recognizably in place today. The main features of it are summarized below.

First, a word about the way Tesco defines 'strategy'. For Tesco, strategy is not a single statement of intent, nor merely an action plan, but an umbrella term for a number of statements that when combined could be described as a 'corporate or strategic framework'. Kaplan and Norton (2008) argue that, to develop the required elements of this 'strategic framework' when developing a 'transformational strategy', which Tesco was trying to do from the mid-1990s onwards, four questions need to be asked:

1 What business are we in and why? (Mission, vision and values.)

2 Where are we going? (Strategic goals.)

3 What are the key issues that our strategy must address? (Strategic analysis.)

4 How can we best compete? (Strategy formulation.)

These four questions can be used to structure our discussion below, which aims to describe and examine the approach taken by Tesco in formulating its own 'strategic framework' during the Leahy years.

What business are we in and why?

First, a business has seriously to ask itself what business it is in. This should not be too limiting, but should encapsulate the broad sense of what the organization does in very simple terms.

What business are we in?

The basic core process employed by any multiple retailer (one having many stores), whether it is in food, consumer goods or any other commodity, is as shown in Figure 3.1.

In essence, the acquisition and resale process consists of these five steps:

1 *Supply:* Suppliers produce the product, whether it be 'branded' and sold with the supplier's name on the pack or 'own label' sold with the retailer's name on the pack.

2 *Buy:* The retailer's 'commercial' team, the buyers, set the strategy for what the retailer is going to sell (what it will *range*, in the retailer's terminology), the cost of goods it is prepared to give to its suppliers and the price it will set for customers to pay. This means in practice that the buyers set the means for the retailer to be successful or otherwise, which is dependent on other functions to do their part fully and efficiently – prompt store deliveries, fully stocked shelves and so on. There is often a separate supply chain department, which sets forecasts for products.

3 *Distribute:* Major retailers now operate their own distribution centre system, because it allows them to range many more

FIGURE 3.1 Multiple retailer product acquisition and resale process

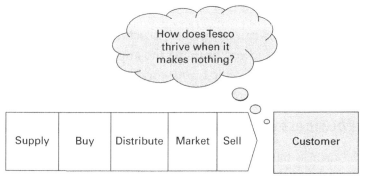

NOTE The 'Market' segment has been added to the way Tesco conventionally used this model, as its inclusion reflects the full 'value chain' idea coined by Porter (1985)

stock-keeping units (SKUs) – a consumer item sold as a single has a different SKU to say a three-pack of the same product – than if suppliers delivered direct to each store.

4 *Market:* The brand image of the retailer – the emotion and trust associated with the company selling the products to the customer – is becoming increasingly important as part of the value mix customers are seeking. However, after all the advertising and hype, the fundamental question is whether the shopping experience matches or exceeds expectations so that the customer wants to return and shop again the next time with the retailer.

5 *Sell:* The retailers' stores, and now online channels, present products to customers to select and buy to meet their needs. A retailer has a benefit if it can offer a wide, appropriate range of goods that are wanted by consumers, as this will help it secure a bigger proportion of individual consumer spend. Given that the major supermarkets offer the same assortment of branded products and very similar own-label ranges, it can be argued that the ranges are essentially commoditized, with few or no unique selling points.

This in essence is the business Tesco is in. It's a retailer, yes – but also more than that. It is about managing and coordinating its logistics as well, across the whole supply chain, from raw materials right through to the customer. Thus systems that allow retailers, like Tesco, to:

- understand what consumers want, and sense changing wants as they arise,
- ensure timely reordering and deliveries to store to replenish shelves to avoid any stock-outs, and
- ensure the whole supply chain is optimized from raw material, or packaging production, through to final product delivery at the end of the chain of supply

– will cause consumers to differentiate the service offered by an individual retailer if it develops the capabilities to do this better. This in turn may tempt customers to become more loyal, it can be argued.

The customer may also appreciate clean stores, rapid checkout, the range of facilities and the wider shopping experience offered, in addition to the products on sale, of course.

Thus, the business of retailing is just the customer face of the business of managing the supply chain. It is the output of the supply chain that the customer sees, and if the chain of supply can be managed in a superior way then this has the potential to become a source of competitive advantage if it enables a more 'convenient' (however this may be defined by each customer) shopping experience in terms of range of goods on sale, shelves stocked so product is available, a great in-store or online experience, and prices customers feel offer them a good deal.

Therefore, we can conceive of Tesco, as well as being a retailer, as actually being the operator of a retail supply chain. The retail supply chain, in short, can be conceived of as a 'convenience factory', and that is the business Tesco is ultimately in: sensing and providing convenient solutions to customers' needs.

And why?

Leahy was passionate about the *why*. At the heart of Tesco's thinking is this very simple belief. In essence it surrounds the premise that Tesco *will* compete on understanding and providing customer value, *not* with trying to beat its competitors, *nor* with optimizing short-term profits. This means, as we have seen, that the only inhabitant of its core purpose is *the customer*. It can be asked how many other organizations can actually claim this. So, for Tesco, its primary reason for existence is encapsulated in its overall mission statement, its 'core purpose': 'to create value for customers to earn their lifetime loyalty'. Critically, this means that effectiveness (providing what Tesco sets out to do and thus what the customer expects) is never jeopardized when chasing efficiency gains.

As briefly touched upon in Chapter 1, this core purpose was remarkable in that it was different from that of most other companies at the time. Kaplan and Norton (2008) suggest that the mission statement is a 'brief, typically one-sentence, statement that defines the fundamental purpose of the organisation... it should include what the organisation provides to its clients and inform executives and employees about the overall goal they have come to pursue'.

By these criteria Tesco's statement of core purpose articulated that the customer was at the heart of the business, around which all activities and decisions would be oriented, so executives and employees were clear about the overall goal. It did not mention profit, nor the needs of other stakeholders, the inference being that if customers were served well then their repeated custom would ensue, and increased top-line and then bottom-line rewards would consequently flow. It stated firmly that the company had to be about sensing and delivering effective solutions for customers. Finally, it left any detailed definitions out, so was flexible in terms of how 'value', for instance, could be defined or identifying the fields of business that Tesco might choose to operate in.

In an era when customers were beginning to be provided with more choice, through the acceleration of globalization, and were about to get more informed through the spread of the internet, it was beginning to be acknowledged that customers were going to develop a more powerful voice in terms of what products were provided for them and how those products were supplied. By acknowledging this and placing the customer at the heart of the Tesco mission, a defining step to articulate what Tesco was now about had been taken.

Underpinning the statement of core purpose, Leahy also confirmed two company values: 'No one tries harder for customers' and 'Treat people how we like to be treated.' These were explained further (see Table 3.1) and were a key aspect that Leahy felt strongly represented what the culture of Tesco should be all about, irrespective of the strategy of the day. These two values addressed Tesco aspirations for customers and people (employees). They reflected that in Tesco everything starts with the customer, with the passion to provide customers with value and service overriding all else, and that Tesco employees should be well managed and work in an environment that is based on trust and respect. Tesco believed that 'well motivated and managed staff will give customers great service: by living the people values we create a good place to work and one where great service is delivered'.

In his book *Management in 10 Words* (2012), Leahy devoted a whole chapter to the subject of values, stating that 'strong values underpin successful businesses. They give managers a sheet anchor, something that holds that position and keeps them from being

TABLE 3.1 Tesco's values in the Leahy era

'No one tries harder for customers'	'Treat people how we like to be treated'
Understand customers better than anyone.	All retailers, there's one team... the Tesco Team.
Be energetic, be innovative and be the first for customers.	Give support to each other and praise more than criticize.
Use our strength to deliver unbeatable value to our customers.	Ask more than tell, and share knowledge so that it can be used.
Look after our people so they can look after our customers.	Trust and respect each other.
	Strive to do our very best.
	Enjoy work, celebrate success and learn from experience.

smashed against the rocks and caught in the storm. Values govern how a business behaves, what it sees as important, what it does when faced with a problem', and that 'companies usually fail when they lose sight of their values and start to make decisions solely on the basis of short-term gain and profit'.

The Tesco culture of old was dominated by power struggles between colleagues: he described it as 'brutal, tough and uncultured – but full of energy and drive'. Leahy was determined through these new values not only to support the company's core purpose, but also to signal that the company was now very different: a company with a 'sense of equity and confidence', he stated.

So, for Leahy, the *why* was all about getting a better deal for customers by way of an organization that would aim to do the right thing for them in a confident and fair manner. This subject will be covered more fully in Chapter 4.

Where are we going?

Most firms operate in a largely unbounded landscape, so it is vital that leaders clearly state the scope that they feel their company should operate within.

In Chapter 2 we explained the areas of business Leahy intended Tesco to be in during his reign as CEO. This 'statement of primary strategy' (in Tesco's terms, its 'goals') addressed the question 'Where are we going?' Tesco was going to be:

- '*The number one choice [retailer] in the UK:* At the time we [Tesco] were still second behind Marks & Spencer and had only recently overtaken Sainsbury's. Most observers thought that our lead was temporary – particularly with the Walmart whale swimming our way.'

- '*As strong in non-food products as food:* In 1997 non-food represented only 3 per cent of overall sales.'

- '*Developing a profitable retail services business* (such as finance or telecommunications): In 1996, Tesco offered no such services at all.'

- '*As strong internationally as domestically:* In 1997 Tesco only had one per cent of space overseas (and were planning to sell that the next year).'

Interestingly, this was merely a statement of intent in terms of areas that Leahy wanted Tesco to operate in with associated targets; there was no attempt to set out how these aims would be attained in this part of the strategic framework.

Another boundary, which was key to setting Tesco's thinking apart from that of many of its competitors, surrounded how it defined its supply chain interest. During the Leahy era, Tesco was never delimited by its current assets in delivering value for its customers. The question that was always asked was: 'How do we best serve customers with convenient solutions that will be valued by them?' rather than 'How do we best serve customers with convenient solutions that will be valued by them *from the stores we run*?' A crucial difference.

What are the key issues that our strategy must address?

These key issues are addressed in Tesco's operating plan. The operating plan sets out what Tesco aims to achieve over say the ensuing two- to three-year period, changing periodically, while the surrounding corporate framework and statement of primary strategy remain constant, thus providing continuity and a solid foundation for the organization's long-term direction.

Much store was set by selecting the correct objectives for any one period: only the ones that would make the greatest difference were chosen. In any business there are always improvements that can be made, for instance to processes or the customer experience. However, if organizations are not careful they can be drowned by initiatives, losing sight of the day-to-day objective of running the business. Other problems include improvements being made to one area of business but not applied across the whole business and the inability many organizations have to sustain advances, as changes quickly fall away without being embedded into the way the business operates.

Tesco's emphasis was to avoid these problems. Each year only the best few projects were chosen to be taken forward, with as a consequence an appropriate sum of investment being made available to go into making these changes happen on time and across the business. Clear accountability would also be given to a named individual to deliver each improvement, with the roles of all colleagues who would be either directly or indirectly involved in each project being made clear through the RACI idea (see the box below).

To select the best projects, in what became known as the 'Step Change Plan', the three business principles characterized in the slogan 'Better, simpler, cheaper', derived from three seminal books introduced in Chapter 1 (*The Loyalty Effect* by Frederick F Reichheld, 1996; *Simplicity* by Edward de Bono, 1998; and *Lean Thinking* by James Womack and Daniel Jones, 1996, 2003) were used to evaluate the merits of each one. So for each prospective project the question was asked – was it:

- better for customers?
- simpler for colleagues?
- cheaper for Tesco?

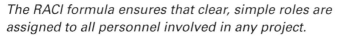

RACI

The RACI formula ensures that clear, simple roles are assigned to all personnel involved in any project.

Tesco has found that having more than one person accountable for a project can lead to the possibility that the project is not seen through to a successful end. So singular accountability is an important aspect of project delivery – **A**.

The accountable leader then has a team who are responsible for carrying out the project – **R**. The team could be spread over multiple locations and functions or divisions across the company.

Other roles include those who need to be consulted, but who also do not need to take an active part in the project – **C**.

There are also those who need to be informed of how the project is progressing and of any outcomes – **I**.

Role clarity ensures time is spent productively with wasted effort minimized!

If new initiatives did not satisfy all three of these principles, they were not taken up as business projects for the coming period.

Importantly, this meant that the pursuit of efficiency alone did not become an obsession. Ensuring customers were satisfied was deemed to be critical, another testament to the way Tesco thought and acted differently at the time: it was more about improving effectiveness rather than efficiency.

To ensure that operating plan goals and associated projects were balanced across the spectrum of the organization over any set period of time Kaplan and Norton's (1996) balanced scorecard approach, which Tesco has termed the Steering Wheel, was adopted. This ensured that the views of all stakeholders were incorporated into the way Tesco conducted itself. As well as customers, core stakeholder segments of this balanced approach included people (Tesco employees), operations, shareholders (financial) (see Figure 3.2) and from 2007 a fifth increasingly important element – the community and environment. This was to reflect the growing importance of acting responsibly in all aspects of business – being a good neighbour at stores and distribution centres, the environmental impacts of operations,

FIGURE 3.2 The Tesco Steering Wheel – the original four-segment format

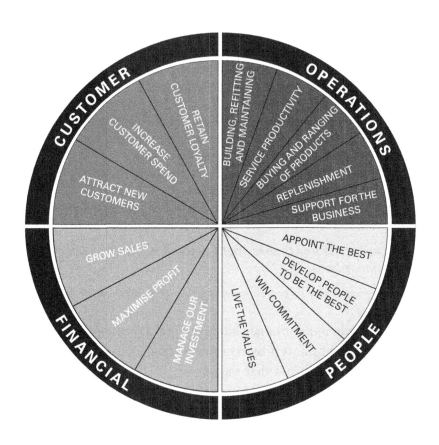

and minimizing or eliminating Tesco's contribution to global warming. The modified Steering Wheel is shown in Figure 3.3. For each segment, short-, medium- and long-term statements of intent and improvement objectives were set, occasionally being refined so they fitted into the overall corporate framework.

For planning purposes clear decisions were taken to select initiatives that would have the biggest impact on the objectives at the heart of each of these segments of the balanced scorecard and effort and resources dedicated accordingly. Through the 'Better, simpler cheaper' test, if an initiative did not contribute to these Steering Wheel objectives, or even did not contribute enough, it was not pursued.

FIGURE 3.3 The Tesco Steering Wheel – incorporating the additional 'Community' segment from 2007

In this way, as well as employees' ongoing focus on the core operation, priority tasks that all fed into the strategic development of Tesco were identified and pursued. Tesco could thus be confident in focusing on effectively meeting customer needs, with the capability to deliver for them as well as securing consequent effectiveness and efficiency improvements. In short, the Tesco Steering Wheel was a smart mechanism to avoid the 'unintended consequences' that bedevil the improvement activity in many businesses.

How can we best compete?

Developing a strategy and setting out how a company wishes to operationalize itself is one thing. Ensuring the company is constantly on track in achieving what it aims to do, whether that is in its conduct of day-to-day business operations right across the organization or delivering strategic projects on time and on budget, is another significant challenge for a company the size of Tesco. Again, the Tesco Steering Wheel helped to indicate to everyone whether Tesco was on track.

Some organizations use a balanced scorecard method to monitor their business, and others to help strategically manage it. Tesco however use it both strategically and operationally – to strategize and refine, as we have seen, and to implement and manage.

Whether targets set for each segment of the Steering Wheel were being achieved or not was indicated visually by utilizing a 'traffic lights' mechanism for reporting progress against each objective and each project or programme aimed at delivering these objectives. Thus:

- green indicated 'on track';
- amber indicated 'caution', that a correction was needed;
- red indicated 'warning', that significant deviation was likely and review with major remedial action was required; and
- blue indicated a significant over-performance, which could be causing a red in another area of the Steering Wheel.

This colour coding gave very rapid visual leads both to the reader of Steering Wheel reports and to Tesco staff who were greeted by the large wall-mounted versions as they entered their respective places of work.

The Steering Wheel also acted as a critical communication device, as it is cascaded hierarchically, with Steering Wheels tailored to each audience (containing only the information relevant to that part of the business) throughout the organization, visible to every employee. Thus there were for example corporate, store and distribution centre versions containing information tailored to the specific roles and responsibilities. This ensured that the decisions and actions of all employees were well aligned with the overall objectives of Tesco.

So Tesco's corporate framework was fundamentally supported by Tesco's Steering Wheel, which stood the test of time and remained virtually unaltered throughout Leahy's 14-year tenure as CEO.

The key message asserted here is that Tesco took a holistic view of how it wished to compete. There was an appreciation that there are inherent trade-offs in managing any enterprise system that need to be understood and managed as a whole if the stated core purpose is to be consistently achieved. So, while there was a very singular core purpose focused on the customer, it would be wrong to conclude that the company was dangerously myopic. While the primary emphasis on providing superior customer value was paramount, this aspiration was integrated with Tesco's need to provide for all its other major stakeholders, which it regarded as critical if it was to be able to sustain its ultimate purpose.

In summary, the 'Tesco Way', which has been described here, developed and followed during Leahy's tenure as CEO, showed that Tesco had moved a long way during the 1990s in designing, developing and implementing an integrated set of mechanisms to deliver its strategic focus. This can be seen schematically in Figure 3.4.

So Tesco's management of its standard retail supply chain should be conceived of within this overarching corporate framework, which guided all decision making. The capability to deliver continual

FIGURE 3.4 The Tesco Way – delivering value for customers

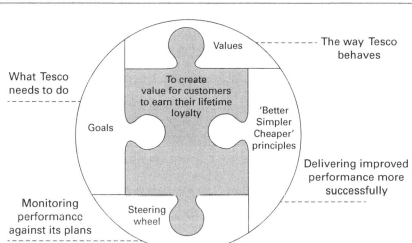

improvements in value during the Leahy years was possible only because of the strength and resilience that this corporate framework provided. The corporate framework was used then to shape Tesco's approach to managing its core business model, which is the five-stage process, introduced earlier – its supply chain – while the mechanism that holds everything together is the Tesco Steering Wheel.

Through the Leahy years, by being highly disciplined in not departing from this overall corporate framework, Tesco remained focused on how it identified its organizational boundaries and how it conducted its business. Tesco's business model, as has been described, is a standard supply–buy–distribute–market–sell retail value chain, yet Tesco competes by surrounding this with its corporate framework, which contains haloes of differentiation potential. From 1997 to 2011 Tesco did not reinvent this corporate framework, but concentrated on learning how best to refine it so that it could be applied to maximum effect. This approach provided the continuity of united purpose from which the organization hugely benefited, a core strength that was at the heart of the Tesco philosophy (Figure 3.5).

FIGURE 3.5   The Tesco corporate framework that surrounds its business model

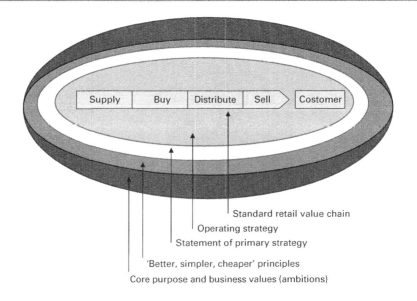

Standard retail value chain
Operating strategy
Statement of primary strategy
'Better, simpler, cheaper' principles
Core purpose and business values (ambitions)

Conclusion – the Leahy era

So, for Tesco, strategy in its widest sense was and is a multi-dimensional concept, better described as a 'strategic framework' – Tesco termed it the 'corporate framework'. As we have seen it contained:

- a hierarchy of statements flowing from Tesco's core purpose and values (why we are here and what we believe in);
- a statement of primary strategy (what the scope of our business is), which largely remained in place year after year;
- the operating plan (how we are going to achieve our ambitions), which articulates a series of goals that are updated periodically;
- the Steering Wheel, which acted as a strategic, monitoring and communication tool to support the strategy in a disciplined way and to ensure it was balanced across the business.

Tesco's corporate framework has commonalities with the 'Hierarchy of Company Statements' articulated in Collis and Rukstad's seminal 2008 paper 'Can You Say What Your Strategy Is?' They suggest that 'Organizational direction comes in many forms. The mission statement is your loftiest guiding light and your least specific. As you make your way down the hierarchy the statements get more concrete and more practical and ultimately unique.' Tesco's framework follows this pattern.

Collis and Rukstad (2008) also argued that all firms should have a statement of ultimate purpose and ethical values by which they operate. This indicates: doing things right, in terms of employee behaviour; and the right thing to do, guiding a firm's actions. But, they assert, 'your competitive advantage is the real essence of a strategy'. In many ways it is how Tesco does things that is the real essence of its advantage in our view. Collis and Rukstad put forward the following analogy to highlight this. Imagine your business as a mound of iron filings, each one representing an employee. By passing a magnet over the filings they line up, all pointing in the same direction. Tesco's strategy lined everyone up so that they were aligned behind a common goal. The power of this approach in allowing the company success-fully to compete and grow proved to be considerable. What Tesco provided in the Leahy era was an excellent example of how this could be interpreted and applied successfully over an extended period.

Evolution or revolution in Tesco's strategic approach

From March 2011, when Leahy was replaced by Philip Clarke as Chief Executive, the question most commentators asked was whether there would be fundamental changes to the 'Tesco Way'. On one hand, for Clarke, with a background of working solely for Tesco and closely with Leahy for many years on the board, suggested the answer would be no. In addition, Clarke's early statements that there would not be a change of direction added weight to this conclusion.

However, it is clear that, after Clarke's three year's tenure as Tesco CEO, certain quite fundamental changes in strategy emerged. The next section of the chapter tries to identity them and to ask how they affected Tesco's supply chain thinking and operation management.

How did Tesco's strategy change?

A 'strategic framework' was still deployed, with a few structural changes, as we will point out. In content too, there were some alter-ations. For example, Tesco's revised core purpose and values were revealed in 2012, and the changes are shown in Table 3.2.

Core purpose

The first change that became apparent is that the headline mission for Tesco altered: 'Our Core Purpose is a clear and simple statement of what we do and what we stand for: *We make what matters better, together*.' This was a substantial change that occurred right at the heart of the Tesco business. In some ways it reflected the reality that any company has many stakeholders, not one, the customer, and thus

TABLE 3.2 How Tesco's core purpose and values changed over time

Original as at 2000	Revised, as in annual report 2012
Core purpose:	*Core purpose:*
To create value for customers to earn their lifetime loyalty.	To make what matters better, together.
Tesco values:	*Our values help us to understand how to put this into practice:*
Our values are our code of conduct – they are the way we have chosen to work at Tesco and drive the whole way we do business. They are:	As one of the world's largest retailers with over 530,000 colleagues, we serve millions of customers a week in our stores and online.
1. *No one tries harder for customers.*	1. *No one tries harder for customers.*
– Understand customers better than anyone.	– Understand customers.
– Be energetic, be innovative and be first for customers.	– Be first to meet their needs.
– Use our strengths to deliver unbeatable value to our customers.	– Act responsibly for our communities.
– Look after our people so they can look after our customers.	Understanding people – customers, colleagues, communities – and what matters to them, and then trying to make those things better, is at the heart of Tesco. It's about listening to people and talking to
These customer values reflect that in Tesco everything starts with the customer and that our passion to provide customers with value and service overrides all else.	them using all the tools at our disposal, from Clubcard data to social media, and then acting by changing and innovating to meet their needs.

(continued)

TABLE 3.2 (continued)

Original as at 2000	Revised, as in annual report 2012
2. *Treat people how we like to be treated.*	2. *We treat everyone how we like to be treated.*
– All retailers, there's one team… the Tesco Team.	– Work as a team.
– Trust and respect each other.	– Trust and respect each other.
– Strive to do our very best.	– Listen, support and say thank you.
– Give support to each other and praise more than criticize.	– Share knowledge and experience.
– Ask more than tell and share knowledge so that it can be used.	We know that looking after our colleagues in a culture of trust and respect is essential to the success of Tesco. Where colleagues feel
– Enjoy work, celebrate success and learn from experience.	recognized and rewarded for the work they do together, where they
We want our people to be well managed and to work in an	have the opportunity to get on and where they are supported in their
environment that is based on trust and respect. We have	development as they move through their careers in the business –
learnt over the years that well-motivated and managed staff	they in turn try their hardest for customers.
will give customers great service: by living the people values	
we create a good place to work and one where great	
service is delivered.	

3. *We use our scale for good.*

- Creating new opportunities for millions of young people around the world.
- Helping and encouraging our colleagues and customers to live healthier lives and through this helping to tackle the global obesity crisis.
- Leading in reducing food waste globally.

Our scale means that we can provide affordable, high-quality food to people around the world and create value for customers. We want to use this scale to create greater value for society as a whole. In many ways we do this already, whether it's by creating thousands of jobs or working with thousands of farmers to provide world-class products. But now we want to scale up our efforts and make a positive contribution to some of the most pressing challenges facing the world.

the core purpose should be more adaptive to address all stakeholders' expectations. Tesco itself argues that the change reflected 'how much business has changed in recent years – more scepticism about corporations, more desire to see business demonstrate it has a purpose beyond profit, a sense that large companies should be contributing more to tackling some of the big challenges. The world has changed from a culture of "more is better" to "making what matters better"'.[1]

Tesco went on to say: 'Our new Core Purpose is true to where we came from but more relevant to today and to the kind of company we want to be.' The obvious concern is that the singular focus that Tesco had, 'to create value for customers to earn their lifetime loyalty', had gone. We have argued that this focused mission gave Tesco an ability to be fully aligned with a purpose that chimed with the marketing concept and the goal of supply chain management excellence. However, even in Leahy's era a fifth segment had been added to the Steering Wheel, which highlighted that modern corporations should conceive of themselves in terms of why they exist in a wider sense than just doing good for their customers; they must give as much back to wider society than they take too, and this new core purpose allowed room for this view to be incorporated into what the modern Tesco was all about.

In addition, there is an argument that the mission for any business is in fact to maximize shareholder value. If it is to attract more investment, a company like Tesco has certainly got to show that it is responsibly managing itself from a financial perspective and showing the degree of capital discipline that is sought. The company arguably had a reputation that it was too aggressively spending on expansion. But now, guided by this broader core purpose, decisions such as the ones to withdraw from the United States and enter an interesting joint venture agreement in China showed that Tesco was able to rein back on capital expenditure on expansion.

Company values

Two of Tesco's values remained unchanged, and even the underpinning statements, although slightly different, could really be explained by Tesco's ongoing obsession to state things as clearly and as simply as possible. So, for instance, 'All retailers, there's one team... the Tesco Team' became 'Work as a team.'

Beyond this tidying up of the first two company values, a third value was now added.

'We use our scale for good'

This extra value reflected the aim that Tesco should continue, perhaps redouble, its efforts to contribute to the societies in which it traded to make a really positive difference. Tesco viewed that given its success it now could and should not only generate value for its customers, but enlarge this aim 'to create value for society as a whole'.

A vision for Tesco

Clarke added a 'vision' statement to Leahy's original 'strategic framework'. In some ways this reflected how big and dispersed Tesco had now become and the need to articulate more clearly what the business stood for. In other ways it illustrated the changes that occurred during the Leahy years and indicated the aspirations of what Clarke wanted Tesco to represent in the future (see Table 3.3).

The theme of growth had clearly emerged during the Leahy era and now became formally adopted as a core aspect of the vision of what Tesco aspires to be. The vision statements also set out a whole range of qualities that Tesco should aim to be associated with, such as being 'modern and innovative' and 'full of ideas'. The concept that the skills learnt across the business should be applied locally and adapted to each market in which it traded was also highlighted.

In addition, the vision statements helped guide the direction and decisions that Tesco would take and thus in some ways were a replacement for the 'Better, simpler, cheaper' principles that had guided the direction and decision making in the Leahy era.

Statement of primary strategy – Tesco's goals

Here too Clarke refined and added to Leahy's four original goals. This is summarized in Table 3.4. The four goals established by Leahy remained, albeit slightly altered. To these, three new goals were added.

TABLE 3.3 Tesco's vision as at spring 2014

'Wanted and needed around the world'	'We see it as essential not only to be the shop of choice for customers but also the place people want to work, a business that communities welcome and the retailer in which every shareholder wants to invest.'
'A growing business, full of opportunities'	'Whether it's food or general merchandise, books or digital entertainment, banking or eating out, our business is full of opportunities for both customers and colleagues. We want our business to offer something new every time.'
'Modern, innovative and full of ideas'	'Tesco's success has always been based on trying to understand customers' needs better than anyone else – and then innovating to make their lives that little bit easier. This attitude, which brought online grocery shopping, extended shopping hours, Finest, Everyday Value, a range of formats from Express to Extra – and all the other things that make us who we are – is as central to our Vision now as it ever has been.'
'Winners locally whilst applying our skills globally'	'Retail is local because cultures, tastes, climates, regulations are all different. But the core skills that we have learned in one place can be applied in others. For example, setting up our grocery home shopping operations from scratch in eight international markets across the Group wouldn't have been possible without what we've learned in the UK.'
'Inspiring, earning trust and loyalty from customers, our colleagues and communities'	'We want Tesco to be a company that earns trust, not just respect, through everything we do – be it our in-store shopping trip, our Price Promise, or our determination to assure customers on food quality. We want to be a business that customers, colleagues and communities trust and are loyal to.'

SOURCE Tesco (2013b)

The first, 'To put our responsibilities to the communities we serve at the heart of what we do', reflected this wider new value for Tesco that had emerged over recent years, which was now been fully endorsed

TABLE 3.4 Comparison of Tesco's statements of primary strategy (goals) under Leahy and Clarke

Under Leahy	Under Clarke
'The number one choice [retailer] in the UK: At the time we [Tesco] were still second behind Marks and Spencer and had only recently overtaken Sainsbury's. Most observers thought that our lead was temporary – particularly with the Walmart whale swimming our way.'	To grow the UK core, the largest business in the Group and a key driver of sales and profit, is a priority. Our "Building a Better Tesco" plan has been restoring growth to the business through a comprehensive series of improvements for customers.'
'As strong in non-food products as food: In 1997 non-food represented only 3 per cent of overall sales.'	'To be as strong in everything we sell as we are in food. Food is our heritage but as the business has grown and diversified over recent years, we have added an ever-wider range of products and services in-store and online, bringing Tesco value and quality to many more categories.'
'Developing a profitable retail services business (such as finance or telecommunications): In 1996, Tesco offered no such services at all.'	'To grow retail services in all our markets. Consumers are increasingly spending a bigger proportion of their income on services – whether it is in telecoms, eating out or financial services. In the UK, we have built some strong, successful new businesses and our ambition now is to take that experience to all of our markets.'
'As strong internationally as domestically: In 1997 Tesco only had one per cent of space overseas (and were planning to sell that the next year).'	'To be an outstanding international retailer in stores and online. We have established profitable businesses in Asian and European markets. Today, 32% of our Group sales and 29% of profits are made internationally and our goal now is to take the performance of these businesses to higher levels.'

(continued)

TABLE 3.4 (continued)

Under Leahy	Under Clarke
	'To put our responsibilities to the communities we serve at the heart of what we do. The changes we have made to our Core Purpose and Values to reflect Tesco's wider social purpose are clear signals that we put our responsibilities to the communities we serve at the heart of what we do.'
	'To be a creator of highly valued brands. Brands are about giving customers confidence in the quality, value and reliability of the things we sell. We aim to be a creator of highly valued brands across our offer, whether it is Finest, F&F [Florence and Fred Clothing] or Tesco Bank.'
	'To build our team so that we create more value. As Tesco continues to grow and diversify we need more leaders to run the broad range of businesses, operations and support functions. We are investing in the development of more leaders and a bigger, more diverse talent pool to support the growth of the Group.'

SOURCE Leahy (2012: 80–81); Tesco (2013b)

as part of Tesco's primary strategy. 'Community' was added as an extra segment on the Steering Wheel from 2007. Its inclusion here further validated the importance the company placed on its corporate citizenship role.

The second new goal, 'To be a creator of highly valued brands', reflected how substantial the various segments of business had now become within Tesco. It also signalled that, if each brand were closely managed with a well-thought-through strategy, even more can be gleaned from each one. It reflected how Tesco was aiming to differentiate itself as a 'house of brands', home-grown and tailored to the markets it served, whether they be product brands like Finest and F&F, service brands like Tesco Mobile or Tesco Bank, or store brands such as Express, or Tesco Lotus in South Korea. The coffee house brand Harris + Hoole, the restaurant brand Giraffe and the digital entertainment brand Blinkbox were also examples of this strategy, where virtually unknown brands were brought in and then scaled up as a Tesco offer. Finally, the Hudl could also be classed as a new Tesco brand.

The last extra goal was a people-oriented one: 'To build our team so that we create more value'. Again, 'people' was always a clear segment on Leahy's Steering Wheel, so this was not new. What was different was the emphasis given and the importance Tesco clearly placed on leadership and employee development to manage and operate the future business. After all, the company had grown very, very quickly, meaning that many of its leaders were probably managing bigger portfolios than would have been envisaged 10, 20 or 30 years ago when some may have started in the company. For a service organization, with over 530,000 people in 2014, employee relations were clearly a significant aspect to manage well too.

In summary, the new business goals represented an extension of remit from that of the Leahy era, but they clearly still delineated what the businesses were that the company aimd to be in. For each, the supply chain process was a crucial part of the jigsaw to get them consistently performing in the right way.

The operating plan

We have already reviewed a number of the current 'operating plans' in Chapter 2 when we looked at how Tesco was changing under Clarke. A clear focus and decision making rooted in the core purpose and vision statements of the business could clearly be seen, for instance in its plans to refocus on the UK core business, the development and growth of Tesco Bank, the move to build a digital entertainment business, the relaunch of the Value and Finest ranges, or the international decisions in the United States, China, India and other countries. The same rigour and purposefulness that were a hallmark of Tesco under Leahy can clearly be seen under the new regime too, for the most part.

Beyond the operating plans a new business model had been developed that had clearly been developed from the 'Tesco Way' we highlighted earlier, but now presented in a much more sophisticated manner (Figure 3.6).

At its core was the core purpose, and this was surrounded by the core activities: 'insight', 'buy', 'move' and 'sell'. These replaced the business

FIGURE 3.6   The revised Tesco business model under Clarke

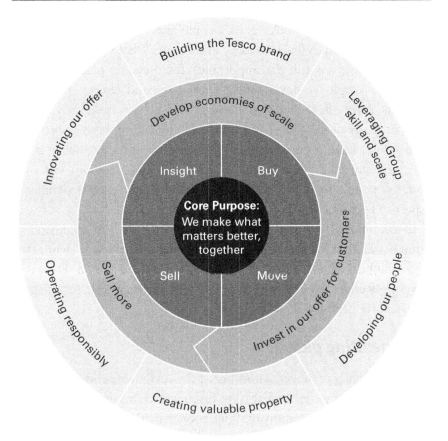

SOURCE Tesco corporate website

model raised earlier: 'supply, buy, distribute and sell', to which we had added 'market'. This shift reflected the focus on customer insight that Tesco had done so much to develop and learn from and acknowledged that predominantly Tesco was not in the 'supply' game. In summary, the core activities of the basic business model had shifted to be closer to the customer.

Interestingly, the next circle of the business model dealt more fully with Collis and Rukstad's (2008) challenge that by spelling out a company's competitive advantage you are dealing with the essential part of strategy. The business model alluded to the fact that a 'virtuous circle' had been developed: if Tesco 'invests in its offer for customers' it will 'sell more'; if it 'sells more' it will 'develop economies of scale' and so will be able to 'invest more in its offer for customers' and so on. Finally, to enable all this, six key enablers were identified:

- 'Building the Tesco brand';
- 'Leveraging group skill and scale';
- 'Developing our people';
- 'Creating valuable property';
- 'Operating responsibly';
- 'Innovating our offer'.

Tesco now had over 500 directors, and the group felt it was developing the in-house experience to be able to translate the inherent experience that had been amassed to projects and programmes across its businesses.

Conclusion – the Clarke era

In the three years Clarke led Tesco, the 'strategy framework' evolved considerably. Many of the hallmarks that were evident in the Leahy era were still evident. For instance, much of the basic structure of the 'framework' was still apparent: core purpose, company values, statement of primary strategy, operating plan goals and so on.

But added to this was an extra level of sophistication. This partly reflected the size that Tesco had become. It also indicated the need to show all stakeholders that they were valued – there could be a debate whether this meant that customers were not quite the absolute focus of the business that they once represented; nevertheless, perhaps in the cycle of any system a balance has to be regained if it was going off-kilter, and this could be an argument for saying that this was a good thing although as authors we would debate this. Finally, the extra sophistication could reflect that a deeper understanding of what the Tesco business had become was being developed. Interestingly, as far as this book is concerned the following statement makes a powerful point: 'Striving for continuous improvement in operations and in the shopping trip, as well as staying close to customers, are fundamentals but the engine of the Tesco business model has always been a combination of scale and growth.'[2]

Much of this book is about continuous improvement of a core process: Tesco's supply chain. But the importance of growth and, following from this, scale should not be forgotten in the assessment of Tesco's fundamental competitive advantage capabilities.

Key chapter summary points

1 The Tesco strategy framework has been developed as a hierarchy of statements.

2 The highly focused 'core purpose' in the Leahy era has been replaced by a more flexible and more widely applicable mission under Clarke.

3 The statement of primary strategy remained constant throughout the Leahy era, providing a great platform of continuity for the group. Although this has been added to, the four pillars of Leahy's statement remain intact today.

4 Tesco is very clear what business it is in, where it is going and what is the source of its competitive advantage. This provides a secure platform from which the group can plan and execute

the management of people, processes and assets to generate continuous improvement.

Notes

1 tinyurl.com/pf633sq, accessed 11 February 2014
2 tinyurl.com/lswd7kh, accessed 12 February 2014

Customer insight, to drive the Tesco supply chain

A company's primary responsibility is to serve its customers. Profit is not the primary goal, but rather an essential condition for the company's continued existence. **(DRUCKER, 1954)**

Introduction

It can be argued that, in retail, a crucial ingredient of success is having an absolute customer focus – that is, being able to identify shoppers' requirements and from this insight make decision after decision to change things to make shopping easier or more convenient for those customers. For Tesco this idea actually defines *why* it exists. So Tesco management and employees would fully agree with Drucker's words in recognizing that its 'primary responsibility is to serve its customers'. By fully taking on this mission Tesco has developed expertise in what it means to be customer driven. This chapter reflects on this.

Tesco understands that without customers its organization would not survive for long. But it is not the fear of losing customers that spurs its ambitions on. Under Leahy's leadership, continued under Clarke and now Lewis, Tesco strove to get better and better at proactively identifying customers' needs, hearing even what they did not say, and more and more capable of quickly delivering actions that offered improved value to win over more and more customers.

Thus, aiming for customers' long-term satisfaction so that they will return time after time would seem to be a laudable goal: hence the core purpose slogan, used throughout the Leahy years, 'to create value for customers to earn their lifetime loyalty'. Tesco is not perfect – the horsemeat scandal in 2013 and the accounting problems in 2014 are testament to this – but can pass on many lessons learnt from its real commitment over many years to being primarily customer driven. For other companies that again and again find that talking the talk in this regard is easier than putting a customer-driven ethos into practical effect, Tesco's experience in putting a customer orientation into action across its group can provide valuable insights into what can be achieved.

'Value' is a fundamental term in management. As a concept it 'is an ancient one that has existed for many centuries, largely developed by philosophers and economists' (Brennan and Henneberg, 2008). Today, the goal of providing value for customers is an ideal that is at the heart of many management disciplines; for instance, it is the core objective of supply chain management, logistics management, Lean thinking and agile management, to name but a few domains and paradigms, as well as, of course, the marketing discipline. Indeed, it is this shared objective that can help bring many departments within a company together, aligned around a common endeavour.

This united focus is what Tesco began to achieve in the Leahy era when the stakeholders with competing needs from those of the organization were asked to take a subordinate role in the objective hierarchy to the primacy of providing continuously improved customer value propositions. The argument proposed was that, if customers were happy, they would return time after time with their custom and would thus buy more with Tesco; the extra volume of business through the turnstiles of Tesco's tills would generate increased profits, if margins were maintained at a fairly constant rate.

This chapter examines the issue of identifying and delivering customer value. It first sets the scene by asking the simple question 'What is customer value?' This includes a discussion on what value looks like in the grocery supermarket sector, and how Tesco chooses to define value for its customers. We then focus on Figure 4.1, which step by step allows us to shed light on the Tesco approach. In essence this follows the sentiment expressed by Russell Ackoff (2010), who in the

FIGURE 4.1 Turning data to wisdom: sensing and meeting customer needs at Tesco

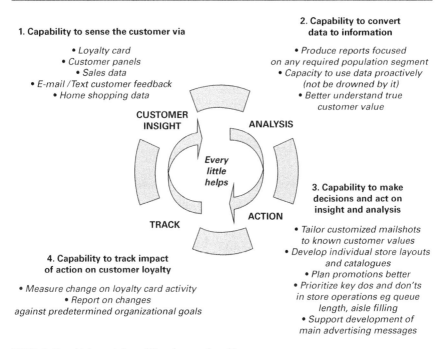

1. Capability to sense the customer via

- *Loyalty card*
- *Customer panels*
- *Sales data*
- *E-mail / Text customer feedback*
- *Home shopping data*

2. Capability to convert data to information

- *Produce reports focused on any required population segment*
- *Capacity to use data proactively (not be drowned by it)*
- *Better understand true customer value*

CUSTOMER INSIGHT

ANALYSIS

Every little helps

3. Capability to make decisions and act on insight and analysis

TRACK

ACTION

- *Tailor customized mailshots to known customer values*
- *Develop individual store layouts and catalogues*
- *Plan promotions better*
- *Prioritize key dos and don'ts in store operations eg queue length, aisle filling*
- *Support development of main advertising messages*

4. Capability to track impact of action on customer loyalty

- *Measure change on loyalty card activity*
- *Report on changes against predetermined organizational goals*

NOTE Authors' interpretation of Tesco's way of working

chapter 'Data to Wisdom' describes the journey of turning a 'planetful of data into a thimbleful of wisdom', summarizing this journey as:

Data → Information → Knowledge → Understanding → Wisdom

We show in this chapter how Tesco has attempted to move along this spectrum and faced up to the challenges the spectrum represents in the attempt to really act on its customers' behalf.

First, we examine how Tesco senses customers' needs and values. We then look at its capabilities to turn this insight data into useful information, before examining its capability to make decisions that act on this insight analysis. Finally, we look at how Tesco checks the effect of its decisions and consequent actions on its customers' behaviour.

In the Preface, we highlighted the marketer Theodore Levitt (1960), who stated: 'Management must think of itself not as producing products, but as providing customer-creating value satisfactions. It must push this idea (and everything it means and requires) into every nook and cranny of the organization. It has to do this continuously and with the kind of flair that excites and stimulates the people in it.' Tesco strives to do just this. Orientating the company around the customer has been the fundamental bedrock of Tesco's period of dominance as the UK; number one retailer since the mid-1990s. This chapter helps to uncover how Tesco organizes itself to sense the customer and meet the customer's needs.

What is customer value?

Today, in many sectors, customers have a greater number of choices available to them than arguably they have ever had. Ultimately, customers pay only for what gives them, in their perception, value, and their choice of supplier is dictated by what they perceive, in their acquirement–consumption experience, offers them the best overall value (Kotler *et al*, 2001). Customers, whether they are business customers or end consumers of products and services, are widely seen as the 'kings' or 'queens' of the product of supply chains, where optimizing their perceived value is the currency of their transaction thinking. Providing value for customers is the lifeblood of the organization – it is what customers expect and the reason for their custom.

But what customers consider of value to them is much more than the product. The customers' experience of value is made up of multiple dimensions. But what are these dimensions? Despite its central role in practice and in theory it would be incorrect to assume that an indisputable halo of understanding pervades the defining and conceptualizing of the value idea: far from it. For instance, in a study published in 2011 entitled 'The Value of Value', Gallarza, Gil-Saura and Holbrook (2011) state this: 'Despite the wide range of relevant theoretical and empirical works, the study of customer value continues to suffer from numerous remaining lacunae.' They go on to argue that this is because theorists face a range of conceptual, methodological and measurement problems. On the conceptual side they suggest that the notion of value is 'multifaceted and complex with different meanings not only among consumers and practitioners but also among researchers themselves'. Methodologically, they argue that primarily because of the multi-dimensionality of the value concept and because no consensus exists as to what represents these dimensions, 'the resulting proliferation of types and categories reflect as much about the imagination of the various researchers as they do about the fundamental nature of the value concept itself'. Finally, from a measurement perspective they suggest that as it is such a complex subject there has been a paucity of studies that have attempted to model and measure it. So much remains to be done in fleshing out the conceptualization, understanding and theorizing of the value concept.

However, although in a broad sense much needs to be done it should not be concluded that there have not been successes in developing the value concept. As noted earlier, although it is a nebulous and multi-faceted notion it is still core to many domains and as such has attracted much interest and thought. Developments of understanding have included some of the following ideas and associated topic areas.

Levitt (1968) identified the importance of understanding that products supplied to provide customer value can be broken down into two elements: tangible and intangible (Figure 4.2). Tangible

FIGURE 4.2 Using service to augment the core product

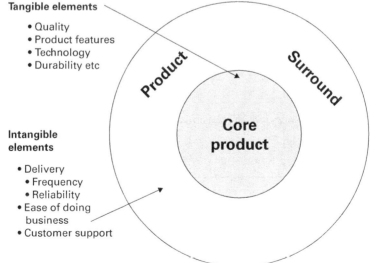

SOURCE Christopher (1992: 31) (after Levitt, 1968)

elements include the core product values, while the augmented product of the intangible elements includes the service surround that is provided along with the core product. This was picked up and developed by Christopher (1992), who argued that this is where the value of logistics and supply chain management lay and that it was in this intangible element that competitive advantage truly could be found – the product itself was more easily copied than the service provided.

Another important dimension was that of taking a holistic view and conceiving that cost minimization might not necessarily equate to value maximization. This can be explained through Johansson *et al*'s (1993) 'customer value criteria' (Figure 4.3). Value is composed of four elements, the aim being to increase quality and service, while minimizing costs and cycle time.

FIGURE 4.3   The value equation showing customer value criteria

Meeting customer requirements
Fitness for use
Process integrity
Minimum variances
Elimination of waste
Continuous improvement

Customer support
Product service
Product support
Flexibility to meet customer demands
Flexibility to meet market changes

$$Value = \frac{Quality \times Service}{Cost \times Cycle\ time}$$

Design and engineering
Conversion
Quality assurance
Distribution
Administration
Inventory
Materials

Time to market
  —Concept to delivery
Order entry to delivery
Response to market forces
Lead time
  —Design
  —Conversion
  —Engineering
  —Delivery
Materials
Inventory

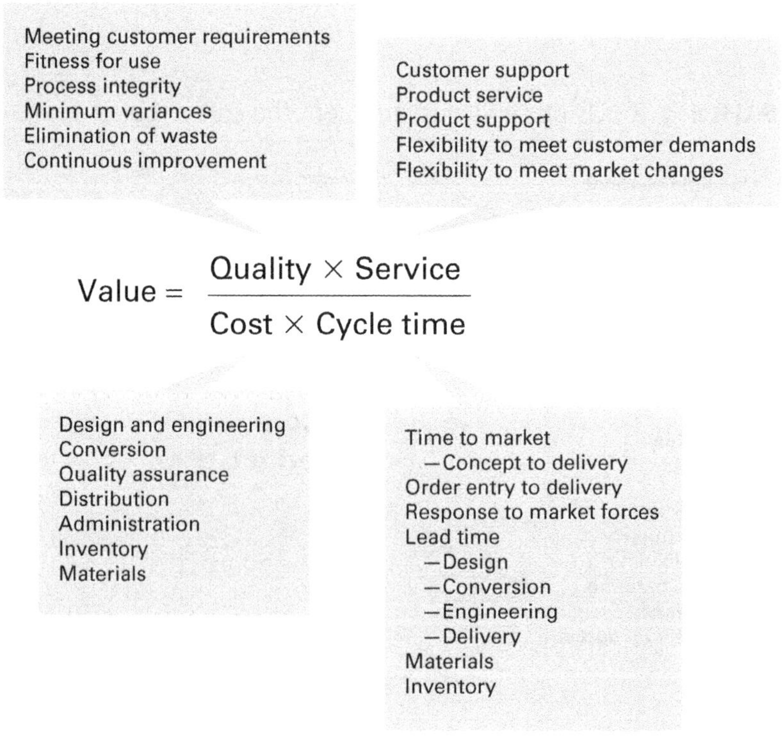

SOURCE Johansson *et al* (1993)

An alternative perspective on value was provided by Bowersox, Closs and Stank (2000), who stated that 'value is the measure of desire for a product and its related services'. They proposed that end customers have three value perspectives: low price, provided through efficiencies (*efficiency value*); *market value*, achieved through product service positioning, ie assortment and convenience; and *relevancy value*, providing value where, when and how the end customer wants it, accommodating the business and lifestyle of the consumer. They concluded that 'the provision of these combined values can be considered as the purpose of the firm'.

This argument is extended by the view that customer value is set within the multi-layered aspect of the customer experience. Meyer and Schwager (2007) suggest this understanding is vital to better appreciate the meaning of value, asserting that 'the customers' experience of value is made up of many dimensions'. Indeed, it is the customers' perception of value that is critical here, and thus many researchers propose that value should always be considered from the customers' viewpoint, not what suppliers consider their viewpoint to be.

One idea that is helpful here comes from Jobber (1998), who argues that customer value is simply this:

Customer value = Perceived benefits – Perceived sacrifices

Perceived benefits categories include the product, service, personnel, image, ease of business and so on. Perceived sacrifices include not only money, but time, energy and psychic costs. He proposes that customers estimate the value and costs and thus the overall capacity of the supplier to meet their needs for any particular product or service.

This is just to give a flavour of the rich terrain that could be covered in exploring the notion of value. Others may include the whole relationship marketing concept, the idea of co-creation of value, the understanding of customer satisfaction and the provision of service, the role of value in the development of customer loyalty and so on.

In the end, at the core of the debate surrounding value is the fact that no consensus exists around its definition and constituent parts, so there is room for different companies to adopt different interpretations of what value means. And it is in this area that Tesco has seemingly stolen a march on many of its competitors, taking a much wider and more holistic view of customer value than had been the norm in the sector.

Customer value in grocery shopping

Porter (1980), the strategy specialist, famously proposed two extremes of strategies that he advocated companies should take up in order to compete in markets with a broad scope: cost leadership and differentiation. Companies should not be caught in the middle, he argued. Conventionally, in the UK grocery sector this is exactly how customer value had been conceived by the leading retailers. For instance, in the UK cost leadership for many was the way to go. The aim was continually to offer value in terms of unbeatably superior prices for the customer as the competitive proposition. Tesco was probably most commonly seen in this way up until the 1980s. At the other extreme, there were those who saw differentiation as the key, developing innovative products that continually pushed the boundaries in creating a difference. For example, Marks & Spencer was commonly regarded as a trailblazer on this front.

Of course, in reality customers judge grocery retailers (although unconsciously) on whether a whole range of expectations are met. Table 4.1 sets out some of these value parameters.

In the UK during the latter half of the 20th century this broader understanding of what value meant to grocery customers was beginning to be appreciated by the leading grocery retailers. Sainsbury's, in particular, had developed a reputation for a certain quality of product at reasonable prices: 'Good food costs less at Sainsbury's' was its corporate slogan from 1959 to 1991, which 'elegantly blended goodness and cheapness in one simple, everyday phrase, without resorting to double-barrelled contrivances like "Sainsbury's for Quality, Sainsbury's for Value"'.[1] However, Tesco's image was still tied up with Jack Cohen's business motto, 'Pile it high and sell it cheap.'

Of course, customers are not an amorphous group with identical desires; most customers (unexcited by shopping for food, which is undertaken many, many times during life) would, in Kano model terms, regard their shopping trip as either a 'basic' experience, at best feeling neutral if all went well or annoyed if there were

TABLE 4.1   Customer expectations when shopping for groceries

Product	Price
	Quality
	Taste
	Wholesome and safe
Shopping basket	Product range available
	Choice within each range group
	Non-food as well as food
	All items included in basket 'wish list' available on-shelf
Shopping experience	'One-stop' shopping convenience, for example:
	– parking available
	– plentiful trolleys or baskets
	– uncluttered aisles
	– speedy checkouts
	'Top-up' shopping convenience, for example:
	– store location that minimizes travel time and distance
	– fast service
Summary	*'Serving all my needs'*
	'Solving all my problems'

problems (queues, product unavailable, difficult parking), or a 'performance' experience – ease of completing their shop, speed through the checkout. Delays will lead to a negative view about the retailer. Some who enjoy shopping may see it as a 'delighter' experience, for example if they find new and relevant products or receive excellent service. What Tesco began to unlock in the Leahy era was how to do the basics consistently well and begin to score on the delighter mode for performance experience for certain customer groups. It also showed it could challenge convention and compete in a broad market through both cost leadership and differentiation – the opposite of what Porter had advocated.

How Tesco defines customer value

Tesco under Leahy codified what this wider interpretation of value meant for Tesco under the slogan 'No one tries harder for customers.' This was expressed by the statements:

- 'Understand customers better than anyone.'
- 'Be energetic, be innovative and be first for customers.'
- 'Use our strengths to deliver unbeatable value to our customers.'
- 'Look after our people so that they can look after our customers.'

Basically, it expressed plainly what Tesco wanted to be about and gave all Tesco employees a powerful steer towards what Tesco stood for. In a company as big as Tesco this was an important development. It was all brought together, for customers and employees, by the advertising slogan 'Every little helps', which reinforced in everyone's mind this core value.

The value statement included price, which is always a vital part of the value equation in grocery shopping, suggesting every saving Tesco made in its processes and operations would be passed on to customers, but also widened what value could mean to include manners, courtesy, product availability, till queues, clear aisles and so on.

However, Tesco also went further in broadening the scope of how value could be defined and thus created. In supplying customers with grocery solutions, it might have taken a myopic view and worked on just improving operations so the in-shop experience for customers was optimized. Tesco went further than this. It took a holistic view, defining the whole shopping experience from the point customers think of going shopping and leave the home to when they arrive home with shopping bags. So, instead of delineating the supply chain at the shop shelf, Tesco conceived it as embracing the full customer consumption experience.

Today, as shopping on the internet has increasingly become the norm, this interpretation of how full the definition of customer value could be may seem more obvious. However, in the mid-1990s this was a ground-breaking development. By conceiving of how Tesco could improve value for customers in their whole shopping experience, rather than being confined by their in-store experience, Tesco leapt ahead of most of its competitors just in its way of thinking of what was possible – a considerable source of differentiating potential that they have arguably attempted to exploit ever since.

So customer value for Tesco was conceived of on a much wider platform than low-cost provision, although the price customers paid for their goods was clearly seen as a vital ingredient in the grocery value offer. Value was understood from a much fuller perspective, incorporating the customers' time, psychic issues such as how customers perceive or feel about Tesco, the amount of personal energy used to search for, select, purchase and deploy the goods Tesco provides, and so on.

To provide value, Tesco had to be ultra-efficient to provide lower prices. It had to be effective too, to provide optimal value solutions across a wide range of dimensions. Indeed, this view dictated that low prices, delivered by efficiency, were just one part of the value equation. What Leahy argued was that Tesco had to ensure that effectiveness was defined and delivered, and then through continual improvements in efficiency this effectiveness should not be compromised but rather could be provided at lower and lower prices. Table 4.2 shows the value mix that Tesco strove for in the Leahy era and beyond, and what they look like they are refocusing on again at the outset of the Lewis era.

'Total shopping convenience' can be used as a shorthand for the customer valuing and receiving all of these effective attributes – a powerful reason to prefer Tesco as their 'shop of choice'. This is particularly true when considering that most purchases are repeat items offering little intrinsic 'purchase excitement', as they have appeared in the customer's basket possibly 1,000 or more times (50 shopping visits per year over 40 years equals 2,000 opportunities to purchase).

What this has meant for Tesco's supply chain strategy, discussed more fully in Chapter 5, is summarized in Table 4.3. In terms of store format, range, availability and quality, as well as value for money, Tesco aims to sense what the customer values and provide order-winning effective solutions.

TABLE 4.2 Total shopping convenience: Tesco strives to provide effective solutions for its customers, not just efficient ones

		Efficiency delivers	Effectiveness delivers
Product	Price	✓	
	Quality		✓
	Taste		✓
	Wholesome and safe		✓
Basket	Range		✓
	Choice within range		✓
	Available on shelf		✓
Customer experience	Convenience		✓
	One-stop shopping		✓
	Local shopping		✓
	'Serving all my needs'		✓
	'Solving all my problems'		✓

This discussion leads to the conclusion that the augmenting 'halo', introduced earlier, derived from the value in the tangible product or its associated intangible qualities, should now be perceived differently. Here it is the assortment of selected products in the basket itself that is the core product, and hence an additional halo around the basket assortment can be envisaged (Figure 4.4).

Developing convenience means understanding what this halo around the physical basket really means and translating ideas derived from this into action. If this halo area around the basket is probed into, it can be seen that the customers' experience of value is made

TABLE 4.3 An effective supply chain strategy for a retailer like Tesco

Attribute	An efficient solution	An effective solution
Store format	Standard large store format. Restricted opening hours.	A range of store formats and online options to better suit customer needs. Extended opening hours.
Product range	Few SKUs. Each SKU – high demand. Single product range.	Wide assortment of SKUs. Spectrum of demand – high, medium and low volume. Multi-product range – branded, own label, premium (eg Finest), normal, value.
Product availability	Store orders once a week from supplier or distribution centre (DC). Each SKU received into DCs in full loads. DC receives goods in 9–5, Monday–Friday. Fixed case quantity regardless of store format and size. Store delivery in full pallets of each SKU. Large store backrooms to accommodate pallet remnant stock – insufficient room on store shelf.	Store orders twice a day from supplier or DC. SKUs arrive in DCs in mixed loads. DC receives goods in 24/7, ie aligned to retail store opening hour cycle, reducing 'bullwhip'. Variable case quantity to suit store format and variable day-of-week demand. Store delivery in product-grouped transit units. Store deliveries – 'retail ready (shelf-ready) packs', no 'remnant' stock; room for all product delivered on store shelf.
Product quality	Long shelf life – ambient and frozen. Fresh is a nuisance – waste etc.	All regimes accommodated – ambient, fresh (chilled) and frozen.
Value for money	Within a niche.	Across a multi-array.

FIGURE 4.4 Extending the customer service dimension to the assorted basket

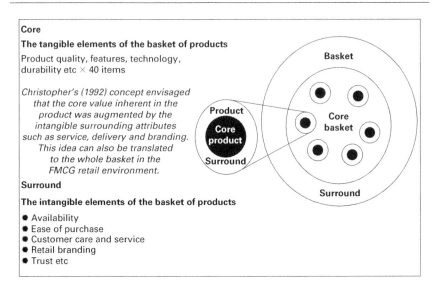

Core

The tangible elements of the basket of products

Product quality, features, technology, durability etc × 40 items

Christopher's (1992) concept envisaged that the core value inherent in the product was augmented by the intangible surrounding attributes such as service, delivery and branding. This idea can also be translated to the whole basket in the FMCG retail environment.

Surround

The intangible elements of the basket of products

* Availability
* Ease of purchase
* Customer care and service
* Retail branding
* Trust etc

SOURCE Developed from Christopher (1992)

up of many dimensions: customer care, ease of purchase, quality of the product, the service experience, trust and emotion tied up in the brand, packaging, advertising features, end-of-life management and so on (developed from Meyer and Schwager, 2007). All need to be managed as an integrative whole but require the core foundation of a highly effective stock fulfilment process. Chapter 5 will focus on how this is being achieved through Tesco's management of its supply chain. The supply chain is key: properly controlled and executed it ensures Tesco's goods are consistently available for a minimum price, so is a core element of the company's primary mission.

Now we have discussed what value looks like in the grocery supermarket sector and how Tesco chooses to define value for its customers, we will focus on the Tesco approach summarized earlier in Figure 4.1. It encompasses four steps:

1 to gain an insight into customers' needs and what they value;

2 to turn this insight data into useful information;

3 to make decisions to improve value for customers from the analysis of this information;

4 to check the effect of these decisions on customers' behaviour.

Each will be looked at in turn.

Gaining insight into what customers value

At the core of this approach are the capabilities Tesco has identified as strategically important to 'understand customers better than anyone else'. Leahy argued passionately that Tesco's secret was its capability to listen carefully to the customers and give them what they want. First, what does Tesco do to listen to its customers?

Great emphasis is placed on being able to sense accurately what potential customers value and how customers perceive the Tesco experience. Authoritative data and information are continually sourced from a range of avenues to provide a dynamic and segmented picture of customers' perceptions and actions. This goes beyond monitoring store or product sales. It includes feedback from customer panels, and regular store visits and attachments by company directors and senior managers, which are combined with the highly detailed insights Tesco gains from its loyalty Clubcard and home shopping systems.

Tesco today is highly sensitized to the key ways in which enhanced value can be generated and conversely the issues that can drain value if the organization gets them wrong.

One of the primary customer sensing activities that Tesco organizes is the customer focus groups, also called customer question time. Leahy (2012) stresses that, 'by knowing your customer... getting behind their views on everything about a product or a service, ... you discover any frustrations they might have about what is on offer, and understand what really makes them tick'. Thus, on a regular basis customer question time sessions are conducted with all types of customer (and with employees too) so that Tesco hears first-hand what the viewpoint of customers really is. For example, in one year, 2003/04, Tesco ran 177 sessions, interviewing 9,000 customers and 2,000 staff.[2] Sometimes this is uncomfortable, but provides a concrete knowledge base of what customers are feeling and whether their needs are being addressed.

Probably the most famous tool that Tesco has developed to gain customer insight is the Tesco Clubcard. Simply, the Clubcard scheme provides money-back vouchers based on the amount of spend to reward loyal customers. It was launched on 13 February 1995 and, although it was not the first loyalty card, its benefit to Tesco went well beyond that of a basic reward card. Tesco was able to develop and exploit its potential to new levels in terms of both earning the appreciation of customers and, crucially, generating invaluable data about its customers.

In 1995, as retailers developed ever bigger superstores in their quest for more efficient retailing, Tesco realized that customers were becoming anonymous. Any relationship grocery supermarket retailers had once enjoyed with customers was being lost. The Clubcard enabled Tesco to overcome this. Information messages could be provided for its customers, personalized to their individual needs.

At the same time the Clubcard provided Tesco with a big competitive weapon: information about its customers. Tesco could see where customers were spending and where they were not. This capability of learning about its customers' purchasing behaviours was put to good use, with data obtained being fed directly into the decision-making processes.

The Clubcard is scanned at the checkout each time the customer shops (there is a screen prompt to the checkout operator to ask for the customer's card at the start of processing the basket scan). The customer receives a discount, which is paid as lump-sum total-money-off vouchers mailed each quarter, plus product-specific offers that are tailored to individuals by selecting what is most appropriate to each customer from thousands of options. The lump-sum vouchers can be spent in-store to reduce a basket spend by that amount, or alternatively the customer can choose to get up to four times their value off the cost of say a theme park visit or a car-ferry return trip. A range of companies are keen to be associated with Tesco and accept the Clubcard money-off vouchers.

The data from each specific shopping visit are captured basket by basket (rather than by averages) on a Tesco database. In this way Tesco can analyse customer behaviour, emerging trends and changes of habit. Suppose that a customer is seen as someone who 'used to buy meat but has not done so in recent visits'. The next Clubcard mail-out will contain not only the money-off vouchers but almost certainly something like '£1 off when you spend £5 or more on meat'.

Tesco continued to refine its use of the Clubcard. In 2009 it introduced Clubcard 2 to spearhead its new drive for market share growth in the UK. Instead of customers gaining one point for every pound they spent, Tesco doubled the incentive to two points. And in December 2009 Tesco announced it was bringing forward its payment of £67 million in loyalty vouchers to its almost 15 million Clubcard holders from February 2010 'to help customers with the cost of Christmas'.

Beyond the Clubcard and customer focus groups, Tesco has also generated a real understanding of what customers seek when they come to a store through home shopping, launched fully from 1999 after trials that began in 1996. As a spin-off, Tesco was able to glean information from their customers that previously could only have been guessed at. As Tesco picked the orders customers sent to them (from their home via the internet) in-store, it was able to establish, for the first time, true on-shelf availability rates – what proportion of each customer's basket was actually available to be picked.

Previously, availability rates were established from information systems that highlighted the proportion of goods available in-store (*but* not necessarily on-shelf) and at snapshots of time. Now accurate ongoing pick rates by customer were readily available. Improved product availability, with the goal of 100 per cent basket fulfilment, became a key performance indicator for Tesco, which Tesco could measure through its home shopping pick rate.

Finally, there have been a number of other initiatives to gain insight. The 'Every comment helps' initiative was launched in 2009[3]. It invited customers from every store to e-mail or text in with feedback, to highlight when things were upsetting them or going wrong, or to suggest new lines that their store currently did not catalogue. In 2009/10, 60,000 comments were fed in suggesting ways in which the product offer or service could be improved. This feedback is taken very seriously and provides a rich picture for the group on how Tesco is perceived by the customer on a regular basis.

The capability to convert insight data to information

Clearly, customer insight is one thing. What needs to happen is to convert the insight data into information and to analyse it to provide useful knowledge and understanding. When Tesco first launched Clubcard it really did not have the skills or the know-how to manage the vast volume of data that was created. Partly, this was because no technology available at that time was able to process the huge number of shopping trips and basket contents that Clubcard was exhibiting for the first time. The marketing consultants Dunnhumby, which had partnered Tesco in the launch of Clubcard, took the lead in beginning to make sense of all the data.

In their book *Scoring Points* (2003), which charts the story of how Tesco successfully launched the Clubcard, Clive Humby, Terry Hunt and Tim Phillips summarized the journey Tesco went on to gain market intelligence from this data mountain. Initially, 10 per cent of the sample was used to create the first useful information, and then in 1997 a Customer Insight Unit was created to see what could be learnt from the patterns of data that Clubcard created. The trick was to present the data in a way that made decisions obvious.

So loyalty was measured using various criteria: 'recency', 'frequency' and 'value' of the shopping trip (amount of money spent) and so on. Even so, making sense of the raw data was very challenging. Setting up and managing the data warehouses so that meaningful information was available was a ground-breaking endeavour. Gradually, with a certain degree of pragmatism, a huge amount of experimentation and a not inconsiderable level of investment in hardware and analytically skilled personnel, useful information began to be drawn out of the data.

Combined with the insight Tesco was gathering through its other sources, a fuller picture of how customers perceived Tesco emerged. Over the years this insight has been further and further refined, with fuller understanding of customers' lifestyles and shopping patterns emerging.

The capability to make and enact customer-orientated decisions

We have already quoted Sir Terry Leahy, who argued that 'Tesco's secret was its capability to listen carefully to the customers... and give them what they want.' We have reflected on how Tesco listened; this section concentrates on how Tesco from the mid-1990s onwards began to really focus on being the first to meet its customers' needs. Having accurate antennae to understand how the customer perceives Tesco is only part of the equation. Indeed, it is Tesco's ability to 'give them what they want' that Tesco prides itself on most and arguably sets it apart.

Through Clubcard, customer focus groups such as the question time sessions and other feedback mechanisms Tesco had gained more and more customer insight. In 2001, in its annual review, it was able to state that it was getting better and better at understanding its customers and responding to their needs: 'the relationship is direct and effective, enabling us to respond quickly and innovatively to changing customer requirements'.[4]

The range of initiatives that ensued illustrated the kind of learning that was being developed. For example, in its 2005 annual review, Tesco highlighted:

- the launch of a new healthy eating range with clearer labelling;
- increased Asian lines;
- a new Kosher range of wines and ready meals.

In 2010 Tesco announced[5] that the fresh food quality drive had been supported by improved technical standards, and 1,000 technical support advisers for larger stores had been put in place.

In recent years this drive to develop targeted initiatives with real investment to see them through has continued, with in 2012 a substantial increase in store staffing numbers, and an increase in the numbers of trained, skilled employees working in the dedicated fruit and vegetable teams in stores.[6]

As well as these kinds of targeted improvements, Tesco has learnt from customers to ensure that the basics of shopping are continually in focus and constantly at the forefront of what Tesco cares about delivering. Under the title of 'Tesco shopping list', five goals are kept in mind. From year to year these basics do not really change. They are:

- The aisles are clear.
- I can get what I want.
- The prices are good.
- I don't queue.
- The staff are great.

Every decision that was arrived at was judged during the Leahy era against the principles of the slogan 'Better, simpler, cheaper'. The Tesco Annual review 2006 powerfully argued: 'Every operational decision we make is judged against these principles... Deceptively simple, but the key to understanding Tesco is to see our obsession with delivering these promises. It is what we are all about. Unless it improves the basics of shopping, we're not interested.'

This relentless focus on the basics was probably summed up by Tesco's approach to perhaps the longest running of these shopping list campaigns: the One in Front initiative to reduce till queues. Launched in 1994, still in 2008 it was being reported on[7] as follows: 'an extra 22.5 million customers did not have to queue thanks to the hard work and effort put in by stores and our extra investment in hours at the checkout'.

So from pre-sorted deliveries so aisles were clear for more of the time, to ongoing price-cutting campaigns, to continuous efforts to improve on-shelf availability (which will be reflected on in Chapter 5), to revamped ranges of own-brand groceries, Tesco tried to focus on the things that customers had told it really mattered on their shopping trip.

The capability to track the impact of actions

The circle of learning from actions is completed by Tesco's obsession with tracking the impact of its actions. Much revolves around the Steering Wheel introduced in Chapter 3. For any initiative the results are meticulously tracked against targets. Following reflection and analysis the actions are often fine-tuned through a further learning cycle, and again the results obtained are reviewed against the estimate, an example of applying Chris Argyris's (1997) idea of 'double-loop learning' or, indeed, the differentiating 'smart' behaviour advocated by Steven Spear in his book *Chasing the Rabbit* (2009).

For example, after the launch of Clubcard, Tesco decided to embark on direct mailing on a quarterly basis to its Clubcard holders with the offers they had earned and information that was felt to be pertinent to them. Over the years Tesco learnt more and more about how these mailings were received by customers, to what extent vouchers were used or the information stimulated fresh buying behaviour, and so on. Today, rather than customers being placed in customer segments of like-minded people, individually tailored offers are sent out with offers of lines that the customer is most likely to buy.

Conclusions

Striving for the goal of achieving the lifetime loyalty of customers means that few mistakes can be allowed. Tesco strives to understand that when a customer transacts with it this occurs within the wider context of the emotional bond that has been developed by the organization with the customer through consistently matching or exceeding the customer's expectations. The perceived benefit must exceed the perceived sacrifice from each customer's perspective for every transaction.

There are various levels of loyalty that Tesco strives for. Butz and Goodstein (1996) describe this in their paper 'Measuring Customer Value: Gaining the Strategic Advantage' (Table 4.4).

The ultimate for Tesco is that customers view it as their favourite retail supplier for the products it provides. Understanding how this can be consistently achieved when competition is as fierce as it is and Tesco does not make anything physical itself to differentiate its offering is what has underpinned Tesco's sustained competitive advantage over the last 15 to 20 years or so.

Effective and innovative marketing has clearly been very important in the rise of Tesco. But the promises put to customers could not have been achieved without excellent supply chain practice. Indeed, the supply chain represents the key to delivering an ever-improving

TABLE 4.4 Five increasing levels of bonding

1	Preferential	'Let's try them this time.'
2	Favouritism	'All things being equal they get the order.'
3	Commitment	'They are our supplier.'
4	Referential	'You ought to buy from these guys.'
5	Exclusive	'No one else has a chance to get an order.'

value offering without letting the customer down. Properly controlled and executed, it ensures Tesco's goods are consistently available for a minimum price, so is a core element of the company's prime mission.

For the most part, Tesco has become better and better at offering customers more and more value, in its widest sense, from its operations by providing its consumers with a wide range of products, excellent quality, good value for money, complete availability in convenient locations, and optimized use of both online and physical retail channels. Interestingly, the good-value-for-money element of value is currently being re-examined, with Tesco launching a new campaign, 'Down and staying down'[8] to ensure its basic products are recognizably competitively priced.

In simple terms, Tesco has shown that the grocery retailer has to be able to present each unique customer with the capability of assembling the customer's required basket (of constituents that are unknown to the retailer). What is required is the range, the availability, the quality (in terms of reliability) and the value for money. This must also be achieved time after time after time so that through the repeated shopping experience a reputation is developed.

This is analogous to Toyota's reputation for quality and reliability achieved through consistent, capable and reliable processes. Clearly Tesco is going through some very tough time recently, but the strength built up in their core supply chain logistics processes provides a confidence that ultimately they will be able to return to a pattern of growth once more. Chapter 5 will explore this and show how Tesco can claim to be the Toyota of retail.

Key chapter summary points

1 Tesco conceives of understanding customer value from the widest possible stance, that is, how shopping can be improved, from the start of the customer's process right through to the end. It is not limited just to giving the best value at the supermarket shelf.

2 Tesco understands that it is the perception of the customer it must account for when sensing the customer, not Tesco's assumed view of the customer's perception.

3 A range of techniques is used by Tesco to generate this customer insight, not just Clubcard information.

4 Tesco emphasizes that, while listening to customers is important, taking action to do something about the insight it gleans is what in the end makes the difference.

5 By constantly re-examining what customers feel about the Tesco offer and how value in their eyes can be improved, Tesco keeps updating its approach and is clearly a long way into the journey of moving from data to wisdom in understanding and serving its customers better.

Notes

1 Tom Albrighton, Sainsbury's slogans through the years, *ABC Copywriting*, 19 September 2011
2 Tesco Annual Review 2004
3 Tesco Annual Review 2010
4 Tesco Annual Review 2001
5 Tesco Annual Review 2010
6 Tesco Annual Review 2012
7 Tesco Annual Review 2008
8 Prices down and staying down, Tesco website, accessed 8 March 2014

Lean and the Tesco supply chain

Mastering the supply chain

Introduction

It could be argued that Tesco is as much a logistics company as it is a retailer, which is how it is more commonly perceived and defined. Tesco largely makes none of its own products, whether they be 'branded' or 'Tesco own label', although they do 'add value' to some of their range, eg in-store bakeries, hot chicken counters. What Tesco strives to do well is provide an assortment of products (and increasingly services too), sourced from a myriad of suppliers, so that customers can save time, energy and money in accessing them. How Tesco organizes its chains of supply is thus at the heart of its competitive offering. This chapter focuses on this and asks: how has Tesco gone about trying to master its supply chains?

Tesco can be considered, in essence, to be little more than a very sophisticated supply chain bringing together literally thousands of products, grown and/or manufactured by numerous suppliers, for consumers to assemble their chosen basket of products. Tesco stores are in a sense like the 'T' layout factories described in the Lean literature, with thousands of 'raw material' components on-shelf from which consumers assemble their limited basket of say 10, 20 or 50 stock-keeping units (SKUs). However, unlike the 'T' layout factory, Tesco invariably does not know the 'parts list' of products that each of its individual customers wishes to purchase.

So the significant challenge for Tesco, or any grocery retailer, is to achieve perfect or near-perfect on-shelf product availability to meet the needs of these unknown customer shopping lists. Tesco's seemingly trite core purpose – 'To create value for customers to earn their lifetime loyalty' – is in fact a huge goal for Tesco to achieve. Tesco envisages that effective provision of what its customer wants always takes supremacy over internal efficiency improvement. This counter-intuitive idea, simple to state and hugely difficult to achieve, guides all of Tesco's actions in delivering current operations, improving them or developing new approaches. So why is this counter-intuitive approach so important? Simply, it puts efficiency improvement in its place.

Effectiveness is about identifying and delivering a purpose – what matters to customers. Efficiency is about improving an output/input ratio such as a resource utilization ratio. But efficiency improvement can have unintended consequences; all too often it worsens effectiveness (you might like to ask yourself how often this happens in your business). Giving effectiveness the primary role helps avoid these unintended consequences of efficiency improvement.

This chapter will reflect on this, in summary, appraising Tesco's focus, over the Leahy, and Clarke and now Lewis eras as Tesco CEOs from 1997 up to 2014, on the optimization of its process systems in the pursuit of 100 per cent on-shelf availability (OSA) of all goods and services for its customers. It is the belief that effectiveness is what matters to customers, rather than efficiency, that drives this endeavour. After the background developments in Tesco's supply chain up to 1997 have been briefly highlighted, the key elements of Tesco's supply chain improvement plans since then will be identified and discussed.

To help us with this exploration, the basic system model (Figure 5.1) introduced in Chapter 1 will be used to illustrate simply how everything fits together. We can conceive any supply chain as a basic system model similar to this. The whole supply chain system has a declared purpose, with inputs and outputs. A feedback loop is integrated into the system so that it becomes intelligent and is capable of learning.

FIGURE 5.1 A basic model of a supply chain system used to support the research undertaken with Tesco by Cardiff Business School

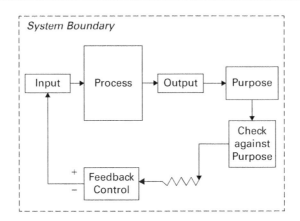

The chapter will also show how the achievement of better on-shelf availability has had a key internal benefit for Tesco as well, allowing it to further improve its supply chains in order to deliver better value. This is because full product availability ensures sales history data are not corrupted by sell-outs and switch buying. Once certainty in supply chain operations improves, this allows for significant efficiency improvements to be made without the risk of denaturing value delivery. We argue that these improvements in effectiveness followed by efficiency are significant factors in Tesco's profit growth and global expansion up to recent times.

Note: We will examine whether this price-versus-value delivery premise is still valid given the current economic circumstances of many consumers – whether price is so dominant that it negates all other attributes – in Chapter 7.

Background

By 1997, when Leahy became Tesco CEO, the company was already beginning to build a reputation for its management of the supply chain. The realization that the supply chain was a critical part of the company's strategy stemmed from the times when supply operations were far from the controlled and capable systems that are evident today. The criticality of supply chain mastery was starkly revealed at the time of the switch from Green Shield stamps to lower prices in the 'Check-out' relaunch of Tesco some 20 years earlier, in 1977.

The success of this initiative had been dramatic, lifting Tesco's market share at the time in a single stroke from 7.8 per cent to over 10 per cent in the ensuing month, with year-on-year sales growth of almost 40 per cent. However, as David Powell said, 'the campaign exposed the weaknesses that bedevilled the whole organisation... taken unprepared, Check-out was threatening to overwhelm its creator... dwarfing its aging systems with its insatiable demands... the problem was how to manage it out of outdated shops and with a distribution system that was close to breaking point'. 'Possibly for the first time in its history, the company recognized that it was as much in the business of distribution as of retailing' (Powell, 1991).

Tesco, from this period, through a series of steps, began to reform the structure, strategy, culture and people connected with what was then called 'distribution' and now is better known as 'logistics'. Smith and Sparks (2004) segmented the change over the next 20 years into two main eras: the move to centralization, which involved the development of a network of distribution centres to coordinate suppliers' deliveries and assemble store-specific combined loads, to replace much of the 'direct to store' delivery method from suppliers that had been common up to the end of the 1970s; and the introduction of 'composite distribution' in the early 1990s, one system of multi-temperature warehouses and vehicles.

These campaigns had helped radically transform the way in which Tesco managed its logistics. For example, 'from 1984, the percentage of sales via central facilities had increased from 30 percent to 95 percent by 2002' (Smith and Sparks, 2004), and inventory cover (in stock days) had been reduced from over 40 days at the end of the 1970s to around 11 days by 1997 (*ibid*). Above all, it was recognized that the management of the supply chain had to be dealt with hand in hand with the development of the entire business. Central control had been established from the ad hoc fiefdoms that had characterized the business at the end of the Cohen era, and although there was much still to do a foundation had been clearly established by around 1997.

Tesco's supply chain improvement

In this chapter the system that we are looking at is the Tesco supply chain, from approximately 1997 onwards. The approach taken for improvement from that time involved a number of aspects, which will be explored and discussed in this section. This section of the chapter is structured around four themes:

1 Identifying the constituents of Tesco customers' expectations of 'value' (we examined this in detail in Chapter 4 – a summary discussion focusing on what this means for supply chain purposes is presented here).

2 Defining strategic improvement goals for the supply chain. They include:
   – the pivotal objective of striving for 'perfect' on-shelf product availability (100 per cent OSA);
   – the importance of supply chain synchronization in delivering superior performance.

3 Using Lean principles and thinking to support the development of a strategy to identify, prioritize and deliver improvement to Tesco's supply chain.

4 Implementation: developing a consensus around the key priorities on which to focus and delivering sustained progress, step by step.

Throughout, we will support the discussion with some of the detailed means by which supply chain improvement has been achieved.

Identifying the constituents of value

In Chapter 4, we presented a summary of what customers may expect when shopping for groceries. Clearly, there are many aspects to what each customer conventionally values, and the mix of these values is dynamic too, changing over time, with other values invariably being introduced as well.

In summary, customer value is realized by either reducing customer sacrifices, such as their time, money energy or psychie costs, or creating added-value benefits such as providing extra convenience or a one-stop shop.

TABLE 5.1 Supply chain improvement has a role in the efficiency/effectiveness agenda in providing customer value

How are customer expectations met?		Efficiency 'value'	Effectiveness 'value'	Role of supply chain improvement
Product	Price	✓		Yes
	Quality		✓	Yes
	Taste		✓	
	Wholesome and safe		✓	Yes
Shopping basket	Product range available		✓	Yes
	Choice within each range group		✓	Yes
	All items included in basket 'wish list' available on-shelf		✓	Yes

Shopping experience in-store or buying experience online	Convenience, for example:	
	– parking available	✓ Yes
	– plentiful trolleys or baskets	✓
	– uncluttered aisles	✓ Yes
	– speedy checkouts	✓ Yes
	One-stop shopping: food, non-food, electronics, basic clothing etc	✓ Yes
	Home shopping:	
	– Click & Collect	✓ Yes
	– home delivery	✓ Yes
	– omni-channel	✓ Yes
Summary	*'Serving all my needs'*	✓ *Yes*
	'Solving all my problems'	✓ *Yes*

A properly managed supply chain can affect both these dimensions, and thus it is clear that the effective and efficient management of the supply chain has a huge bearing on value provision. For grocery shopping this can be summarized as in Table 5.1, which shows how supply chain improvements map on to the efficiency/effectiveness agenda covered in Chapter 4: the supply chain has a bearing on most of the dimensions of value listed.

However, while there are many drivers of value, one can be identified as being key in the mix for all grocery retailers: the ability to stock the shelves consistently with no sell-outs.

Tesco in the Leahy era defined by its quest to achieve its customers' lifetime loyalty, identified that a proxy for value could be argued to be the customers' 'time'. 'Don't waste my valuable time' summed up the feelings of many, especially those customers who were becoming increasingly time poor and cash rich. As a result, full on-shelf availability, where the customer can select what he or she wants every time, became a key constituent of what effectiveness meant when it came to grocery shopping: a pivotal objective for the business to strive for.

Defining strategic improvement goals for the Tesco supply chain

Goal 1: 100 per cent on-shelf availability

While 100 per cent OSA was agreed as a pivotal objective (as it both supported the aim of achieving customers' lifetime loyalty and provided the certainty required in terms of a full sales history base to be able to forecast more accurately and thus manage the future supply chain), measuring on-shelf availability was seen as a notoriously difficult activity. For instance, do you measure OSA at a snapshot point of time during the week or day, or do you try to measure it more often? It may seem surprising, but companies like Tesco generally did not know what their on-shelf availability performance was through the entire week.

There are circumstances when Tesco does know its availability performance, though, from customers' shopping lists. This is when Tesco is doing the 'assembly' itself, as with home delivery of online grocery orders, launched at the end of the 1990s. Thus, more visible actual shopping baskets of individual products (known in the industry as stock-keeping units), selected online by the customer and assembled by a Tesco employee, either in-store or in one of the new 'dark stores' that were later developed, provided Tesco with a highly valuable source of new information. The various assembly and collection options being offered by Tesco will be covered later in this chapter. Possibly the most interesting business aspect of these 'assembled by Tesco employee' options is that it provides Tesco with accurate data on products, SKUs and availability, ie from these orders Tesco can tell what its customers want and what it has available to fulfil these orders – a more continuous OSA measure than it ever had before.

This knowledge provides a powerful, competitive measure of a key aspect of effectiveness. What Tesco found in the early days of Tesco .com online grocery ordering was that, despite being held up as one of the leaders in the field in terms of management of its supply chain, it in fact was not able to fulfil its own online customers' shopping baskets to a consistently high standard. Aiming for complete basket fulfilment, as measured by its ability to service online orders, became the new standard that drove supply chain improvements and further elevated full availability as one of the key constituents of effectiveness that Tesco strove to achieve through its supply chain prowess.

The impact of less-than-perfect product availability is huge when viewed at the shopping basket level. Conventional thinking deems that a service level of say 98.5 per cent is acceptable and that any increase on this would not be justifiable on a 'law of diminishing returns' basis, because a retailer would be gaining only a marginal benefit by increasing service levels to say 99.5 per cent. According to this conventional thinking, Toyota and other companies would be bankrupt as a result of building cars at near-perfect quality levels. The logic behind the law of diminishing returns is flawed and is an economic premise that depends on a key factor staying constant – capability.

If process capability improves, then achieving superior service levels actually results in little or no increase in cost and has the potential to reduce total costs, as, for example, sales will improve and rectification costs will reduce. For a retailer there is a further reason to aspire to improve service levels as indicated above – its impact on shopping

TABLE 5.2 On-shelf product service level and the impact on fulfilment

Assume:

- Weekly shopping basket = 40 items
- 52 weekly shopping trips per year
- Lifetime association of say 40 years

Terminology:

- Basket fulfilment = Probability of all items being available on-shelf
  = Line availability $^{\text{(No. of items in basket)}}$

- Annual fulfilment = Probability of all items being available during year
  = Basket fulfilment $^{\text{(No. of shopping trips during year)}}$

- Lifetime fulfilment = Probability of all items being available over life
  = Annual fulfilment $^{\text{(No. of years shopped)}}$

If on-shelf availability target = 98.5% (= efficient solution based on law of diminishing returns)

Basket fulfilment = $98.5^{(40)}$ = 54.6%
Annual fulfilment = $54.6^{(52)}$ = 0.00000000000022
Lifetime fulfilment = $0.00000000000022^{(40)}$ = 0.00000... *then 547 zeros...* 00784

Thus it is absolutely certain that the retailer will let down every customer who shops with it over 40 years

basket service fulfilment. This is demonstrated in the example in Table 5.2, which looks at the impact of an on-shelf product availability of 98.5 per cent on a basket of 40 products – 'basket availability', or what the consumer experiences.

By any measure of satisfaction the basket availability performance demonstrated in the example is not consistent with a core purpose of 'creating value for customers to earn their lifetime loyalty'. Why, if this is the case, do customers still shop at Tesco?

Quite simply, no retailer is consistently achieving the on-shelf availability levels that Tesco is already achieving. The objective for Tesco is to achieve levels of on-shelf availability that capable and consistent replenishment processes can deliver – not just on-shelf in-store, but

TABLE 5.3 Fulfilment performance improvement with Six Sigma capability

With Six Sigma performance, on-shelf availability target = 99.9997%

- Basket fulfilment = $99.9997^{(10)}$ = 99.988%
- Annual fulfilment = $99.988^{(52)}$ = 99.378%
- Lifetime fulfilment = $99.378^{(40)}$ = 77.9%

end to end through the supply chain. Thus, if Six Sigma process capability can be achieved this will provide Tesco with the benefits that companies like Toyota obtain through their quality performance, although still not near-perfect on a lifetime basis – see Table 5.3.

Goal 2: supply chain synchronization

The aim of capable, synchronized supply chains is to deliver products to customers reliably, time after time, at minimized costs. Supply chains are only as strong as their weakest link, and consistent performance requires all the supply chain links to be capable.

In the mid-1990s Tesco was acknowledged to have an efficient and competitive supply chain (a substantial achievement compared to what had existed around 15–20 years before). However, its exposure to the ideas and approaches espoused by Lean thinking made it aware that perhaps it was not as capable as conventional yardsticks might indicate.

At this time Graham Booth of Tesco, with some of its key suppliers, joined the Supply Chain Development Project (SCDP), a research project being run by the Lean Enterprise Research Centre (LERC) at Cardiff Business School. SCDP brought together blue-chip sponsors from the automotive, electronics, process, distribution, health care, public transport, and grocery manufacturing and retailing industries and was led by Professor Dan Jones, who had come to be well known through his contribution to two seminal works on Lean thinking – *The Machine That Changed the World* (Womack, Jones and Roos, 1990) and *Lean Thinking* (Womack and Jones, 1996). The purpose of the programme was to implement Lean thinking in these disparate industries in order to help them achieve world-class performance and sustainable competitive advantage and in the process help the team from Cardiff Business School learn more about the implantation of Lean.

Through its work with SCDP, Tesco began to see and understand that it manifested three symptoms of a less-than-perfect supply chain, namely:

- It didn't have end-to-end performance excellence in its supply chain, although there were 'islands of excellence' in parts of the chain. Thus, the proportion of total cost expended in store replenishment accounted for almost half the total end-to-end supply chain cost (see Table 5.4). This so-called 'last 50 metres' was strong evidence of a poor degree of internal collaboration with the store personnel having to deal with supplier and DC efficiency measures that totally ignored store colleagues' needs for shelf-replenishment-friendly product deliveries.

- There was widespread evidence of 'bullwhip', also known as demand amplification, as stock moved between each tier of the supply chain. Tesco realized that most inventory (stock) was clear evidence of process failure and poor collaboration or information sharing between the partners in each tier of the

TABLE 5.4   Tesco UK supply chain cost (1995)

Supply chain activities from supplier's gate to Tesco store shelf			
	Supplier delivery to Tesco DC	Tesco DC and delivery to store	Store shelf replenishment ('last 50 metres')	Replenishment systems – store orders and supplier orders
Percentage breakdown of costs incurred (total 100%)	18%	28%	46%	8%

FIGURE 5.2 'Bullwhip' – demand amplification in the Tesco supply chain

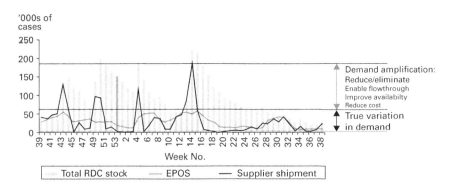

chain. Thus, it had exactly the same experience as those who have played the MIT 'Beer Game', namely huge fluctuations in stock movement but considerable inability to meet customer orders consistently. See Figure 5.2 for 'bullwhip' plots for a Tesco top 10 SKU (ie a significant, very high-volume product).

- Researchers, along with Tesco and supplier senior managers, 'walked' complete supply chains assessing where and how much value-adding work was being delivered. They identified that less than approximately 1 per cent of the total time that the products spent from creation to on-store shelf was value-adding. Most time was in storage, delay or transport – in Lean terms a great deal of waste (difficult to eliminate, but a target for the Lean pursuit of 'perfection'). The results of this 'walk' are shown in Figure 5.3.

Womack and Jones (1996), in *Lean Thinking*, give a similar example for a can of cola on its journey to a Tesco store shelf, pointing out that 'world-class' companies achieve up to 5 per cent value-adding time – still much potential on the journey to 'perfection'.

These SCDP research project findings were regarded as a wake-up call within the business. Tesco managers determined systematically to improve their supply chain, seeking an effectiveness goal – their core purpose 'to create value for customers to earn their lifetime

FIGURE 5.3 Value-adding work as a proportion of total end-to-end time in the supply chain for a sample supplier branded grocery product

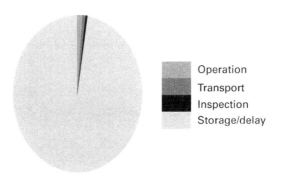

Operation
Transport
Inspection
Storage/delay

Current state: ThroughputTime = 230 hours
Value adding time = 2.7 hours = 1.2%

loyalty' – rather than conventional efficiency targets. Any efficiency improvements gained would be welcome, provided they didn't degrade or destroy effectiveness.

We have described the *what* and *why* of Tesco's improvement. We now turn to the plan for *how*, supported by examples of what Tesco has achieved. (For more about the SCDP research project, see Hines *et al*, 2000).

Using Lean to underpin the strategy for sustainable supply chain improvement in Tesco

Tesco has been a great advocate of using Lean thinking in its business. Sir Terry Leahy is quoted on the cover of the 2003 edition of *Lean Thinking* (Womack and Jones, 2003): 'Lean Thinking has been an enormous influence on my business thinking. It is not just about improving efficiency, it shows how you can fundamentally transform your business.'

Following his retirement as Tesco Chief Executive, Leahy wrote a book on his time and experiences with Tesco – *Management in 10 Words* (2012). He devotes Chapter 8 to 'Lean thinking'. Although he uses 'Lean' in its widest sense, he chooses to use examples of how it has been used by Tesco in pursuit of sustainable consumption objectives. Thus he writes: 'Sustainable consumption depends on desiring goods and services that use fewer natural resources. By thinking Lean, we can go green – and do more for less.' He goes on to give many examples – from Tesco and from other organizations – of the counter-intuitive logic that 'more for less' has been achieved.

In this chapter, we will describe how Tesco set about using Lean thinking in a planned, prioritized and coordinated manner. Tesco set out principles for how its supply chains (DCs, deliveries, stores etc) were to operate. They were:

- to be customer-focused;
- to be responsive;
- to be planned;
- to be disciplined, with clear standards applied; and wherever possible
- to have 'one-touch' replenishment mechanisms as the goal.

The principles set out map well on to the five Lean principles. Furthermore, they align to the effectiveness/efficiency agenda discussed above. They are shown in Table 5.5.

Turning Lean theory into practical and sustainable improvement activity within a supply chain can be difficult: for example, how does one apply ideas sourced from a manufacturing environment? This was a key objective of the SCDP. Graham Booth (then the Supply

TABLE 5.5 How Tesco operating principles link with Lean thinking principles

Tesco operating principle	Lean principle	Sequence
Customer focus	Value	
Responsiveness	Flow and pull	Effective first
Planning holistically	Value stream	
Disciplines and standards	Perfection	Efficient second
One-touch replenishment	Attacking waste	

Chain Development and Planning Director of Tesco Stores Ltd) was a key member of SCDP and describes this dilemma in 1999 in his foreword in *Value Stream Management*, the book describing many of the findings from SCDP, as follows (Hines *et al*, 2000):

> When the programme started lean production ideas had only really been applied within a factory environment. This was the first time they were being tried across whole supply chains outside the auto industry. As we began to explore these lean ideas, it became clear they opened up new possibilities for improving supply chain performance and were as relevant to grocery distribution and retailing as in the auto industry. Indeed some of the work carried out within SCDP has had a significant impact within Tesco and its supply chain, which we are continuing to this day.

Building on a piece of research carried out by LERC on sustainable improvement in car after-sales (Kiff and Simons, 2002), and described in a chapter in *Value Stream Management* (Simons, 2000), Simons set out and described a sequence of four stages for supply chain improvement, as follows:

- *Step 1: control.* Ensure every replenishment decision in the supply chain is consistent in timing and logic. Improve the algorithm eliminating unnecessary safety stock. Apply standard operations to physical distribution.
- *Step 2: time.* Order more frequently, and remove delivery delays from the system.
- *Step 3: centralization.* Introduce visibility of stock throughout the supply chain. Rationalize ordering to one decision point, ideally at the production stage.
- *Step 4: structure.* Eliminate unnecessary echelons in the supply chain.

The research identified that adopting this sequence of improvement actions in car after-sales supply chains was associated with the most sustained improvements.

These sequential stages became the basis for a 'road map' for supply chain improvement in Tesco. Two modifications were made to the SCDP research findings, which were: 1) 'centralization', which had a particular meaning in retail, namely the use of regional distribution centres as an alternative to suppliers delivering their goods direct to retail stores, was replaced by the term 'collaboration' (ie central logic); and 2) steps 2 ('time') and 3 ('collaboration') were deemed to be iterative and needed to be repeated many times in order to seek improvement through growing capability. One of the authors of this book, Barry Evans, in his role at the time as Lean Process Manager in Tesco, was tasked with identifying Lean improvement opportunities in Tesco operations in its supply chain. This included maintaining an ongoing relationship with LERC, which wished to provide a mentoring role to Tesco's Lean aspirations. The LERC representative was David Simons. Evans and Simons populated the 'road map' structure with detail relevant to Tesco. The original was published in *Logistics and Transport Focus*, the journal of the Chartered Institute of Logistics and Transport (CILT) (Evans and Simons, 2000). Over time that original was modified to reflect various feedback comments. This is as shown in Table 5.6.

TABLE 5.6 A 'road map' sequence for Tesco supply chain improvement

Step	Objective	Method	Examples in Tesco
Establishing process control	Stable and predictable processes	Map core repetitive processes.	Standard operations – 'routines'.
Time compression	Elimination of non-value-adding time – 'waste'	Mapping identifies waste – take steps to eliminate waste.	Lean replenishment systems: – continuous replenishment (CR) for stores; – product grouping; – flowthrough for suppliers.

(*continued*)

TABLE 5.6 (*continued*)

Step	Objective	Method	Examples in Tesco
Collaboration	Visibility	With suppliers: – share data; – end-to-end KPIs. Work across industry through agreed common standards.	Stock management. Tesco Information Exchange (TIE). Tesco Knowledge Hub. Industry-wide collaboration: – Efficient Consumer Response (ECR); – World Wide Retail Exchange (WWRE); – Consumer Goods Forum.
Structure	Strategic stock that addresses demand variability	Align networks to value streams. Eliminate 'process' causes of stock.	Logistics product management: – shelf-ready packaging; – factory-gate pricing; – flowthrough; – reducing bullwhip; – design and implementation of end-to-end holistic supply chain solutions.

SOURCE After Evans and Simons (2000)

Thus the strategy for Tesco supply chain improvement was complete in terms of what, why and how and a sequence established for when. Tesco's 'plan–do–review' approach can be linked to this 'road

FIGURE 5.4 The supply chain goal of optimized product shelf availability identified as the purpose with the four stages of the iterative 'road map' indicated on the basic model of a supply chain system used to support the research undertaken with Tesco by Cardiff Business School

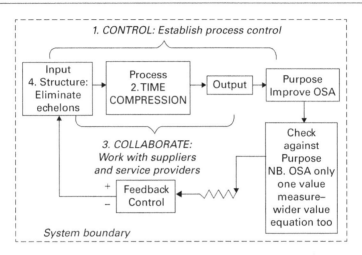

map' and can be indicated in terms of how it fitted together on the basic system model (Figure 5.4) the researchers at Cardiff Business School used for their work with Tesco. As each improvement initiative increased capabilities it would be reviewed and the results used to add to or modify the system as appropriate.

In the next section we will look at some of the detail of the supply chain improvements made (as shown in Table 5.6).

Implementing Tesco supply chain improvement

The first three themes of this discussion have centred on how Tesco went about the 'plan' phase of its supply chain improvement campaign from the end of the 1990s onwards. We now focus on the 'do' phase: how Tesco went about the implementation of the process improvement of its supply chain.

The implementation followed the sequence introduced above, which was designed to provide for sustained benefit. By following a logical path of improvement that built a growing capability of people, process and systems, the 'road map' sequence was key to Tesco unlocking real benefits from its supply chain operations. As a reminder, the sequence was:

- step 1: establishing process control;
- step 2: time compression;
- step 3: collaboration;
- step 4: structure.

This sequence will guide the ensuing discussion, each step being highlighted with examples of some of the project work that was carried out in progressing each stage, as indicated in Table 5.6.

It is perhaps important to reflect too, at this stage, on a common theme that applies to all of the following detail: the supply chain strategy and sequenced implementation plan aligned with Tesco's principles, to be 'better for customers, simpler for staff, cheaper for Tesco' and observed the 'effective first, efficiency follows' requirement.

Step 1: establishing process control

When an aspect of what was to become known as Lean, the just-in-time (JIT) delivery principle, was taken up by non-Japanese automotive companies in the late 1980s, it brought about immediate benefits in stock reduction. However, as it invariably was not matched with the development of the underpinning quality ethos required, the supply chain just fell over, all too frequently, when product or service defects occurred. The buffer stocks that had been relied upon to fall back on at these times had been removed following the introduction of JIT. The key lesson learnt was that JIT could not be introduced in isolation.

TABLE 5.7 Step 1 in the 'road map' sequence for Tesco supply chain improvement

Step 1	Objective	Method	Examples in Tesco
Establishing process control	Stable and predictable processes	Map core repetitive processes.	Standard operations – 'routines'.

A holistic system-wide introduction had to be conducted, what became known as 'Lean', which included at its base the need to establish a total quality ethos and process control. In practice, what this meant was that supply chain processes had to become stable and predictable.

Tesco supply chain operations include a range of activities and tasks in its core supply chain processes that are repeated literally millions of times every year. Tesco segments a large part of its supply chain into three elements: primary distribution concerns the movement of product from the supplier to a Tesco distribution centre (DC); secondary distribution concerns the product movement through the DC and on to stores; and store operations cover the activities undertaken at the store. Table 5.8 shows examples from the journey along the supply chain from supplier to store shelf.

The tasks listed in Table 5.8 are not a comprehensive list of all these highly repetitive activities, but instead indicate that a large number exist and, as stated above, each occurs millions of times every year in Tesco's operations. Tesco, therefore, has a huge improvement opportunity if it can master each of these process activities, and it realizes this is the case. However, to maximize any potential benefit from improvement, it has two 'must do' requirements. First, each repetitive

TABLE 5.8 Examples of highly repetitive tasks in the Tesco supply chain

Primary distribution	Secondary distribution	Store operations
Load palletized product at supplier's premises.	Unload palletized product at Tesco DC. Place pallets in storage. Let down pallets to pick location. Pick individual cases of product to meet store order. Load store delivery cages to vehicle.	Receive unloaded cages to store backstore area. Unload cases at shelf location and decant product if appropriate. At checkout, scan customer's selection through scanner, take payment for products etc.

core task is the subject of a standard operation – what Tesco terms a 'routine'. This details the standard way the task is to be performed in any location where it is carried out (for example, in several thousand stores, a hundred or so DCs etc). Second, local change to a routine is not permitted. Tesco wants to ensure that any improvement is made at every location where the routine is used. Therefore, a suggested improvement is fed to a central team, where the suggestion is evaluated against any other suggestions. An improvement suggestion that is seen to have merit will be trialled, probably at the site from which it originated, and if successful will be rolled out to all sites where that routine is performed. In this way Tesco ensures that only the best suggestions are taken forward and that the standard remains just that – used at every relevant location time after time.

Routines are, in typical Tesco fashion, displayed on very visual documents intended to be read quickly and easily. A typical routine is generally shown on a one-page document available to Tesco personnel. It contains information as follows:

- a title, brief description and purpose;
- a step-by-step explanation of how to carry out the task;
- a RACI listing (see the box headed 'RACI' in Chapter 3);
- a fishbone problem-solving help guide showing possible causes and cures if a site is having a problem with carrying out a particular routine; and
- an indication if there are, for example, any relevant health and safety regulations.

Additional pages will be added if there are specific legal, health and safety, hazard analysis and critical control points (HACCP) or other requirements to be added.

In summary, the routine becomes a means to train, communicate and utilize current best practice, capture and roll out improvements, and adhere to any statutory or regulatory requirements.

Importantly, it provides the company with stable and predictable operations in all of its core supply chain activities, which as a consequence can be relied upon. This paves the way for the next step in the sequence: the compression of time to eliminate non-value-adding time.

TABLE 5.9   Step 2 in the 'road map' sequence for Tesco supply chain improvement

Step 2	Objective	Method	Examples in Tesco
Time compression	Elimination of non-value-adding time – 'waste'	Mapping identifies waste – take steps to eliminate waste.	Lean replenishment systems: – continuous replenishment (CR) for stores; – product grouping; – flow-through for suppliers.

Step 2: time compression to eliminate non-value-adding time

The seven classic Lean 'wastes', identified in Womack and Jones (1996), provide a very helpful way to examine the opportunities that Tesco used to make large and sustainable improvements within this phase of its 'road map' journey. Table 5.10 shows how Tesco time compression initiatives map against the seven wastes.

Each of the key initiatives highlighted in Table 5.10, which were rolled out right across Tesco's operations in a planned and very deliberate manner over a number of years from the late 1990s to the early 2000s, most as part of what Tesco called its 'Step Change' plan, is summarized below.

Continuous replenishment (CR)   The origins of store replenishment ordering lie in manually compiled orders with product delivered to each store by suppliers – a time-consuming and very inaccurate process. Thus the store manager or appointed deputy would review store shelf and backstore stock, assess likely sales and existing supplier orders in the period up to the likely delivery of any new order and

TABLE 5.10 How Tesco initiatives map on to the time compression phase of the 'road map'

Seven wastes		Tesco initiatives – brief description
Over-production	Making more than is needed	Continuous replenishment (CR) – aimed at bringing the right amount of shelf replenishment stock into stores and to leave no residue stock in the store backroom.
Transportation	Materials, parts, vehicles	Flowthrough – aimed at bringing in fast-moving SKUs that equalled a full vehicle load on an 'as needed for today's store orders' basis.
Excess operator motion	Unnecessary movement	Flowthrough – also avoided the need to put away to storage or let down to pickface. Product grouping – store deliveries were in 'sorted' rather than random assortment cages.
Time spent waiting	Parts etc not ready when required	Flowthrough – again, avoided delays waiting for product to be let down to pickface.
Over-processing	Doing things not required by the customer	CR and flowthrough – aimed at bringing the right amount of shelf replenishment stock to each store – avoided residue stock that won't fit on the shelf and has to be returned to backstore holding until needed.
Unnecessary inventory	Should only meet JIT needs	CR and flowthrough – aimed at bringing just the right amount of shelf replenishment stock to each store.
Defective products	Corrections, scrap, waste	Flowthrough – less putaway and letdown reduces the potential for damage to stock.

then place a new order. On-shelf product availability was a long way below 100 per cent.

Store congestion was made worse by the need to hold stock in a backstore holding, perhaps many days' stock of an individual SKU, and the arrival of a large number of supplier delivery vehicles on an individual day, delivering direct to each store from numerous factories. These factors put a limit on the number and range of SKUs that a store could offer, which impacted on any desire a consumer might have for 'one-stop shopping'.

Thus, the move to central distribution (introduced earlier in the chapter) – pioneered in the UK by Tesco among other retailers at the end of the 1970s and into the 1980s – helped to solve this limit on what range of products a store could hold. Each store now received all of its replenishment deliveries on dedicated delivery vehicles from the network of Tesco distribution centres. Over time this DC network was refined to have DCs handling different ranges of products. Typically, in the UK, this was:

- Ambient grocery:
  - fast-moving ambient product via local DCs very close to the stores they served (handling Pareto 'A' category products);
  - medium-moving ambient product via regional DCs (handling Pareto 'B' category products);
  - slow-moving ambient product via a national DC (handling Pareto 'C' category products).
- Fresh food:
  - large-volume suppliers via local DCs very close to the stores they served;
  - smaller-volume regional suppliers supplying perhaps regional speciality products delivering into the nearest consolidation centre, where product was aggregated into a full load for delivery to each fresh food local DC.
- Frozen food was originally co-located in the fresh food DCs. There is now a national frozen food DC.
- Beers, wines and spirits via a national DC – fast-moving SKUs may move to local DCs to meet peak volume demands, eg at Christmas.

- Non-food and clothing via a national DC.
- Certain products were (and are) still delivered direct to stores from suppliers, such as:
  - high-volume perishable products such as bread and milk;
  - prescription drugs for Tesco in-store pharmacies.

This move to centralized distribution away from delivery direct to stores also permitted some backstore space to be repurposed as selling floor area. The remaining backstore was intended to receive deliveries for sale over the next 24 hours rather than be a stockholding area.

This was all supported by a simultaneous change in moving to automated store ordering protocols based on electronic point of sale scans (EPOS checkout scans), stock on order from DCs, and shelf bookstock calculations to enable new orders to be raised on supplying DCs.

However, there was a significant factor that impacted upon the confidence that could be placed on the accuracy of replenishment orders. Stores were 'polled' on a once-per-day basis to collect data on sales, shelf stocks etc. There were no data available on what might be termed 'fulfilment performance', ie whether an individual SKU was always available when a customer tried to select it from the store shelf. Store data might show that particular SKUs were available in the store, but that did not necessarily mean that they were on-shelf – they could have still been in the backroom awaiting shelf filling.

The problem is similar to that when actions are based on averaged data rather than time series data – the daily poll gives no indication of what may have happened during the day concerned.

However, if EPOS data are polled on a more frequent basis, then a picture begins to emerge of what may have happened. For example, assume the following:

- Store EPOS is polled a number of times in a day.
- An individual SKU is selling regularly, appears to be on stockout and then resumes regular sales.
- The stockout did not coincide with a period awaiting the store replenishment vehicle to deliver. The only explanation

is that the product was available in the backstore but not replenished to the store shelf in time to avoid 'not available for customers'.

- This 'not available to customers' may coincide with an uplift in sales of a similar product – different pack size, alternative brand etc.

These time series data allow a different interpretation of the data to be made, such as what sales might have been if shelf replenishment performance had been more timely.

Continuous replenishment does this. After its introduction, which was phased in during the late 1990s and early 2000s, EPOS data were polled several times in the day. This permitted richer time series data to be collected and in turn allowed problems to be explored, process improvements to be identified and appropriate decisions to be made. The revised data also became a more reliable dataset for future forecasting.

A further benefit was that big-selling SKUs could be replenished on twice-daily deliveries – a main fill and a top-up in a single day. This reduced pressure on backstore operations by matching delivery volumes more closely to rate of sale.

Product grouping (known as 'family grouping' in the United States and Canada) Table 5.4 referred to the original research carried out in the SCDP project and showed how 46 per cent of the total product replenishment cost incurred from supplier factory gate to Tesco store shelf was actually in the 'last 50 metres', ie from backstore to in-store shelf. The end result of improved efficiency in maximizing vehicle fill, warehouse fill and warehouse product-picking performance was reduced distribution unit costs, but large costs were incurred in transporting individual roll cages around stores, unloading cases to the appropriate shelf location. This was made worse by the practice that developed of 'spotting' – leaving individual cases on the floor at the shelf for a return later to decant product to the shelf.

By taking a more holistic, system-wide view an alternative was developed based on categorizing products into a relatively few product groupings, eg canned vegetables, cereals, detergents etc. This change had the following impacts:

- Warehouse capacity was reduced, as products could no longer be located in random pick slots and location had to be within a certain set of pick slots.
- Cage fill was marginally worsened whenever the end of a product group pick did not coincide with a full cage.
- Marginally worsened cage fill had a marginal impact on delivery vehicle fill.

But these adverse impacts were more than compensated for by a significant factor: the consequent major benefit to store shelf replenishment. Cage contents could be decanted straight to store shelf with far less travel and no spotting – a much simpler operation.

This shows the potential for adverse impacts to arise from efficiency initiatives that do not assess the situation end to end. Once the needs of the end user are considered, a different – truly optimized – solution is the result.

Flowthrough (for 'time compression' reasons) Table 5.10 showed that the flowthrough initiative mapped against six of the seven wastes (all except over-production). Warehouse systems were originally the root cause of this 'waste', because they were originally designed when the prevailing capability was to work on semi-manual forecasting and picking systems managing stock.

Over time, Tesco capability had become better and better, with disciplines ensuring automated replenishment, better forecasting and more rapid replenishment 'supplier order–delivery to DC–delivery to store' cycles. This improved capability enabled the development of flowthrough. Flowthrough was a virtually stockless system that aimed to bring in, from the supplier, the right amount of stock needed by a DC to meet the orders, for that day, for the stores it served.

Data analysis of fast-moving ambient product SKU volumes delivered to stores from an individual DC met the lesser-known aspect of Pareto's law. This is that 10 per cent of the SKUs equated to 50 per cent of the total DC volume. Thus, relatively few SKUs accounted for half the DC volume handled. Essentially, flowthrough amounted to cross-docking this 10 per cent SKUs/50 per cent total through-put rather than supplying it from stock. The benefits were huge, namely:

- There was a 50 per cent reduction in the volume of pallets put away and let down to the pickface:
  - reduced labour requirement;
  - reduced potential for product damage;
  - the freeing up of much-needed DC space for range expansion.
- The remaining 90 per cent SKUs/50 per cent of DC volume was handled traditionally by putaway and letdown.
- A small amount of additional stock of the flowthrough SKUs is stocked in case of unexpected increases in demand above the anticipated daily flowthrough volume. However, this stock is not held under a traditional 'first in, first out' stockholding rule – it remains in stock until either it is used or it reaches say half of its shelf-life period (which is a year on many ambient products). At the 'half of shelf-life' trigger, the small safety stock is replaced by some of the incoming flowthrough order.

Summarizing, the flowthrough initiative had a pervasive impact, addressing the following 'wastes':

- Transportation: bringing in fast-moving ambient SKUs on an 'as needed for today's store orders' basis.
- Excess operator motion: reduced putaway to storage or letdown to the pickface.
- Time spent waiting: less delay waiting for product to be let down to the pickface.
- Over-processing: bringing the right amount of shelf replenishment stock to the store avoided residue stock that would not fit on the shelf and had to be returned to backstore holding until needed.

- Unnecessary inventory: bringing just the right amount of shelf replenishment stock to each store.
- Defective products: less putaway and letdown reduces the potential for damage to stock.

Note: Flowthrough also had an impact on the 'structure' phase of the 'road map' – this will be discussed in the section 'Step 4: structure'.

Step 3: collaboration

Stock management Basic stock management is about ordering replenishment product to arrive in DCs in time and in sufficient quantity to be delivered to stores to replenish shelves ready for customers to select what they wish to buy at the time of their visit. If only it were that simple. It would imply, among other factors:

- Basic demand for product was relatively constant and predictable.

TABLE 5.11 Step 3 in the 'road map' sequence for Tesco supply chain improvement

Step 3	Objective	Method	Examples in Tesco
Collaboration	Visibility	With suppliers: – share data; – end-to-end KPIs. Work across industry through agreed common standards.	Stock management. Tesco Information Exchange (TIE). Tesco Knowledge Hub. Industry-wide collaboration: – Efficient Consumer Response (ECR); – World Wide Retail Exchange (WWRE); – Consumer Goods Forum.

- Suppliers' suppliers received what they needed in a similar manner – static demand, reliable food and packaging supply, plant and equipment totally reliable, and delivery vehicles always delivering on time.

- Consumer demand for products was relatively static – not influenced by seasons, weather, events (Christmas, Easter, Halloween) or the state of the economy.

- There were no promotions.

- Promotional uplift in volume was predictable.

Clearly, the foregoing is a totally incorrect representation of what actually happens in grocery retailing. In short:

- demand is not stable;

- demand is impacted by seasonal and weather factors as well as the state of the economy;

- promotions are a significant and frequent occurrence affecting demand;

- competition between retailers adds to uncertainty.

Thus, it is impractical for stock managers to rely totally on their own means to attempt to ensure that the replenishment process – the right products in the right stores in the right quantities and at the right time – works effectively. A typical superstore might have 40,000–50,000 SKUs in-store at any given time – a major challenge to get them all correct all of the time.

Therefore, it is clear that collaboration between supply chain partners – suppliers, retailers, packaging suppliers etc – has a huge potential to ensure the replenishment process works effectively to meet customer needs. Collaboration involves a range of means that facilitate a full dialogue, including:

- Joint planning and execution – plan, do and review the transactions used to deliver replenishment, but also learn from existing replenishment processes and develop improvements to increase competence and capability.

- Data transfer mechanisms – one-way such as electronic data interchange (EDI) and two-way such as Tesco Information

Exchange (TIE) or the World Wide Retail Exchange (WWRE).

- Vendor-managed inventory (VMI), where the supplier takes the responsibility to manage the total replenishment process on behalf of the retailer.
- In some instances, co-location of supplier and stock management staff to facilitate better performance. This is not always a permanent arrangement; it could occur perhaps over a critical trading period.

One area where joint planning is particularly critical is in managing promotions. Promotional campaigns for products can be developed over a long time as part of a strategic focus on a range or item or, on occasion, can be more reactive, a response to a category missing its budget, for example. Promotional management can be segmented into three phases, each being challenging to manage:

- the pre-promotion phase, where estimated sales uplifts need to be worked out and stocks need to be built up, often in anticipation of higher sales, so that authoritative feature displays can be set out by stores in advance;
- the promotion phase, where lessons need to be quickly learnt about the actual sales and the need to manage sales and consequent stocks that are either ahead of or behind estimate; and finally
- the post-promotion phase, where stocks need to be scaled back to the level of new post-promotion sales levels as quickly and as smoothly as possible. In addition, there needs to be an evaluation of what worked well and what needs refining, to be fed into the next promotional cycle.

In a broad sense, what Tesco was leading was a recognition that there was no point in optimizing the company's internal operations if the interface between itself and its suppliers was not also optimized. By aligning objectives, processes and learning using shared information, the culture of collaborative behaviour that Lean thinking encouraged, and Tesco began to lead the way on from this time, became evident in the way Tesco engaged with its supply chains[1].

Tesco Information Exchange Key to this development was the Tesco Information Exchange launched in 1998. TIE is an online mechanism that allows suppliers to access daily and time series data relating to sales, stocks etc of the products they supply to Tesco. A variety of menus and screens provide this in both numerical and chart format. For example, information can be viewed as follows:

- Daily sales of an SKU at national and individual DC level.
- Participation – how an individual SKU contributes to the total sales of a particular group of products. For example, a supplier can see data and graphs showing its liquid biological cleaner in a 500ml pack against a total for all suppliers providing a similar product (but not the individual data for each competitor supplier).
- Data are available as daily, weekly and year-to-date data versus last year's data etc.
- Information that both supplier and Tesco can use to monitor and evaluate promotions and adjust inventory levels accordingly.

Brand managers from suppliers, rather than working in isolation from retailers like Tesco, perceiving retailers as merely distribution channels or barriers to their customers, were having to adjust to the world where they were having to work more in concert with retailers and to develop marketing campaigns jointly that would build both the suppliers' and the retailers' brands.

Tesco Knowledge Hub In more recent years the Tesco Knowledge Hub was established. The Tesco Knowledge Hub is a supply chain sustainability collaboration mechanism, providing an online knowledge-sharing platform for members, including people from Tesco's largest suppliers, Tesco staff and external experts. The Knowledge Hub is a key pillar in Tesco's work to reduce the carbon footprint of the products it sells.

Tesco has set a target to reduce its carbon footprint by 30 per cent by 2020. The Knowledge Hub enables suppliers to work with Tesco, allowing each party to accelerate efforts to reduce greenhouse gas emissions throughout their supply chain, while at the same time unlocking resource efficiency savings and building trusted relationships between them.

As well as collaborative initiatives that were focused on supporting the development of inter-organizational relations between Tesco and its supplier base, Tesco was also among the pioneers in developing industry-wide collaboration forums. These are discussed below.

Efficient Consumer Response (ECR)   Tesco was one of the main supporters of the ECR movement in Europe, which began in the mid-1990s and continues to this day, notably in Europe, Asia and Australasia. ECR's mission is 'working together to fulfil consumer wishes better, faster, at less cost and in a sustainable way'.[2] It has proved to be an effective and pioneering forum in facilitating and focusing retailers, manufacturers and service providers to act together on non-competitive issues to bring about transformative change to the whole sector. Leahy himself was co-Chair of ECR with Frank Riboud, CEO of Danone, for a period in the movement's early years, underlining Tesco's belief in working productively with other players across the industry.

World Wide Retail Exchange   This section is about the development of industry-wide approaches to improving the end-to-end supply chain by developing a shared view between retailers and their suppliers on a range of topics – product identification, standards, supply chain improvement etc.

The WWRE was founded in March 2000 by 17 international retailers, all market leaders. It was based in the United States but was internationally oriented and included retailers such as Tesco, Ahold, Boots, El Corte Inglés, Kmart, RadioShack, Toys R Us and J C Penney.

The original membership included retailers and suppliers in the food, general merchandise, textile and home, and drugstore sectors. Their goal was to enable participating retailers and suppliers to:

- simplify,
- rationalize, and
- automate supply chain processes

by eliminating inefficiencies in the supply chain.

WWRE was set up to operate as an open, independently managed company that generated benefits for its members, suppliers and, ultimately, the consumer through improving supply chain efficiency within the retail industry.

It identified the following sources of value:

- *efficiency* – simplify, eliminate and automate existing business processes;
- *service* – improve existing business processes in an efficient and innovative way;
- *innovation* – new facilities for collaborative commerce.

Today, these services are offered by NeoGrid. NeoGrid, formerly trading as Agentrics, was created from the merger of World Wide Retail Exchange (WWRE) and the Global Network Exchange (GNX). It offers solutions created by many of the world's largest and most prominent retailers to meet their supply chain service needs. The solutions include:

- demand planning and replenishment;
- retail and distribution intelligence;
- strategic sourcing solutions;
- logistics and financial exchange.

NeoGrid describes its services in the paper 'Retail Supply Chain Collaboration: Down to the Store Shelf'.

Additionally the Global Commerce Initiative (GCI) is aimed at facilitating dialogue and bringing manufacturers and retailers together to simplify and enhance global commerce and improve consumer experience in the retail supply chain. It aims to drive implementation of GSI standards and best practice. GSI standards include, but are much more than, the individual bar codes that identify different SKUs. GSI standards provide a framework for supply chain visibility as follows:

- standards for the identification of items, locations, shipments, assets etc and associated data;
- standards for encoding and capturing data in physical data carriers such as bar codes and RFID tags;
- standards for sharing data between parties.

Note: GSI identification standards do not provide identification of country of origin for a given product. Member companies may wish to manufacture products anywhere in the world. GSI focuses on three sectors – consumer goods and retail, health care, and transport and logistics.

The Consumer Goods Forum Tesco also works with the retail industry to tackle industry-wide problems through the Consumer Goods Forum (CGF), which is a global network of over 400 retailers and manufacturers, established in 2009. In 2010 the CGF members pledged to help achieve zero net deforestation by 2020, and they are working to increase the production and purchasing of sustainably sourced commodities associated with deforestation such as palm oil, soy, beef, and pulp and paper. These targets are being addressed through the CGF's 'sustainability pillar'[3] (one of their five strategic pillars). It will achieve the following purpose for the consumer goods industry: 'drive and communicate sustainability improvements throughout the value chain of the… Industry by:

- addressing sustainability challenges that impact the industry;
- bringing global alignment and voluntary standards to non-competitive areas such as ethical sourcing;
- developing and agreeing methodologies and metrics that measure sustainability improvements in the industry'.

The CGF's website describes its initiatives, which include:

- A Climate Change Initiative to deal with a major threat of climate change to customers, businesses, the economy and society. It has three elements:

- sustainability measurement: understanding the environmental and social impacts of consumer products;

- developing a global system for carbon measurement of company business activities and the products sold;

- an extension to include other issues, such as water use.

- Addressing supply chain hotspots:

- Deforestation accounts for 20 per cent of all greenhouse gas (GHG) emissions – mainly as a result of reuse for soya and palm oil cultivation, timber logging to produce paper and board, and cattle rearing. A target of zero net deforestation by 2020 has been set.

- Refrigeration is a significant and increasing source of GHGs caused by the inclusion of hydrofluorocarbons (HFCs). Currently these account for 1.5 per cent of warming potential and are forecast to represent 6–9 per cent of total GHGs by 2050 if no action is taken. The CGF has decided to begin phasing out HFC refrigerants by 2015 and replace them with non-HFC natural refrigerant alternatives.

- A common language. The CGF has developed a glossary that defines the terms used in environmental sustainability. It has also developed a packaging sustainability protocol.

Finally, the Consumer Goods Forum has published an 'Activation Toolkit', which can be downloaded from the Consumer Goods Forum website.[4]

Step 4: structure

Logistics product management Automated store replenishment systems when they were introduced by retailers in the 1980s had a very beneficial impact on on-shelf availability performance, ie consistently making product available for consumer selection. The main reasons for this were:

- The starting-point performance was not very good.

- The automated systems introduced logic and rigour, which were better than human 'emotional' responses – 'play safe', 'just in case' etc.

TABLE 5.12 Step 4 in the 'road map' sequence for Tesco supply chain improvement

Step 4	Objective	Method	Examples in Tesco
Structure	Strategic stock that addresses demand variability	Align networks to value streams. Eliminate 'process' causes of stock.	Logistics product management: – shelf-ready packaging; – factory-gate pricing; – flowthrough; – reducing bullwhip; – design and implementation of end-to-end holistic supply chain solutions.

- Automated systems have more capability to deal with large numbers of SKUs.
- Appropriate automated systems handled different types of products, namely:
  - 'Pick by store' systems for stocked, ambient or frozen product;
  - 'Pick by line' systems for fresh, short-shelf-life product. These pick stock in the DC to zero residue each day, although they may have a reallocate capability to revise the store allocation close to vehicle-despatch-to-store deadlines.

However, having achieved this improvement, OSA had reached a plateau. Thus, automated store replenishment systems had reached the limits of their capability, mainly because they were designed as 'one size fits all' systems:

- All products were made available for delivery to store on a daily basis. Thus, whether they were fast-moving or slow-moving, seasonal or all-year-round products, they had one rule – daily replenishment!

- Ambient or frozen – always delivered from stock using 'pick by store' algorithms.
- Fresh – always delivered using 'pick to zero' algorithms.

There was a need to remove this limit on OSA, by using systems that were:

- better matched to the demand dynamics of individual SKUs;
- capable of recognizing that dynamics change at different times of the year – seasons, promotions, events etc;
- capable of switching products between systems to suit the dynamics at any given time.

In fact, the need was to have the ability to choose, at any given time, the most appropriate replenishment system for the demand dynamics of an SKU, but to handle it through a DC that had an appropriate temperature regime. The demand dynamics are as depicted in Figure 5.5.

So individual SKUs are 'interrogated' to establish their demand dynamics and then delivered from the DC as shown in the examples in Table 5.13.

FIGURE 5.5 The three axes of logistics product management

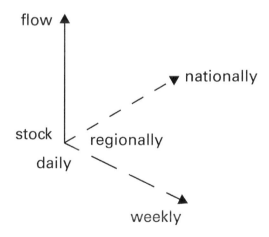

TABLE 5.13 SKU DC to store delivery options

Temperature regime	Fast-moving	Medium-moving	Slow-moving
Ambient	Daily flowthrough	Daily from stock	Weekly from stock
Fresh	Eg daily potato merchandise units Pick to zero	Daily pick to zero	Daily pick to zero
Frozen	Daily from stock	Daily from stock	Weekly from stock
Options	Eg fast-moving wines in merchandise units at Christmas, cross-docked via any DC, ambient or chill Eg seasonal clothing launch, cross-docked from ambient DCs at launch, with replenishment from national DC daily or weekly		

Shelf-ready packaging The conventional journey for product destined for a store via a DC is as follows:

- Pallets of product arrive from the supplier into the Tesco DC.
- DC handling:
  - for ambient or frozen product, pallets are unloaded from supplier delivery, put away to storage, let down to the pick slot or picked to a store delivery roll cage in cases;
  - for fresh product, pallets or wheeled dollies are unloaded from supplier delivery and picked to a store delivery cage or wheeled dolly at the DC store assembly point in cases or plastic trays.
- Roll cages or dollies containing cases or trays of individual products are delivered to the store.
- Cases or trays are decanted to the store shelf.

This journey involves a huge amount of double handling – or 'waste' in Lean terms!

However, for faster-moving products, alternative, 'waste-free' methods have been developed that combine the transit mechanism with the store display mechanism. This reduces to a minimum the amount of double handling. One can walk around a Tesco store (or indeed other retailers, as these mechanisms have become commonly used) and observe examples such as:

1 Wheeled dollies, which can be wheeled from supplier packaging (can or bottle filling etc) through to store merchandise (see Figure 5.6).

FIGURE 5.6 Wheeled dolly merchandise unit

2 Potato dollies – like 1 above. Bags of potatoes are filled at the supplier packaging location, placed in potato dollies and delivered via the DC to the store. They become the store merchandise unit (MU) from which customers select their purchase (Figure 5.7).

3 Paper goods (kitchen towel, toilet rolls etc) in large transit and display outers. The outer is placed at the merchandise location; the outer front is removed and it becomes the merchandiser.

4 Promotional dollies – during periods of high demand, as in promotions, individual SKUs can be handled via the appropriate mechanism as described in 1 to 3 above.

FIGURE 5.7   Potato dolly

Initially, suppliers expressed concerns as to their capability to handle MUs via their automated systems. However, they are now commonplace (see Figure 5.8) and seen as a way for the supplier to grow its sales volume, as they contribute to improving OSA.

Table 5.4 disclosed that back in 1995 46 per cent of the costs in the supply chain were actually incurred in the 'last 50 metres', within

FIGURE 5.8 Auto filling on to a wheeled merchandise unit

the store itself. The examples listed above improved this position enormously for the fast-selling products. But there remained much that could be done to generate efficiencies for slower lines. This was due to many factors, such as the low volumes involved in filling any one product up on the shelf, the need for date rotation, the amount of rework that needs to be undertaken if product amounts delivered do not actually fit on the shelves and so on.

The product grouping initiative discussed earlier began to help make improvements, but beyond this suppliers were encouraged to supply in packaging that would reduce the amount of decanting single products from transit packaging at the shelf fill operation. Thus, increasing volumes of goods began to be developed with suppliers that had transit packaging that permitted direct merchandising to the selling shelf, which allowed a whole case of product to be put on to the shelf in one go from the delivery pallet.

Factory-gate pricing As Tesco has consistently reduced its need for 'structural' stock (stock that buffers less-than-capable processes), so it has needed to adjust the volume of product moving on primary transport (ie inbound from suppliers to DCs). What is required to support lower inventories of each product is smaller and more frequent deliveries of these products. This need keeps volume movements aligned along the supply chain and reduces the potential for 'bullwhip' (demand amplification).

Thus, with the need for more frequent and smaller individual deliveries, it was no longer acceptable for a supplier to fill a lorry with a single product: Tesco wanted only enough stock to cover the next period of sales, with a minimum of buffer stock.

As Tesco became Leaner in terms of its inventory-holding policies, suppliers, no longer able to transport in full shipping loads, as they had done in the past, began to consolidate mixed loads of products. Sometimes this occurred with ranges of products all supplied from a single large supplier, and sometimes it was managed through inter-supplier agreements, with the use of consolidation centres that were co-managed through supplier agreements.

Tesco recognized that the way the primary supply chain was being managed was fairly ad hoc and far from being optimized. It established that to rectify the situation what it essentially needed was to establish fuller control of this inbound supply chain itself.

Consequently, in 2001, Tesco launched its factory-gate pricing initiative, ie paying for goods on an 'ex factory' basis without any distribution costs. Control of the inbound transport leg from the supplier to the Tesco distribution centre network then passed from the supplier's control to Tesco, which set up its own network of consolidation centres to manage consolidation of part loads from virtually all its suppliers in the UK more holistically.

Effectively this gave a single point of control for the whole inbound logistics network, which allowed many synergies to be realized. Potter, Mason and Lalwani (2007) segmented these into operational, tactical and strategic benefits, and there is no doubt that the move to factory-gate pricing had the effect of significantly strengthening Tesco's ability to compete through its supply chain prowess. With this single change Tesco was able to generate major operational savings in distribution costs and be clearer about exactly what it was paying for when purchasing goods from its suppliers (before this, the combined goods and shipment purchase price clouded what exactly was being paid for), and it permitted greater synergies to be developed with backloads from secondary distribution activities (deliveries from Tesco DCs to stores). The change also removed volume from competitor inbound supply chains, having the effect of making them less efficient, particularly the lower-volume players, which compounded the strategic advantage for Tesco.

The concept, once successfully implemented in the UK, was then repeated in other parts of the Tesco business, notably for inbound European supply chains, the servicing of Tesco's eastern European stores and in Asia, both for the store networks and where suppliers were delivering to ports for onward shipment to Europe, for example.

Flowthrough (for 'structure' reasons) DCs exist for two reasons: 1) to handle natural variation in demand; and 2) to buffer less-than-perfect process. Improved process capability and repeatability reduce this dependence on DCs. Because flowthrough is a stockless operation, it requires only a suitable space to receive daily inbound volumes for reassembly and delivery to store. The result is that available

DC space – ambient or fresh DC – can be fine-tuned to handle flow-through volume, particularly the seasonal high-volume lines such as wine, cooking foil etc.

Removing bullwhip As noted above, Tesco recognized that the natural phenomenon of bullwhip was occurring in its supply chains. By means of going Leaner, reducing inventories, lowering case sizes, increasing the frequency of orders through the CR initiative and decreasing lead times through policies such as flowthrough, the demand amplification effects were being subdued compared to former levels. However, Tesco was still concerned that store ordering systems were too sensitive to sales levels being either ahead or behind target for a product over a specific time period.

In a study conducted by Cardiff Business School (Potter and Disney, 2010), the research team identified seven replenishment algorithms that existed in Tesco's ordering systems and demonstrated that, of those, three (representing 65 per cent of sales) were generating excessive bullwhip. By applying bullwhip reduction principles, in particular reducing order variability to 75 per cent of sales levels on one algorithm, the range of amplification was then reduced, resulting in considerable ongoing improvements in the performance of the affected supply chains.

Given that Tesco was now controlling the inbound flow of product after the factory-gate pricing initiative, Tesco was able to observe and directly benefit from the smoother inbound flows.

Design and implementation of holistic supply chain solutions

Once these measures had been established, which overall took many years, control, predictability and better product flow became a characteristic of the Tesco supply chain. This provided the foundation for a new wave of initiatives driven by the quest to better optimize the wider supply chain, ie to think and act holistically and invariably also to include the objective of reducing supply chain emissions over six years by 50 per cent as part of Tesco's sustainability pillar agenda, introduced above.

One illustration of this way of thinking was given in the BBC television programme *Christmas Supermarket Secrets* on 15 December

2013.[5] The aim of the programme was to go behind the scenes and uncover what the customer does not usually see of how the supermarkets and their suppliers work to improve the products the customer buys and the supply chains used.

The example that really exemplified the way Tesco now thinks and acts in how it manages its supply chains came in the episode that looked at how Tesco supplies wine to its stores. Tesco is now the biggest wine retailer in the world and has looked hard at how it moves wine from vineyards around the world to supply its stores. It has opened a dedicated bottling plant in north-west England to support this, but up to 2007 was dealing with over 3,000 lorry loads a year in shipments from east coast ports. In a project that took 18 months to develop, by directing shipments to the port of Liverpool instead and then running a twice-weekly service by barge along the Manchester Ship Canal to Irlam in Greater Manchester, where the bottling plant is located, a carbon reduction of 80 per cent compared to the original road solution was achieved, combined with significant demurrage savings by moving the containers to the plant from the port. The programme also highlighted that the wine is moved in huge bags stuffed into containers, which means weighty and fragile glass is not involved in global shipments from suppliers either and Tesco can ensure higher levels of quality and consistency in terms of its bottling and labelling standards, a further advantage of this postponement supply chain strategy. Parts of this case study are also written up in an IGD case study series.[6]

The example illustrates how invariably today Tesco is trying to identify wastes in the wider supply chain and is beginning to unlock real and substantial upgrades in performance by radically reconfiguring what has been accepted as normal practice up until now.

Conclusions

In this chapter we have aimed to present the key principles that Tesco has tried to deploy in developing its capacity to compete through the mastery of its supply chains, essentially up to the store shelf, which it controls. The results achieved by Tesco have been all about making the supply chain (1) *simpler for stores* – the 'internal' customer at the end of the supply chain; and (2) *better for customers* – the 'external' beneficiary of the supply chain improvement in effectiveness and efficiency.

We have shown how Tesco has used Lean thinking to develop and continuously improve a customer-focused supply chain by implementing a structured and sequenced improvement agenda. Over time, a population of improvements in capability have been amassed, which when combined have radically enhanced Tesco's performance as an organization.

What is clear is that Tesco's improvements in this area have been no accident. They have been developed through a purposeful campaign that has been aligned with Tesco's overall business strategy. With hindsight, it may all now seem quite intuitive, but in reality each step of the sequence has needed substantial investment, business focus and discipline, as well as the support of Tesco employees, in what is a very labour-intensive activity. Tesco has achieved consistency by combining skilled people with a focused process and market-leading systems capable of regularly meeting customer aspirations, as shown in Figure 5.9. Over a period, Tesco has developed a core engine within its business that can be relied upon as an underpinning strength.

FIGURE 5.9 Consistency – repeatedly meeting customer aspirations

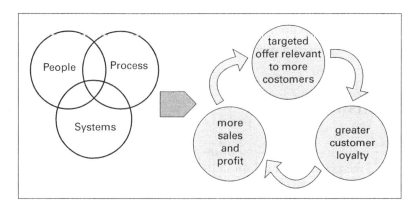

And, perhaps, the journey Tesco has been on, in developing its business and supply chain strategies, was more than attempts to improve its physical supply chain management prowess. What this gave Tesco was a mindset, now woven into the very fabric of what it stand for, which is fundamentally the belief that effectiveness is what matters to customers, rather than efficiency. This continues to drive Tesco's endeavour. It has provided a way for the organization to think and behave that predominantly has allowed it to stay ahead of the chasing pack of competitors. This is a theme that will be expanded on in Chapter 6.

However, time moves on. As a result of various forces, the supply chain recipe that may have worked needs to be refined, sometimes incrementally, sometimes radically. Tesco today is having to deal with arguably the most challenging conditions it has faced for over two decades at least. Can it cope with this change and still retain its core strengths and beliefs, which could fuel it to another period of impressive growth? This will be the story of Chapter 7, which looks at the challenges of today and of the future for Tesco as a company and for the way it manages its supply chains and logistics.

Key chapter summary points

1 Tesco supply chain improvement demonstrates that 'effectiveness' should be the system purpose.

2 Efficiency can follow provided it does not diminish or destroy effective delivery of value in the process.

3 The Tesco supply chain is an example of Russell Ackoff's (2010) challenge to focus on effectiveness ('doing the right thing') rather than efficiency ('trying to do the wrong thing righter').

4 Lean thinking has provided principles and a framework to support the development of the Tesco supply chain.

5 The principles Tesco used to guide it were:

- to be customer focused;

- to be responsive;

- to be planned;

- to be disciplined, with clear standards applied; and wherever possible

- to have 'one-touch' replenishment mechanisms as the goal.

6 The framework followed four sequential steps:

- step 1: establishing process control;

- step 2: time compression;

- step 3: collaboration;

- step 4: structure.

7 Through following this process and tackling change initiatives one by one, meaningful results can be achieved that:

- deliver value to customers, improving availability, range etc;

- strive for supply chain efficiencies that permit better prices;

- by consistent delivery support Tesco's goal to earn customers' lifetime loyalty;

- underpin Tesco's 'Better, simpler, cheaper' principles; and in turn

- fuel the growth that Tesco strives for.

Notes

1 Tesco uses technology to tighten supply chain, *Marketing Week*, 5 February 1998

2 http://ecr-europe.org/about-ecr/what-is-ecr

3 www.theconsumergoodsforum.com/sustainability.aspx

4 http://sustainability.mycgforum.com/

5 http://www.bbc.co.uk/programmes/b03lp9rk

6 tinyurl.com/q9njbg2

Tesco and continuous improvement

06

Debunking seven myths of conventional business thinking

Introduction

The journey Tesco has been on, notably over the last 20 years or so, has been a remarkable one. We have argued in this book that, while there are many ingredients that have combined to result in Tesco's performance during this period, one of the key factors has been the way in which Tesco has aimed to master its supply chain systems. This pursuit has contributed to Tesco, during the period from 1993 to 2012, increasing sales and profit every year (see Appendix 5). As a result, this has moved the company from being the number two player in the UK grocery market to the number two retailer in the world. Arguably, only recently, and for the first time since the early 1990s, is Tesco beginning to be questioned as to whether the broad strategy that enabled it to achieve such a sustained period of growth is the strategy that will allow it to maintain this trajectory into the future. This chapter and Chapter 7 reflect on these themes.

First, in this chapter, we take an overview of the 20-year continuous growth period to 2012 and ask what Tesco did that enabled it to differentiate itself from its competitors over that time. Thus we will unveil and examine seven, invariably counter-intuitive, ways of thinking and working that we argue have characterized the Tesco approach. By developing and deploying these ways of working, Tesco has steadily built the capabilities needed to become a smarter organization, capable for the most part of being able to stay ahead of the competition over a substantial period of time, enabling it to get better and better in organizational performance terms. Hopefully, these overarching themes will provoke debate and help to draw out some of the generic messages that make the Tesco story relevant to virtually all types of organizations.

Then, in Chapter 7, we look afresh at the challenges Tesco faces today. We examine whether the strategy and the ways of working that helped it reach where it is now should be the approach that will help it move forward successfully.

What sets Tesco apart?

This chapter reflects on much of the ground that the book has covered and attempts to distil the essence of what separates Tesco from the chasing pack. What is it that has made Tesco different? What is the recipe that allowed Tesco to outdistance the others and resulted in it setting the pace for change in many of the markets in which it competes?

The keys perhaps lie in Tesco's approach and ways of thinking and behaving that have allowed it continually to harness its organizational system to a common goal: to serve the customer better and better. This aligns with the position of the leading advocate of total quality management, W E Deming, who clearly demonstrated that 95 per cent of business problems lie in the organizational system, not with employees. With the business system encouraging all employees to pull together in the same direction towards a common purpose, they are able to work collaboratively and continuously towards perfecting the processes that exist across their business and in their supply chains. Improvement comes through gradually removing adverse system conditions. Toyota took this message to the core of its business model, and clearly Tesco has the same belief in its efficacy. Easy to say, hard to do!

Through the adoption of this philosophy, Tesco has learnt a great deal. In the years 1993–2012 this resulted in it consistently wrong-footing its competitors by applying ground-breaking, often counter-intuitive, 'breaking the mould' thinking in the way it decided to take the business forward. Many of the examples have been introduced in this book and include:

- *The One in Front campaign:* This was introduced by Leahy as Marketing Director in 1994 at a time when all Tesco's competitors were cutting store staffing in difficult trading times, not unlike those of today, and thus were suffering from long till queues, especially at peak times such as at lunchtimes or on Saturdays. By 2010 Tesco was still stating that the 'one-in-front initiative… continue[s] to keep us ahead of the industry on customer measures of checkout service'.[1]

- *The Tesco Clubcard:* This was launched in February 1995, at a time when data-creating loyalty cards were not understood or commonly used by other organizations. Secretly launched, 'it wrong-footed competitors' (Humby, Hunt and Phillips, 2003).

- *The first 24-hour opening:* In 1996, Tesco became the first to open its doors 24 hours a day six days a week. The number of stores open 24 hours a day quickly grew: 200 by 2000, and 365 by 2002 in the UK.

- *Store-based picking for grocery home shopping:* The Tesco.com grocery business was launched in 2000. Rather than adopting the conventional picking solution for the fast-growing development in grocery home shopping, using dedicated warehouses to pick home shopping orders, Tesco chose to pick and deliver internet grocery orders from its local supermarkets. This enabled Tesco to make home shopping available to 90 per cent of the UK population by the end of 2000.[2] (The conventional, 'efficient' specialist DC solution would have taken years to deliver, and its commercial viability was questionable too.)

- *Tesco Express on petrol forecourts:* After experimenting with small Tesco stores on petrol forecourts, Tesco announced in February 2000 that it was investing in a three-year plan to create 150 of these stores on Esso forecourts.[3]

- *Tesco Express neighbourhood convenience stores launched:* In 2002, building on the success of the Tesco petrol station forecourt Expresses, Tesco decided to prioritize the development of Express stores for local communities too. And once the decision was made Tesco was, as usual, quick to enact the strategy, purchasing T&S's 850 stores in October 2002 and opening 270 Express stores in 2005, bringing the total to 550 by that time[4]. This strategy was quite different to that of its competitors, notably Asda, which was fixed on the traditional large supermarket model, a business that was about to go into decline in the ensuing decade as shoppers moved to discount, local and online alternatives.

- *Tesco in a Box:* In 2001, to help Tesco handle its information technology more efficiently, it started identifying best-practice processes across its business, supported by a standard suite of systems, so that the latest version could be rolled out time after time when needed across the business. This internal measure was called 'Tesco in a Box' and was extended so that by 2007 all systems could talk to each other.[5]

- *Factory-gate pricing:* Tesco surprised the whole UK grocery industry in 2001 when it announced that it was changing the way it purchased products. Rather than its suppliers being responsible for delivery to Tesco's distribution centres, Tesco moved to buy products at 'ex-factory' prices (ie paying just for the price of the products, not the distribution as well as was conventional practice across the industry) and took responsibility for most of the UK inbound distribution to its network in collaboration with suppliers, hauliers and consolidators.

- *100 per cent product availability:* Conventional thinking would suggest that striving for 100 per cent product availability does not make commercial sense, as the law of diminishing returns implies that achieving extra availability over a certain point is too costly to be worthwhile. Yet Tesco, which strives for effectiveness above efficiency, thinks and acts differently and strives for 100 per cent availability of all products in its stores and its distribution centres. In 2010, for instance, Tesco stated that, 'by developing more efficient ordering systems, introducing better in-store monitoring processes and changing the way we store our stock we have reduced evening gaps in fresh food by 18%'.[6]

- *Self-scanning checkouts:* In 2004 Tesco introduced the first trial of self-service checkouts,[7] and was one of the first in the industry to put this idea into practice.

- *Tesco Direct:* Launched in September 2006, Tesco Direct was a pioneer in offering a multi-channel shopping solution. Customers could browse online or via a catalogue, they could order items by phone or online, and they could choose to have their goods delivered to their home or collect them from over 200 collection desks in stores by 2008.[8]

- *A supermarket for everyone:* Conventional wisdom suggests that companies should target specific customer segments. Tesco has broken this assumption with a supermarket philosophy that targets everyone. And it works. For instance, Tesco stated in 2005: 'customers love both our Value and Finest ranges. In fact 77% choose to buy from both'.[9]

- *Carbon footprint on products:* From 2008, working with the Carbon Trust, Tesco began to put the carbon footprint on product labels – the amount of CO_2 emissions associated with the supply of each product. By 2011 over 500 products were labelled in this way (Tesco Annual Review 2011: 11).

- *Ordering on smartphones:* By 2011 Tesco customers could scan the bar codes of items and then order groceries on their smartphones for delivery to their homes.[10]

- *Virtual shops in South Korea:* Virtual shops of Tesco goods at bus stops and railway stations allow customers to shop during their commute to and from work.

- *Click & Collect:* Tesco was a pioneer in developing 'collect' booths in its car parks. For example, by 2012 it already had 45 stores that offered Click & Collect groceries.[11]

- *Tesco Facebook:* Tesco saw quickly that integrating a social media presence into its offer fitted with the company's strategy of listening to customers and acting on their feedback. The Tesco Facebook page had grown to more than 680,000 'likes' by 2012.[12]

- *Launch of the Hudl:* The Tesco tablet was launched in 2013, very competitively priced at £119. The 'T' symbol in the bottom left corner allows users quickly to gain access to all Tesco's services: Tesco Bank, Tesco.com, Tesco Direct, Blinkbox and so on.

- *The supply chain Blueprint Team:* Managing diverse and complex supply chains across 12 markets in a standard way is a significant challenge for Tesco. The Blueprint Team comprises a set of supply chain experts brought together to spread best practice to improve operational efficiencies. The idea won the European Supply Chain Excellence Award for 2013, with the judges saying 'they had a clear vision which they were able to demonstrate was aligned to the corporate strategy'.[13]

All these pioneering examples indicate that Tesco is a business not afraid of learning and changing. It is a company with outstanding operational effectiveness and uses this base, together with its ethos to orientate itself around its customers, to innovate continually and to do the right things; indeed 'doing the right thing' was how Philip Clarke concluded his statement in the 2012 Tesco annual review.

Over the 20 years of continuous growth to 2012 Tesco could be characterized as being a 'high-velocity organization' as Steven Spear (2009) liked to term such companies in his seminal book *Chasing the Rabbit*, 'racing from success to success with growing market share, profitability and reputation'. Spear's argument was that every company 'advances over time, improving performance along various metrics such as quality, efficiency, product or service variety, workplace safety, and time to market. The problem for the pack is that the rabbit achieves a certain level before everyone else and, while others close in on where the rabbit was, it has darted away, still to be chased but not captured' (Spear, 2009). Spear cited examples of high-velocity companies from many sectors, but it was Toyota, which came to personify the Japanese way of working, that he recognized as particularly important for an understanding of why some companies managed continually to stay in front. Spear pinned it down to the 'velocity of improvement and problem solving'. Through a process known as *Kaizen* (continuous improvement), companies that were following the Lean way of working had teams of people most closely involved in work activities systematically improving that work with a sense of purpose and urgency. While the Lean way of working was significant, 'copying the tools alone did not generate the paradoxical combination of stability and flexibility that was increasingly associated with Toyota. It was Toyota's way of designing and improving processes that generated both short-term stability and longer-term agility and responsiveness' (Spear and Bowen, 1999, cited in Spear, 2009).

As we have discussed throughout this book, one of the foundations of the Tesco success too has been the adoption of Lean thinking as an underpinning philosophy to guide the business from the mid-1990s until today. Thus Tesco has become an exemplar of the benefits of adopting the Lean approach outside its heartland of the automotive sector. It has fuelled a way of working that, until the last couple of years, has allowed it to stay ahead of the chasing pack, as a high-velocity organization, just as in Spear's summary of Toyota, Southwest Airlines and Alcoa. In the process, Tesco in many ways defied convention and established new ways of working that have led to sustainable success. To gain further insight into the Tesco approach, seven invariably counter-intuitive, myth-debunking ideas to which Tesco adheres are now presented and examined.

How Tesco has defied conventional wisdom

Conventional wisdom says efficiency wins. Tesco's counter-intuitive answer is: No. Effectiveness wins!

As has been emphasized throughout this book one of the key counter-intuitive approaches adopted by Tesco is to strive to improve its effectiveness in providing for its customers, knowing that efficiency will also improve as a result. This can be seen too in the way Toyota operates its production system, and Tesco builds this same 'effectiveness first, efficiency follows' purpose into its business through its 'Better, simpler, cheaper' principles. In summary, Tesco believes that its quest for efficiency should not destroy effective value delivery.

This ideal goes to the very heart of the way the company conceives of itself, the business operating model. If managed and operating well it provides the business with a virtuous circle that fuels the business, driving it forward continuously year after year. Better effectiveness drives sales, higher sales drive volume, and higher volume drives profit growth if margins are held constant, which generally they were over the 20-year period we are reviewing here.

Of course, efficiency improvements can also feed into effectiveness improvement in an extra loop in this virtuous circle: efficiency improvements from developments in the supply chain can be fed into better prices, which leads to higher sales volume, with higher profits again ensuing if the margin is retained (see Figure 6.1).

Tesco does not fall into the trap that many businesses fall into, either by chasing efficiencies as a primary goal and only then trying to deliver effectiveness or alternatively feeding efficiency improvements straight into boosting margins, a temptation that many businesses succumb to.

Retail is in many ways a cyclical business, and momentum counts for a great deal. When the virtuous circle is moving in your favour, with the management of the supply chain constantly delivering effectiveness and then efficiencies each year that can be used to fuel lower prices, then, as Tesco enjoyed for 20 years, this provides for a perpetual period of sustained growth. Many of the Tesco supply chain

FIGURE 6.1 Tesco increase profits through increasing volumes – not by increasing margins

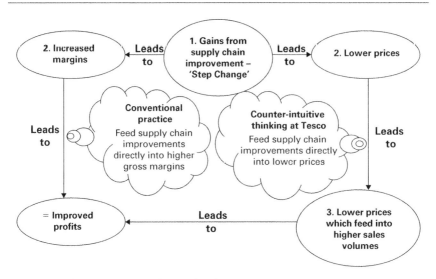

SOURCE Developed from Evans and Mason (2012)

efficiency projects were planned and managed under the Step Change programme, with approximately £500 million of efficiency savings being generated every year and fed in each time to lower and lower prices.

However, as we will discuss in Chapter 7, in the recent past a reverse has begun to occur. For a whole series of reasons, a vicious rather than a virtuous circle has begun to take hold: lower sales, feeding into lower profits, so there is less money to invest in new supply chain efficiency projects, as well as lower volumes to generate economies of scale. This in turn feeds into less competitive prices, hence lower sales and so on. Somehow Tesco has to become a growth business again, which is why we see the company sacrificing some margin and investing heavily in the short term in the core UK business by reducing short-term profits and so on to turn the cycle around in its favour once more.

So Tesco's belief in putting effectiveness as its primary goal and efficiency as a follow-on target as long as it does not negatively impact on effectiveness delivery is at the heart of the Tesco DNA in the way it manages its supply chain (Figure 6.1). The hypothesis that follows is encapsulated in Figure 6.2. If efficiencies are pursued in spite of, rather in keeping with, the effectiveness agenda businesses set, the consequence will be that any successes achieved could be short-lived and therefore unsustainable. As a corollary of this, if what the customer values is understood, and the dominant business logic is to pursue effective solutions to best satisfy these desires, then a more stable platform for sustained success may be achieved. This is not to say the pursuit of efficiency is wrong, but to say that efficiencies should be pursued from within the effectiveness agenda, not at the expense of it.

This is strikingly different to the approach of many publicly listed companies, or public sector organizations for that matter, which put profit or coming in on budget as their primary objective.

It could be argued that in good times Tesco could afford to hold such an ideal, but even when times get tougher Tesco is still prepared even to sacrifice some short-term profit for a stronger medium- to longer-term business, as we have discussed. This has been exemplified in the recent strategy announcements surrounding the reinvestment Tesco has undertaken in the UK business. For instance, in the performance review of 2011/12 Clarke confirmed that 'we decided to forego some short term profit to re-invest in the long term health of the business, with a clear focus on improving the shopping trip for customers'.[14]

FIGURE 6.2 The quest for efficiency should follow effectiveness provision, and efficiency gains should be implemented only if they don't damage effectiveness

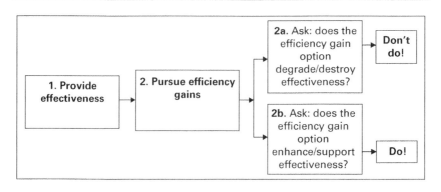

In summary, by developing organizational 'effectiveness' (enhanced quality, improved customer service, professional staff development and *gemba*-based improvement), then, through a process of continuous improvement, efficiency improvement can still be delivered, but as part of the outcome of sustainable success. Critically, the approach avoids unintended consequences *and* can be continued again and again in the spirit of continuous improvement (the approach of one-off improvement initiatives is not adopted, as improvement is everyone's job). Cost reduction and efficiency improvement do not appear in this counter-intuitive approach, but the benefits of cost reduction and efficiency improvement are delivered as part of the outcome of sustainable success.

Organizations such as Toyota and Tesco know that cost reduction and efficiency improvement are outcomes rather than objectives and should *always* take second place in their improvement hierarchy. Effective delivery of customer value has primacy.

Conventional wisdom says get better and better at what we do compared to competitors. Tesco's counter-intuitive answer is: No. Get better and better at providing for customers

Conventionally, business leaders are advised that if they want to improve it pays to look at their competitors and learn from the best. Certainly, having an external focus is not a bad thing. It provides objectivity and an ability to begin to see ourselves and our organization as others see it. However, while the leaders in any field of business should not be afraid of identifying and copying good practice from others, their focus is invariably on self-improvement – getting better and better at providing for their own customers in their own way. This is certainly Tesco's logic, and it is a key element of its operating philosophy.

Businesses are invariably structured around functions, but customers do not see the outcome of one function when they interface with the company. They interact with the output of many functions all joined up by processes. It's the output of these processes that customers witness when transacting with an organization. One of these processes is the supply chain, which is composed of many functional areas of business all working together: marketing, sales, logistics, production, buying and so on. Integrating these functions so they work in concert to optimize value for the customer is the challenge, which some organizations understand and others have yet to grasp.

Tesco gets this. It sees the supply chain system that is at the heart of the retail offer it provides, and that customers can choose to interact with the output of this system, or not if they feel they can get better value from an alternative supply chain system's output. 'Success in today's competitive business environment is largely dependent on the extent that firms are able to integrate across traditional functional boundaries to better serve customers' (van Hoek, Ellinger and Johnson, 2008).

So Tesco, while not being unaware of its competitors, sees that its main purpose is to orchestrate and manage the supply chain system, the core process that flows through the heart of its business, to the best of its ability. To do this it recognizes that progress can only be made step by step, to develop capabilities, hold on to these capabilities and progress to get the system better and better aligned to serve all its customers, whoever they are and whatever they value, with solutions that represent great value for them as individuals.

Tesco has developed a great internal energy and urgency across the business to identify problems that prevent it from achieving this and develop solutions to deal with them. Tesco's way of working in this regard has much in common with the way the Japanese operate and perhaps stems from the Lean thinking mentality that Tesco has used as an underpinning operating philosophy to guide it since the mid-1990s. What becoming Leaner does is remove the buffers of inventory that previously masked inadequacies in how functions integrated in managing the supply chain process. If a machine broke down, if a delivery was late, if too much or too little stock was ordered, or if sales were under- or overestimated it did not matter, as slack in large stockpiles of inventory would cover up the problem. With a Leaner approach, problems are exposed and solutions need to be developed and enacted to deal with them so they do not reoccur.

How Tesco manages this is indicated in the four-stage summary detailed in Figure 6.3.

FIGURE 6.3 Turning problems into opportunities to learn and improve at Tesco

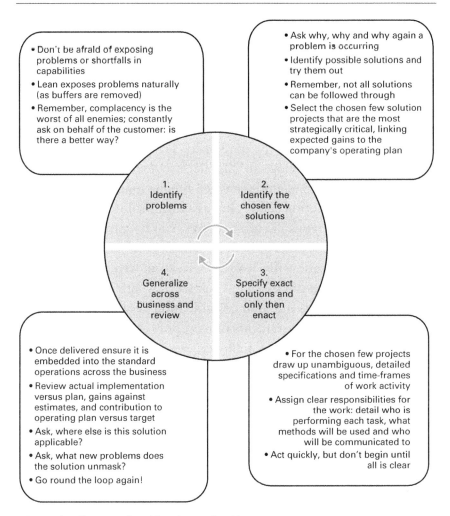

- Don't be afrald of exposing problems or shortfalls in capabilities
- Lean exposes problems naturally (as buffers are removed)
- Remember, complacency is the worst of all enemies; constantly ask on behalf of the customer: is there a better way?

- Ask why, why and why again a problem is occurring
- Identify possible solutions and try them out
- Remember, not all solutions can be followed through
- Select the chosen few solution projects that are the most strategically critical, linking expected gains to the company's operating plan

1. Identify problems

2. Identify the chosen few solutions

4. Generalize across business and review

3. Specify exact solutions and only then enact

- Once delivered ensure it is embedded into the standard operations across the business
- Review actual implementation versus plan, gains against estimates, and contribution to operating plan versus target
- Ask, where else is this solution applicable?
- Ask, what new problems does the solution unmask?
- Go round the loop again!

- For the chosen few projects draw up unambiguous, detailed specifications and time-frames of work activity
- Assign clear responsibilities for the work: detail who is performing each task, what methods will be used and who will be communicated to
- Act quickly, but don't begin until all is clear

NOTE Authors' interpretation of Tesco's way of working

First, Tesco is not afraid to unearth problems. When the system is not working as it should this is where new knowledge can be found. It may also be that the solution to the last problem has created new problems to be solved, as in the 'lowering the water exposes the rocks' analogy often used to explain Lean waste removal.

For instance, the lowering inventory levels in Tesco's distribution centres over many years, after the adoption of Lean thinking into the business, had created a problem with inbound deliveries. The old solution of moving full truck loads from the supplier just did not work now that there were frequent deliveries and smaller batches of product were required. Toyota had addressed this problem with the solution of milk-round deliveries, where a vehicle would tour around local supplier factories picking up components for delivery to the assembly plant just in time as they were required. The problem for Tesco, which now had a similar need at its distribution centres, was that its suppliers were not local to each distribution centre. A new solution needed to be developed. The answer was to set up consolidation centres close to suppliers so loads from part-filled trucks from suppliers could be merged for the longer truck journey direct to the distribution centre. But again this solution unmasked a new problem. The consolidation centres, run by partnering suppliers in a fairly ad hoc way, did not holistically optimize the inbound network of distribution for Tesco. So Tesco moved to the factory-gate pricing solution discussed in Chapter 5, where Tesco took over the management of its inbound consolidation network, making still further significant improvements in its supply chain logistics operations. More iterations again followed, where the idea was refined and refined and the concept was spread across the whole business over many years.

This example has been briefly summarized again to illustrate the Tesco approach. After the problem has been identified, solutions are researched. Often trials are carried out and an evidence-based assessment made to evaluate the ranking of solutions by strategic importance to Tesco. What Tesco realizes is that not all solutions can be enacted straight away. What needs to happen is the identification of the 'chosen few' that will best take the business forward over the coming period to achieve its operating plan priorities. This again marks Tesco out from many other businesses that become drowned by 'initiativitis', if such a word existed, and get drowned by change initiative after change initiative without making any of these changes work in a meaningful or sustained way.

The Step Change programme was a vehicle that helped focus this way of operating. Thus Tesco at any one time focuses on a few strategically important change initiatives that will deliver significant benefits to capability, customer experience, profit growth etc. Again what was remarkable was the way Tesco scoped out and specified these programmes, which ensured Tesco built up a reputation for itself of sure-footedness in delivering what it promised. This attention to detail chimes with what Spear (2009) argues is a key virtue of his 'high-velocity organizations':

> They specify in advance what outcomes are expected; who is responsible for what work in what order; how products and services, and information will flow from the person performing one step to the person performing the next step; and what methods will be used to accomplish each piece of work... everything it knows so far into these specifications to maximize the likelihood that people will succeed.
>
> (Spear, 2009)

This encapsulates the Tesco approach: a 'right first time' mentality that recognizes that change can be hard to manage and can impact many parts of the organization and indeed members of its supply chains. One tool Tesco uses over and over again in this regard is the RACI formula for attributing roles in projects, which was introduced in Chapter 2, but can perhaps be usefully repeated and included here

---

RACI

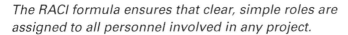

The RACI formula ensures that clear, simple roles are assigned to all personnel involved in any project.

Tesco has found that having more than one person accountable for a project can lead to the possibility that the project is not seen through to a successful end. So singular accountability is an important aspect of project delivery – **A**.

The accountable leader then has a team who are responsible for carrying out the project – **R**. The team could be spread over multiple locations and functions or divisions across the company.

Other roles include those who need to be consulted, but who also do not need to take an active part in the project – **C**.

There are also those who need to be informed of how the project is progressing and of any outcomes – **I**.

Role clarity ensures time is spent productively with wasted effort minimized!

too. We have also used it in countless projects outside Tesco; it really works in ensuring everyone is clear about their job, reducing frustrations and creating in the end a clear demarcation of who is ultimately responsible for what.

The other thing that Tesco does really well here is to act swiftly. For example, the time from when Tesco agrees internally that it is going to do something to the time it goes live with the development is invariably fairly impressive. Examples are manifold, ranging from the rapid development of the convenience Express stores to the launch of Clubcard, or more recently the relaunch of the Finest range, the creation of Tesco's own Hudl tablet, or the move to offer petrol points with Clubcard nationally. Tesco does things without problem (mostly), with marketing, logistics, buying and other departments seemingly working seamlessly together and in complete concert. This is because of the way the company tries to operate with complete focus and commitment behind the chosen few projects. Tesco sets challenging timescales for the attainment of change projects and rewards those that deliver them. Time and again Tesco achieves things that its competitors are only just beginning to wake up to.

And obviously it does not stop there. Once a solution is put in place its results are fed straight into the operating plan and checked against initial expectation, and lessons are learnt. These are then fed back into the next round of projects, with solutions often creating fresh problems to be resolved, as has been discussed, or exposing a frailty in capabilities that needs to be questioned and investigated, and the whole continuous quest for improvement commences again.

Finally, the diffusion of the innovation across the business is taken seriously too: hence the supply chain Blueprint idea highlighted in the list of Tesco mould-breaking ideas at the beginning of this chapter. Again, the alignment with the strategy of the company is what ties ideas like this together, ensuring they are seen to have top management support and thus helping to ensure they work effectively.

So, in summary, yes, Tesco is keeping a close eye on what its competitors are doing, but is more focused on what is right for it in continuing its development to serve its customers better and better. Through this approach, pursued over many years now, Tesco has developed a reputation for real leadership in the sector, which many admire.

And it never stands still. Tesco seemingly has a relentless energy and motivation to identify and conquer the next problem or develop even greater capabilities. Inertia can really hurt a business, but Tesco is constantly committed to do the right things and not succumb to the temptations of an overlarge head office, a stifling bureaucracy and so on. Tesco could never be labelled a grand or flashy organization.

Times are getting tougher perhaps as the retail sector endures significant forces of change, and some internal issues arise that need to be but Tesco in our opinion possesses what it needs to take disciplined, responsible decisions to equip itself for a positive future.

Conventional wisdom says prove the business case before backing an initiative. Tesco's counter-intuitive answer is: No. If it feels right for the customer it can make business sense too

Sometimes decisions are not easy to take for any organization, however. As has been discussed, determining what is pursued is not an ad hoc action at Tesco. Decisions are taken in a purposeful, well-thought-out manner and if possible backed by evidence from trials or hard results before commitments are made to progress.

There are times though when decisions cannot be made by these logical rules, when intuition and judgement come more into play. Often the payback from an investment does not flow back directly on to the bottom line in a linear fashion. Retailing is a highly complex business, and invariably decisions will have to be made more on a hunch than from making hard figures stack up.

On these occasions Tesco uses a simple maxim that fits entirely with its corporate philosophy: if it feels right for the customer then it can make business sense too.

Examples where this thinking has guided Tesco towards ground-breaking decisions were briefly touched on in the list detailed at the outset of this chapter; from moving into the convenience market to launching its Hudl tablet, Tesco has not been afraid of breaking new ground. Perhaps it is worth concentrating on one far-reaching development here to illustrate the kind of thinking and decision making that Tesco has become famous for: the move to home shopping in the late 1990s and its consequent expansion so that today the quest has evolved to one of becoming established in multi-channel leadership. It illustrates, perhaps better than anything else, the opportunities that Tesco sees in an industry confronting huge changes and where Tesco is always guided by the principle of questioning how it can seek ideas to make shoppers' lives easier.

By the mid-1990s the internet was beginning to emerge. Although personal computer use was low, businesses such as Tesco had seen how electronic data interchange (EDI) links with its suppliers had revolutionized how it transmitted forecasts and orders. However, it was considered that, even if personal computer use and internet connectivity increased, they were not an entirely friendly format for managing grocery shopping transactions. Leahy though thought differently, and along with his colleague Tim Mason began to develop the idea of Tesco.com, driven purely on the basis that if grocery home shopping could be made to work their view was that 'customers would love it... because of the novelty and – above all – the convenience it would offer' (Leahy, 2012).

In the United States by the end of the 1990s a number of what were called at the time 'pure-plays' had been set up with e-grocery business models that centred on picking products ordered over the internet from warehouses before delivering them to the homes of consumers. Most of these businesses were to find that their business case was not borne out by reality and went bankrupt one by one early in the following decade.

Simultaneously in the UK, before the failed outcomes of the US pioneers became apparent, the leading supermarkets began to develop business models to move into the e-grocery market. Sainsbury's focused on the pick-from-warehouse model in line with the thinking in the United States. Tesco, however, developed its own way. It was driven by the mindset to try to make lives easier for customers and hence was determined to make e-grocery work for the customer.

A new process would have to be created from scratch, because in Tesco's view the warehouse picking model would never work until considerable volumes of business were being generated through the format, unlikely in the early days. So, going against the conventional thinking at the time, Tesco developed a solution that was centred on picking and delivering from stores, not dedicated warehouses at all.

The key was that stores were closer to where people lived than warehouses and had fixed costs that were already being paid for in terms of day-to-day shopping trips, and through Clubcard Tesco could track how much was entirely new business and how much came from people who already shopped with Tesco.

Leahy, reviewing the success of the Tesco.com model, said:

> Webvan's [one of the US venture-capitalist-funded e-grocery players focused on warehouse picking] failure taught us an invaluable lesson. When creating a new offer, the critical aim – and basic building block of success – is to win custom, not create a perfect process... much better to get cracking by creating a simple process that you can build on and perfect as you go along.
>
> (Leahy, 2012)

Tesco.com quickly became a remarkable success, resulting in Tesco becoming the largest online food business in the world, with sales of over £3 billion annually. Tesco had shown that by trusting its instinct of what it perceived the customer wanted it could deliver outstanding results. It should be noted that the 'Heath Robinson' approach was a cautious, but wise, one to take. Leahy again noted: 'if an organisation really has to do something for the first time, the trick is to make sure the change is incremental and begins with small steps, so the mistakes you will inevitably make won't destroy the organisation (be it public or private) entirely' (*ibid*).

Our interpretation of Tesco's belief is: if it feels right for the customer it can make business sense too. The same thinking is being deployed in refreshing the UK store portfolio today, or investing in the full multi-channel supply chains to integrate them seamlessly to provide great solutions for the way the customer is increasingly wanting to transact with retailers currently. As Philip Clarke argues:

> innovating for the customer is something which has always guided our development... whether Clubcard, Express, Extra, Finest, Everyday Value or the launch of the first supermarket online grocery service in the UK... by taking the time to understand how their [customers'] lives were changing, we had a good idea that they were meeting untapped needs. You'd certainly never dream of taking them away today.
>
> tinyurl.com/pfvgwlu

Conventional wisdom says how to be good at business is difficult to understand but easy to do. Tesco's counter-intuitive answer is: No. It is easy to explain but hard to do

This book has predominantly focused on this issue. It tries to show that a recipe for business has been developed by Tesco that has generally worked and has helped to propel it from number two in the UK to number two in the world in the retail industry, in little under 20 years. The success Tesco enjoyed over this period was built on simple, enduring principles, which have helped guide the business at a time, especially after the financial crisis of 2007, when many businesses found the pace of change to be unrelenting and difficult to cope with.

Leahy (2012) argues that on reflection the company's values provided a 'compass' that ensured the right decisions were taken. By listening to customers, he suggested, much can be learnt: 'heed their advice, however difficult it may be, and you stand a greater chance of success' is how he concludes *Management in 10 Words* (Leahy, 2012). Certainly, this is a key element of the Tesco jigsaw of success. It all starts with an obsessive focus on the customers.

To support this, the full range of ideas within what has been termed the 'House of Lean' (Figure 6.4) is adopted and capabilities developed. The key is that this is done completely rather than through any tendency to pick and choose. Thus, the argument is to focus not just on tools, not just on just-in-time (JIT) and flow, but on both pillars of the 'House of Lean' – JIT and *Jidoka*. The 'House of Lean' has been developed over many years to encapsulate that Lean is not just a set of tools, but a management philosophy that requires a system perspective and thus a multi-faceted approach.

The 'House of Lean' is a reminder that a 'learning organization' achieves 'learning' through many, many, many plan–do–check–act (PDCA) cycles. This is achieved through people who are committed, trained and competent. *Jidoka* is the pillar designed to gain this aspect of a continuous improvement culture. Sustainable improvement

FIGURE 6.4   The House of Lean, illustrating the point that lop-sided improvement, such as just a tools-focused approach, will not lead to sustained capability development

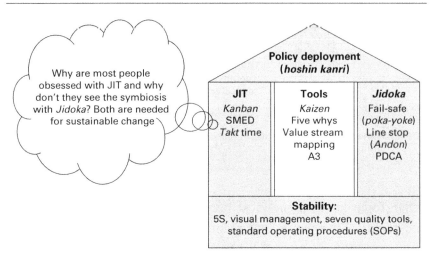

SOURCE Developed from Evans and Mason (2011b)

needs both pillars to be functioning. Obsessive focus on JIT and tools alone is not sufficient to deliver sustainable change.

Essentially, what Tesco, like other Lean exemplars, understands about achieving sustainable improvement is that a business, with its wider supply chain (suppliers, customers and connecting mechanisms), is a complex system. Improvement to that system has to be systemic to become sustained. In other words it has to be holistic, addressing the whole, rather than tinkering with parts in isolation. Indeed, tinkering aimed at efficiency improvement runs the risk of worsened efficiency, unintended consequences and transient improvement at best.

So start by addressing system purpose to avoid this and create a compelling counter-approach to the quick-win mentality favoured by so many. This means expecting to invest in advance of sustained improvement, for example by raising workforce capability and providing better leaders and general skills training, both generic and technical.

FIGURE 6.5 Fluctuating performance that can be expected in typical business metrics – tackle the major recurring issues first

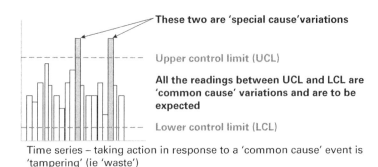

These two are 'special cause' variations

Upper control limit (UCL)

All the readings between UCL and LCL are 'common cause' variations and are to be expected

Lower control limit (LCL)

Time series – taking action in response to a 'common cause' event is 'tampering' (ie 'waste')

What Tesco has (for the most part) been brilliant at is identifying and tackling the major and recurring problems first before more minor, often quite normal fluctuations in performance are considered (Evans and Mason, 2011b). Figure 6.5 approximates any key performance indicator and emphasizes that a degree of variation can be expected in any metric, although there will be more variation in novice organizations and much less in excellent organizations, where capability to control variation is greater. The lesson should be that reacting to common-cause variation within lower and upper control limits is wasteful tampering. An understanding of variation will identify those events that are special-cause and that may then warrant a reaction.

So, put simply, Tesco conceives of its business as a complete system. It is driven by its core purpose, which in turn drives its goals. These are delivered via its strategy, using its values and principles. Its core purpose, derived in the early 1990s, is stated as 'To create value for customers to earn their lifetime loyalty', and this largely remained unchanged, although it was rephrased under Clarke's leadership. In its goals it states the main themes of its business model – food retailing, non-food retailing, financial and related service offers, and its intention to be a global business. Its values describe the type of culture it wants to build and the role of teamwork, trust etc in achieving this. Its principles are simply 'Better, simpler, cheaper', that is:

- better for customers;
- simpler for staff;
- cheaper for Tesco.

It aims, in all its operations, improvement activities and projects, always to focus on delivering all three principles (never one or other at the expense of a third). This simple, but powerful, approach helps Tesco avoid the unintended negative consequences so often associated with much change in the majority of organizations. So the solutions Tesco has adopted are relatively simple to explain, yet not easy to adopt.

In conclusion, our blueprint for Tesco's philosophy of supply chain improvement (Evans and Mason, 2011a) has been rooted in the Womack and Jones (1996) Lean principles:

- Understand what customers value – understanding exactly what customers value and designing effective mechanisms to deliver it are at the root of sustainable success.
- Create value streams – end-to-end, including your suppliers and customers.
- Create flow and pull in the value streams.
- Strive for perfection.

Tesco has delivered sustained success on the back of adopting a sequence of behaviour focused on:

- improving quality;
- improving customer service;
- professional development of staff and *gemba*-based improvement; and
- continuing this again and again in the spirit of continuous improvement (the world of one-off improvement initiatives is not adopted, as improvement is everyone's job).

For Tesco, what is smart here is how the rigorous application of 'Better, simpler, cheaper' principles was enacted through policy deployment to ensure that Tesco was very sure of what 'doing the right thing' meant.

Conventional wisdom says to stand out from the crowd in business you should be the cheapest or the most innovative. Tesco's counter-intuitive answer is: No. You can compete through both innovation and price

For many organizations the classic way to improve is to adopt a business model that facilitates the achievement of competitive advantage through efficiency improvement. For example, Michael Porter (1985) has written extensively on how businesses can choose to compete through low prices supported by highly efficient operations, often spanning organizational boundaries through aligned actions with other supply chain members. This can be visualized as in Figure 6.6, which shows efficiency improvements incorporated into business strategy and deployed into operations.

FIGURE 6.6 Conventional business thinking: driving efficiency improvement into operations

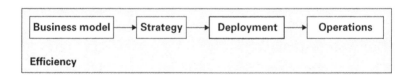

A weakness of this approach is that for many businesses improvement is often not sustained and rarely seems to be reflected in bottom-line gain. This is, as Ackoff (2010) describes, 'doing the wrong thing righter'. Driving business improvement to achieve cost reduction is missing the point.

Instead, what Tesco's experience shows is that improvement is about identifying critical constraints and improving against those to achieve sustainable gain. Cost miraculously reduces as well. This is Ackoff's (2010) 'doing the right thing' and is like hitting gold in archery – it doesn't get any better than this.

This is the counter-intuitive logic behind Lean thinking. Cost reduction is seen as an output, not a measure of success on its own. Hence, as we have argued, it should not be seen as the primary goal of the company at all. Indeed, cost can be removed from any organization, whether it is trying to compete in the low-cost or the premium differentiated game. From Primark to Rolls-Royce it should be effectiveness first, efficiency second, just as in the blueprint Tesco has provided.

Thus we concur with some authors who challenge a narrow conception of business process improvement ideas such as supply chain management or Lean thinking as just a set of ideas or tools to remove inefficiencies. They suggest instead that the ideas should be seen fundamentally as business philosophies, which can provide enhanced effectiveness through continuous improvement of purpose (eg Zokaei and Hines, 2007). Thus a system is developed to achieve both value and waste elimination, yes, but as a secondary by-product of continuous improvement, which should be the primary goal. This echoes Spear and Bowen's (1999) finding in 'Decoding the DNA of the Toyota Production System' that suggested that observers wishing to understand and potentially imitate the success of Toyota needed to 'go beyond the tools and practices... and look at the system itself'.

In practice, as well, Tesco has demonstrated that there are synergies in competing on both of Porter's identified dimensions of competitive advantage, namely price and differentiation. Both can be achieved, contrary to Porter's view that it is an 'either/or' choice. Customers buy from both the Everyday Value range and the Finest range on the same occasion, for example.

Conventional wisdom says think from production forwards. Tesco's counter-intuitive answer is: No. Act from the customer backwards

What is the thinking behind this counter-intuitive stance? In many sectors it was convention that supply chains ran at the behest of the manufacturers, which in effect wanted to supply all that they produced to the market on a high-volume, low-unit-cost, 'push' model. With intensified competition, catalysed through globalization, deregulation, enhancements in technology such as the internet and so on, there is an increasing emphasis on the need for organizations to sense and react to customers' full values and expectations from products and services to earn their custom. Consequently, the view that is argued is that the customer should be placed at the heart of process systems improvement.

This stance is summarized well by Meyer and Schwager (2007), who worry passionately about the 'customer's experience' and suggest that managing the customer should not be left to those who have functional responsibility for customer-facing tasks, but should extend also through to all process and functional leaders. They define 'customer experience' as the 'internal and subjective response customers have to any direct or indirect contact with a company' and argue that each customer's needs and value net are different and contingent upon the situation they face. They are also dynamic, and thus it is vital that organizations can sense and have the capabilities to react rapidly to changes. Thus the voice of the customer needs to be placed centrally in the organization and form the source of all decision making.

Tesco does exactly this, as we have consistently argued, and intrinsically feels it is intertwined with everything the company represents and is about, in improving the value it provides for its customers.

Tesco also takes a broad view of what value means, extending it beyond just low prices, although recognizing that this is an important component of the value equation in a largely commoditized sector such as grocery retailing. Thus Tesco has developed a much more sophisticated appreciation of what the notion means to all its different customers.

Hence, many of the innovations highlighted above are about how Tesco can serve customers, whoever and wherever they are, each with a whole variety of needs, better and better. For example, opening stores 24 hours a day was not a service that benefited everyone, but a segment of the population, such as shift workers who preferred to shop at night, did value this development. The same argument could be deployed to underpin the decision to extend the Tesco home shopping grocery service to the Isle of Lewis in 2014. For that segment of customers, value was improved. The examples can be exhaustively listed, from the development of ranges for Asian customers, to upgrades in the Value and Finest ranges, to the launch of the Goodness brand, providing a range of healthy and nutritious products for children.

Conventional wisdom says business leadership is the art of coping with complexity. Tesco's counter-intuitive answer is: No. Business leadership is the art of simplifying the complex

As we have suggested on numerous occasions in this book, keeping things simple is another key strength that Tesco tries to really focus upon. In short, it believes that making things simple wins, not adding complexity. In many ways this is a counter-intuitive approach, as logical wisdom would countenance that more complicated solutions are harder to imitate. We have mentioned in previous chapters Tesco's principles, which include pursuing simplicity, based on de Bono's (1998) ideas. Leahy felt this was critical in a business as fast-moving and dynamic as Tesco's was becoming: 'Simplicity is the knife that cuts through the tangled spaghetti of life's problems' (Leahy, 2012).

Complexity is the nemesis of modern organizations. What a simplicity ethos does is distil objectives down to their bare essentials, enabling clarity and then consistent evaluation, decisions and implementation. It can be applied to every aspect of an organization and has huge payback when the same task has to be delivered literally millions of times every year in the day-to-day operation of a business like Tesco's.

For enhanced process management therefore, as in the operation of the supply chain, it is a very valuable skill to develop. Tesco has developed the habit of relentlessly questioning every activity and attempting to ensure it is explained in as simple a way as possible so that it can be uniformly understood and performed: this is personified in Tesco's standard work practices ('routines', as Tesco terms them), discussed in Chapter 5.

It may be felt that the fairly disciplined approach Tesco adopts in simplifying and standardizing process activities might stifle the generation of new ideas, but from our experience this does not appear to be the case. Ideas to improve the way of working are highly valued, but the key for Tesco is only to operationalize the ones that will have the most potential, as we have discussed. Mechanisms exist to feed ideas rapidly up through the organization; they are evaluated against all other ideas, and those with the most potential are taken forward for company-wide implementation in Tesco's operational strategy. Thus all stores and distribution centres operate in the same way, with common standard operations. This presents a consistent view of the business to all customers (and other stakeholders). In turn, it also provides a consistent platform against which ongoing review through Deming's plan–do–check–act cycle can ensure continuous operational improvement. This has parallels with Toyota, where the ownership of standards by the workforce, as Tesco also has achieved, has acted as a platform for continuous improvement and not constrained it. So our view is that simplicity is a key building block foundation in the Tesco House of Lean approach.

Conclusion

This chapter has aimed at teasing out some of the factors that have helped to make Tesco special, distancing itself from the competition through most of the last 20-year period. The chapter has attempted to show how Tesco has tried to become a smarter organization, able to sense, think and act more quickly than its competitors in the cutthroat world of retail.

In so doing the chapter has taken a reflective stance and explored how Tesco has been able to challenge some of the accepted thinking on how businesses should be managed and, as a consequence, has become an excellent exemplary source of new thought on how business can be and perhaps should be practised.

Tesco uses its obsession to think and act to improve effectiveness, rather than efficiency, to develop and execute counter-intuitive, innovative and sometimes unconventional ideas orientated around serving its customers better. Over the two decades to 2013 Tesco stole a march on competitors with several such mould-breaking initiatives.

Key chapter summary points

1 There is one critical learning point here: counter-intuitive thinking allows a company to become a 'rabbit' (Spear, 2009).

2 However, making it habitual (part of your organization's DNA) is the key to achieving sustained competitive advantage.

3 What may seem counter-intuitive ideas for many organizations have actually become fairly logical and intuitive ideas for Tesco in operationalizing its three established principles of 'Better, simpler, cheaper'. In this way Tesco has made counter-intuitive thinking habitual.

Notes

1 Tesco Annual Review 2010

2 Tesco Annual Review 2000

3 Tesco Annual Review 2000

4 Tesco Annual Review 2005

5 Tesco Annual Review 2007

6 Tesco Annual Review 2010

7 Tesco Annual Review 2004

8 Tesco Annual Review 2008

9 Tesco Annual Review 2005

10 Tesco Annual Review 2011

11 Tesco Annual Review 2012

12 Tesco Annual Review 2012

13 M Davies, How Tesco is spreading best practice around the world, *Supply Chain Standard*, 8 April 2014

14 Tesco Annual Review 2012

Current challenges

07

Aligning corporate and supply chain strategies to a changing macro environment

Introduction

This chapter focuses on Tesco today (in mid-2014) and into the near future by looking afresh at the challenges Tesco is facing. It explores what these challenges mean for Tesco's strategy and the implications for the way the company manages its supply chain.

Retailing has always been characterized as a dynamic, fast-changing industry, but arguably today it is going through one of the most turbulent times in its recent history. The biggest reason for this is the landscape-changing effect that new technology development and adoption are having, linked to their impact on consumer behaviour. Some of the markets in which Tesco trades, such as the UK and South Korea, are perceived as world-leading in this respect in that the mass take-up of new technological developments combines with mature retail supply markets willing to cater for and anticipate new needs.

But, as well as providing a commercial arena where there are many new opportunities for retailers, it is also an era when traditional business models are being threatened and thus strategies have to be carefully handled so that the pains of transition, which are inevitable, are well managed. What makes this all particularly difficult is the pace of change. If companies' strategies and supply chain propositions cannot be quickly aligned to each new requirement it makes successful adaptation particularly hard.

Obviously, technological advances are not the only issue to be considered. The chapter will examine other external macro environmental changes, such as the challenging economic conditions and the consequent impact on consumer spending that exists in many of the markets in which Tesco trades, the changing needs of the consumer beyond those fuelled by technological change as more convenient shopping solutions are sought, and other issues that will be explored.

The chapter is based around the basic system model (Figures 1.1 and 5.1) that has been used throughout the book and centres on a series of questions that spring from this. They are:

1 What are the main changes in the macro external environment that Tesco trades in?

2 What are the implications of these changes for the way consumers behave and the values they seek from Tesco?

3 How does this affect Tesco's corporate strategy and core purpose?

4 In what ways does a new corporate strategy affect Tesco's supply chain system strategy?

These questions provide the skeleton for the chapter before conclusions are reached. Much of the chapter is focused on the UK, where a significant proportion of Tesco's trade occurs. However, there will be discussion relating to other countries in which Tesco trades as well.

In the UK there is certainly a lot to play for. In a recent IGD report (Gladding, 2014), it was proposed that over the five years to 2019 the UK grocery market is forecast to grow by 16.3 per cent, taking

TABLE 7.1 UK grocery market growth, 2014–19

	Value year to April 2014 (rounded)		Value year to April 2019 (rounded)		Growth or decline 2014–19	
					£bn (not rounded)	% change 2014–19 (not rounded)
	£bn	%	£bn	%		
Superstores and hypermarkets	73.7	42.2	70.8	34.9	−£3.0	−4.0%
Small supermarkets	35.5	20.4	35.7	17.6	£0.1	0.7%
Other retailers	9.4	5.4	9.3	4.6	−£0.1	−0.7%
Convenience	37.4	21.4	49.0	24.1	£11.6	30.9%
Discounters	10.8	6.2	21.4	10.5	£10.6	98.0%
Online	7.7	4.4	16.9	8.3	£9.2	119.4%
Total	174.5	100%	203.0	100%	£28.5	16.3%

NOTE All data are year to April.
SOURCE IGD published research © Institute of Grocery Distribution (IGD).

its value from £174.5 billion to £203 billion, a difference of £28.5 billion (Table 7.1).

A more striking way of looking at this total forecast growth shows that three principal areas will drive this growth – convenience, online and discounters. Together they account for over £4 in every £4 of total cash growth in the market, offset by a decline in superstores and hypermarkets, the largest channel in the market (Table 7.2).

This chapter will explore this assertion and examine whether Tesco is meeting the challenges faced by the rapidly changing supply channel structure that is being anticipated.

TABLE 7.2 For every £4 of market growth the proportion from each channel

	Channel share of each £4 of market growth
Superstores and hypermarkets	−£0.42
Small supermarkets	£0.03
Other retailers	−£0.01
Convenience	£1.62
Discounters	£1.49
Online	£1.29
Total	*£4.00*

FIGURE 7.1 Summary of chapter structure: macro external environment changes impact on customer values, which dictate that the supply chain system purpose alters, and the supply chain system needs to realign to this

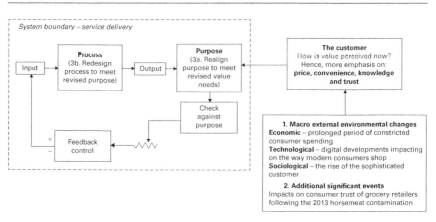

The changing macro external environment

There are clearly many aspects in the macro external environment that have a bearing on how companies perform; sometimes an analysis of this is conducted using the PEST method, reviewing the political, economic, social and technological changes. Here three issues are picked out:

- the economic backdrop;
- technologically led change;
- the rise of the sophisticated customer.

Each issue is currently having a profound impact on the grocery retailing landscape in the UK, and in some ways they are also combining, as we will see, to redefine what value means for the modern consumer. If companies like Tesco want to remain truly market orientated in the way they organize their strategy and their supply chain operations they need to be on top of how the market is changing.

The economic backdrop

A fundamental element of any discussion about the macro environment companies trade in is the state of the economy. For Tesco, which holds such a large market share of a commodity industry, in this case groceries, the state of the wider UK economy has a crucial bearing on trade.

Clearly, the UK economy has been subdued over a prolonged period now following the financial crisis of 2007, the banking collapse of 2008, and issues surrounding rebalancing national finances ever since. After benefiting from an economy that progressively grew over many years from the early 1990s until 2007, Tesco showed that it was able to ride out the early years of the more challenging times after 2007. However, in the last two to three years it has found the economic backdrop much harder to work with.

One of the most significant reasons for this is the compound effect of wage inflation being lower than the inflation rate across the wider

FIGURE 7.2 Since 2008 average weekly earnings increases have run behind the CPI inflation rate in the UK, which has had a compound effect on average householder spending capability

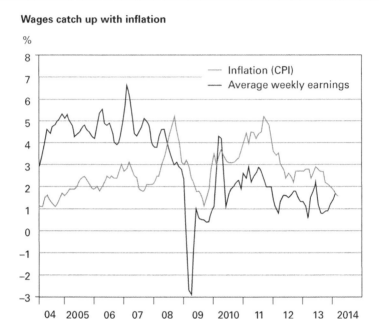

SOURCE ONS

economy. This is indicated in Figure 7.2, which highlights that only by the spring of 2014 had wage inflation matched up to inflation measured by the Consumer Price Index, an approximation of the change in the cost of living year on year, after six years of being behind it.

Progressively, this has had a compound impact on average UK household spending capacity. Effectively, many of those in work have been steadily getting worse off year by year in terms of the spending power generated by their take-home pay. While it could be argued that groceries are a staple rather than a discretionary product, it has meant that increasingly consumers are questioning more and more closely what they are spending.

A decline in spending power for average UK consumers since 2008 has been compounded by increases in other commodities such as fuel and energy. For example, Figure 7.3 shows the rise in the petrol price since 2007. Although this stabilized in 2011–14, its rise over

FIGURE 7.3 Average UK petrol price, in pence, from January 2007 to January 2014

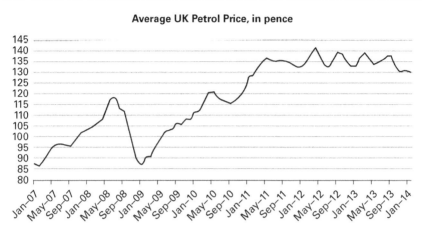

Average UK Petrol Price, in pence

SOURCE Hoffman (2014)

the period when average wages were not increasing at the same rate has meant that average UK consumers are asking how their spending ability can go further – and this pressure only increases year by year.

Technologically led change

Clearly, one of the defining features of the current age is the impact changes in technology are having on customer behaviour. Tesco's CEO, Philip Clarke, stated in a *Daily Telegraph* article in 2013[1] that 'the UK is undergoing the biggest generational change in consumer behaviour since the 1960s'. In particular, it is the hardware and software developments in digital technology, the internet, the smartphone, the tablet and so on that are having a landscape-shifting impact on the way consumers think and behave when searching for, selecting, paying for and accessing goods.

Clarke, in a speech to the World Retail Congress in 2012,[2] showed that he was fully aware of these changes, describing the new challenges and opportunities that are arising from the digital age:

Digital technology – in particular smartphones – has become a lifeline, offering not just untold choice, information, and access to bargains, but acting as a new and more affordable channel for entertainment and socialising. Social media has given rise to the agnostic consumer, whose actions and tastes are heavily influenced by word of mouth, who moves quickly and seamlessly between channels, and who expects retailers to keep pace.

The rise of the sophisticated customer

The third and in many ways connected characterizing feature of the modern age in the wider external macro marketplace is the discernible rise of the sophisticated customer.

Piercy (2000) suggested that 'one of the paradoxes we face is that as we get better at focussing on customers, improving quality, upgrading service level, and so on, we fuel further and higher customer expectations for more of the same'.

The UK retailing market, ironically driven considerably by what Tesco has pioneered, can be seen as an exemplar of this statement. Many forces are combining so that consumers today are increasingly more informed, discerning, knowledgeable and sceptical.

One of the drivers of this change has again been technology advances. Clarke is very much aware of this too and has argued that 'digital technology has empowered consumers to be smart shoppers, who can make informed choices… over half of visits to our Tesco.com website are to check prices – and this is our food site, not our general merchandise site'.[3]

Sophisticated customers are more self-aware of what represents value to their own situation as well. Sometimes this equation is dominated by price considerations, a criterion that may be growing for many, as discussed above, but it will be impacted by many other value metrics too, such as ease of shopping, trust in the brand, brand cachet, convenience and so on.

In conclusion to this discussion on macro factors, these are just three of the external trends that are acting individually and together to change the trading environment for retailers such as Tesco; there are clearly others, which are beyond our focus here.

But what does all this mean for the retailer such as Tesco? This is the theme on which we will concentrate in the next section.

Impacts stemming from changes in the external trading environment

How the concept of value is changing for consumers

It is clear, then, that the way in which consumers perceive value is undergoing significant change. As a result of a number of factors, such as the recent financial crisis, consumers' increasing sophistication and their reaction to developments in the digital age, consumers are re-examining what constitutes value to them.

One of the key themes that is emerging is the growing importance of price in the customers' value demand equation. Driven predominantly by the compound shrinking of wages in the UK, this is producing a fundamental shift in the UK retail marketplace, which is really challenging retailers such as Tesco, as the discounters, in particular, try to exploit this situation.

This is illustrated by looking at how market share is beginning to move to the discounters. Kantar Worldpanel collects weekly till data on a sample basis to create a database to identify retailers' market share, trends etc. It has data that show total grocery spend and within this the spend at multiple food grocers. (Kantar does not include Marks & Spencer in this dataset for historical reasons, so they not shown in Table 7.3.) Tesco and other major UK retailers (apart from Sainsbury's) saw reductions in their UK grocery market share in 2014. Actually for Tesco and Morrisons this decline has been evident for longer (see Table 7.3). (Appendix 4 gives the market share data since 2006.)

Clearly, those trading at the 'value' end of the market – such as Aldi and Lidl – have seen their market share grow substantially. A further illustration of this trend is Farmfoods, which although small was in fact the fastest-growing grocery retailer in the UK at the end of 2013.[4] It would appear that customers are more willing to shop in discount stores, which are increasingly seen to be acceptable to the UK customer.

There is another development that is evident from these figures: the rise in market share of the chains at the opposite end of the industry from the discounters. This is exemplified by the performance of

TABLE 7.3 Multiples' share of UK grocery market

	12 weeks to 25 January 2009	12 weeks to 21 February 2010	12 weeks to 20 February 2011	12 weeks to 19 February 2012	12 weeks to 3 March 2013	12 weeks to 2 March 2014
Tesco	30.7%	30.4%	30.3%	30.1%	29.6%	28.7%
Asda	17.2%	17.0%	16.9%	17.8%	17.8%	17.5%
Netto	0.7%	0.7%	0.7%	2010 Asda purchased majority of Netto stores		
Sainsbury's	16.2%	16.3%	16.5%	16.9%	17.0%	17.0%
Morrisons	11.9%	12.3%	12.3%	12.4%	11.8%	11.1%
Co-operative	4.3%	5.7%	6.7%	6.4%	6.2%	6.1%
Somerfield	3.3%	1.7%	0.1%	2008 Co-operative purchased majority of Somerfield stores		
Waitrose	3.7%	4.3%	4.4%	4.6%	4.9%	5.0%
Aldi	3.0%	2.8%	3.1%	2.6%	3.3%	4.3%
Lidl	2.3%	2.2%	2.4%	2.6%	2.8%	3.2%
Iceland	2.0%	2.0%	2.0%	2.1%	2.2%	2.2%
Farmfoods	0.5%	0.5%	0.5%	0.6%	0.5%	0.7%
Other	2.0%	2.0%	2.1%	1.9%	1.9%	2.1%
Total multiples	97.8%	97.9%	98.0%	98.0%	98.0%	97.9%

SOURCE Kantar Worldpanel grocery market share.

Waitrose, Marks & Spencer Foods (even though it is not listed in Table 7.3) and to a certain extent Sainsbury's, although the most recent reports indicate that its market share has reached a plateau. There has been much deliberation and speculation as to the reasons for this, but clearly their growth indicates that for some consumers trading up is becoming more attractive. It highlights that there are many forces at play, not just a collective desire for more discounted groceries.

In broad terms, what these figures indicate is that there is a polarizing effect occurring in the UK grocery market. The major multiples, which predominantly trade across the middle of the marketplace, such as Tesco, Asda, Morrisons and the Co-op, have been adversely affected. The polarization is now seen as a longer-term trend rather than a blip.

In particular, it would appear that the discount boom is set to continue. Initially consumers were attracted by their low prices, but the discounters have now added quality of offer, which is keeping their strong growth a feature of UK food retailing. Research shows that almost half of all shoppers now regularly shop at food discounters, and one in 10 do their main grocery shop in the discounters' stores. IGD research forecasts discounter sales will almost double and reach £21.4 billion by 2019 (Gladding, 2014).

Tesco needs to be able to compete seriously with the discounters – not an easy task, as Tesco's business model, and the way it manages its supply chain, is quite different to the discounters' model.

The growth of the convenience channel

In the IGD report (Gladding, 2014), highlighted at the beginning of this chapter, 'convenience', the name given to the rise in neighbourhood and express store formats, is the channel that will grow most in cash terms – by over £11 billion in the five years to 2019. Clearly, the IGD anticipates that there is still a lot of potential to be harnessed in this area through accessing new locations and further tailoring ranges that fit with local catchment needs. Customers who are increasingly time poor and relatively cash rich are valuing this kind of offer to make their lives easier.

The emergence of multi-channel (omni-channel) consumers

The last of the big three channel drivers the IGD forecasts will underpin future growth is unsurprisingly the development of trade online, which it predicts will be the fastest-growing channel over the five-year forecast period to 2019 (Gladding, 2014). Customers are seeking ways to optimize solutions that suit their needs. Often this translates to a desire to integrate the virtual and physical worlds in terms of securing retail products. IGD argues that this is increasingly being catered for, so growth in online will be driven not just by demand for it rising but by supply capabilities improving. In the report, the following features are evident:

- Retailers are investing in delivering a more convenient, reliable and flexible service.
- Suppliers are putting more resources behind the channel.
- Morrisons online grocery was launched in January 2014.
- There is grocery click-and-collect development:
  - Tesco and Asda expecting to have over 500 sites between them offering the service by the end of 2014;
  - Waitrose also experimenting with collection from lockers;
  - Sainsbury's trialling click-and-collect groceries from London Underground station car parks;
  - investment in new 'dark stores', which will increase capacity in the areas of highest demand, improving service standards.
- Effective digital engagement and cross-channel marketing will further grow the market.
- The launch of online delivery subscription schemes drive customer loyalty and online shopping frequency.

To this list could be added:

- the growth of online specialist Ocado;
- the increasing level of competitiveness forcing prices down and catalysing various new types of offers, such as the opportunity for customers to sign up over a protected period for a discounted amount;
- the increasing use of smartphones to access online shopping offers.

The development of this area goes far beyond this analysis, however. Digital technology, as quoted by Philip Clarke in his speech to the World Retail Congress in 2012,[5] cited in our discussion on technology change earlier in this chapter, is a pervasive influence, providing a new, attractive, often more affordable channel for consumers, not just for the purchase of goods but also for entertainment and socializing. In a recent Ofcom survey[6] it was found that 16- to 24-year-olds in the UK spend over 24 hours a week online.

So supply chain management and company strategies need to evolve to cover not just the management of the quality and reliability of the physical products and services supplied but also the 'softer' aspects of how it is done.

The decline of hypermarket and supermarket channels

The growth in these alternative channels is putting considerable pressure on the traditional channels, notably the hypermarket and supermarket stores. Up to this period of change much of the growth from which UK grocery retailers had benefited was derived from the move to larger and larger stores, which could exploit the economies of scale of these bigger formats and could accommodate the ever expanding catalogue range that was being developed. Today, as we noted in Chapter 2, Clarke has signalled the end of this 'space race', and certainly with more business being diverted online and through convenience stores the owners of the larger stores are seeing a decline in business share via this format.

Table 7.3 showed that Tesco, Asda, Morrisons and the Co-op had all lost market share, or at best stagnated, in recent years. There are also indications that Sainsbury's period of increasing market share has halted. All these retailers have a significant portfolio of larger-format stores, which leaves them exposed if lower volumes are being derived in this segment of the market. The IGD five-year market and channel forecast predicts that superstores and hypermarkets will actually decline by 4 per cent by 2019 (Gladding, 2014).

Trust

Beyond the movement of supply channel, the emotion around the retail brand is also becoming increasingly important. Driven partly by the rise of customer sophistication, in turn partly driven by the new digital age, it is clear that consumers now have aspirations that cover more than just having their material needs met. They also expect retailers to act with integrity, openness and responsibility – in short to be seen to be transparently meeting their obligations in all the communities in which they operate.

The consequences for retailers that do not meet these standards are significant. Loss of trust is hard to win back and customers, faced with many different easily accessible alternatives, are becoming increasingly fickle. Making a customer loyal to a retail brand is becoming very hard to achieve without absolute integrity, as perceived by the consumer, and is completely locked into the way the retailer is seen to operate. The supply chain, the process at the heart of all retail operations, is hence open to scrutiny as never before, and the highest standards of performance need to be shown as being set and adhered to if customers are to continue shopping with any particular retailer.

It is with this background that Tesco, among other retailers, had to contend when the issues surrounding the 'horsemeat scandal' began to emerge at the beginning of 2013.

Over recent years the consumer has been exposed to a number of events that have shaken their confidence that they can always trust the safety and quality of the food that they buy. To name some of these events, they include:

- *E coli* outbreaks;
- BSE;
- foot and mouth and the mass slaughter of millions of beef cattle;
- the inclusion of harmful extenders in baby milk in China and the subsequent deaths of numerous babies;
- the concerted attempts by large multinationals like Monsanto to introduce genetically modified (GM) foods into the UK (resisted by many consumers).

Given the frequency and severity of the various food-related events, consumers have some or all of the following reactions:

- Why are they doing it?
- What's in it for them?
- Do they really care about the impact on me (the consumer) and my family?

The consumer's suspicion and lack of trust are directed at a range of targets that seem unaccountable based on what has happened in all of the previous food-related issues. These include the chain from farmers and growers to manufacturing suppliers and retailers. And the issue of trust in the operation of the supply chain was finally brought to a head at the beginning of 2013 in the horsemeat scandal.

In early 2013, there was a series of incidents in the UK where various meat-based products (sausages, pies etc) were found to contain meat, notably horsemeat, other than that on the label. Following some random tests of food products in UK supermarkets, it emerged that there were traces – some minute – of horsemeat in various processed meat products such as sausages, pasties and pies. What developed over a number of weeks caused consumers to have good reasons to have even less trust. Events showed that retailers and their suppliers knew little about the actual provenance of some of their meat products. This included products that were ostensibly beef, lamb or chicken. All the major UK retailers, except Sainsbury's, were found to have offending products.

So while of itself not a danger to public health, it was the incidence of ingredients that were not intended to be present and the fact that retailers were not aware of their inclusion that caused the concern. In detail the problems that emerged from the horsemeat scandal were as follows:

- That retailers, including Tesco, did not really know the provenance of all the products they sold. The 'scandal' products were ostensibly beef from the UK and Ireland. It transpired that some meat ingredients originated in other countries.

- This lack of awareness of what was included was despite retailers having stringent quality standards and rigorous procedures to visit suppliers and test their processes and products. To be fair to retailers, the inclusions were often at trace levels, but that is not a mitigating factor – if a specification indicates what is permitted, it therefore provides for what is not permitted!

  - Thus the retailers assumed that their specifications and supplier visits together with product testing would guarantee adherence. They did not.

- Retailers are ultimately responsible for what they sell in their stores and cannot use 'We didn't know' as a defence.

So today the perception of trust that consumers possess in the providers of their food and groceries is arguably more important than it has ever been before. A quality supply chain that can be relied on is at the heart of all of this and must be purposefully managed with this in mind.

Redefining system purpose

Introduction

The changing external macro environment and its consequent impact on what value means to today's variety of consumers has been examined. What all this means for a retailer like Tesco is that it must align its business purpose around this ever-changing demand. This is not easy, as company strategy, supply chain channel assets and so on are often hard to alter as fast as market demands change.

To some extent, Tesco has been at the forefront of anticipating many of these developments, and consequently it could be argued that it is better prepared to cope than many of its competitors. For example, Tesco has been developing online and convenience offers for well over a decade and thus, compared to say Morrisons, which only last year branched into these channels, has a considerable head start.

But the pace of development is exceptionally fast, so it is hard to be ahead of the curve on all fronts. In areas such as being able to match the discounters on price and developing theatre and a fantastic shopping experience in stores Tesco has seemingly lagged behind. And in the area of trust it appears, more than any other grocery retailer, to have been impacted by the horsemeat scandal, despite being so up front and honest in the way it has handled and communicated its stance and approach over the issue.

This section will review the debate surrounding the need and timing of redefining core purpose. In Figure 7.1 we indicate that it is vital that organizations define their core purpose from their customers' perspectives and strive continually to meet these and improve their offering. As we will discuss, it is challenging to stay consistently on top of this.

Tesco 2012 – time for a new corporate and supply chain strategy

By 2012, Tesco, under Clarke's leadership, had made major changes to its core purpose, values and business model. The rationale behind these changes was based on a range of intelligence gathered by the company. Typically for Tesco, it was orientated around what Tesco perceived was being felt by customers, which Clarke outlined in September 2012.[7] He argued that customers were saying:

1 'I want control over my life.'
2 'My life feels busier than ever.'
3 'I want more for my money.'

He proposed that this provided opportunities for companies like Tesco to:

1 develop the ability for digital technology to empower consumers;
2 provide better retail solutions to help them lead simpler, easier lives; and
3 give a better 'brand experience and rewards for loyalty on top of that'.

In summary, he argued that 'retailers need to think more intelligently about how to win and retain loyalty in the new, converged world'. To win, an era of 'mass personalisation' was required, and he also spoke of consumers' expectations of the companies that supply them: 'Personalisation and accountability... integrity, honesty, openness, responsibility: quite simply, people expect big companies to be doing their bit for the communities in which they operate, for their teams, for the wider world. This is not some optional extra that management can ignore.'

Tesco needed to improve its abilities to serve the new generation of customers, but still retain the established customer base. These needs were the drivers for its revised strategy.

Thus Tesco developed and presented significant changes at this time to its core purpose, values and business model, much of which was discussed in detail in Chapter 3. In summary the changes were as follows:

- The core purpose became: 'We make what matters better, together.'
- The new values were:
  - 'No one tries harder for customers.'
  - 'We treat everyone how we like to be treated.'
  - 'We use our scale for good.'
- The business model – composed of the new core purpose, with the following sequentially arranged surrounds:
  - Four core activities – insight, buy, move and sell.
  - A virtuous circle:
    Invest in the offer for customers.
    Sell more.
    Develop economies of scale.
  - Six key enablers:
    building the Tesco brand;
    leveraging group skill and scale;
    developing Tesco's people;
    creating valuable property;
    operating responsibly;
    innovating the offer.

A notable feature was that the fifth segment of the Steering Wheel, which had been introduced by Leahy, focusing on community, was given greater status by becoming the third value: 'We use our scale for good.' Tesco uses the 'Tesco and Society' page on its website to explain its approach in this area:

- Tesco's three big ambitions:
  - to create new opportunities for millions of young people around the world;
  - to improve health and through this help to tackle the global obesity crisis;
  - to lead in reducing food waste globally.

- Tesco's four essentials:
  - to trade responsibly;
  - to reduce the impact on the environment;
  - to be a great employer;
  - to support local communities.

Tesco reports progress against these in half-year and full-year 'Tesco and Society' reports, which can be downloaded in pdf format from its website. The reports include a measurement section, which for example presents the progress it is making against its four essentials, for instance its carbon footprint globally and by individual country where it operates, which is shown in gross tonnes of Equivalent Carbon Dioxide (CO_2e) (in 2014 Tesco was given a top award for cutting carbon emissions from freight transport, demonstrating its ongoing commitment and efforts in this area[8] and its greenhouse gas measurements, which are independently verified by an external consultancy following the WRI/WBCSD Greenhouse Gas Protocol. (A promotional video summarizing Tesco's approach, 'Rebecca Shelley introduces Tesco and society', can be accessed at tinyurl.com/kaqzzvf.)

In conclusion to this section, it seems to the authors that Tesco's way of conducting relationships with suppliers has moved from a perceived autocratic and paternalistic manner to a more reflective and inclusive style. Yes, it still has hard business objectives to meet – sales, profit, growth, and an exacting supply chain to operate – but it is increasingly driven by 'softer' issues as well, issues that represent an acknowledgement that Tesco is striving to be seen to operate in a way that meets the changed aspirations of an inclusive society in the 21st century.

What does this mean for the Tesco supply chain strategy?

As a follow-on from the last section we will now examine some of the remedial actions that Tesco is undertaking to rebuild its capability to meet the challenges in the new retail market and look at the implications for the Tesco supply chain.

First, we will explore how Tesco has taken the long-term decision to ensure customer trust is at the heart of its corporate strategy and supply chain approach.

Rebuilding trust following the 2013 horsemeat scandal – putting trust at the heart of the Tesco offer

It would be possible to write a separate book on the horsemeat scandal, but for the purposes of this book there is one key outcome. Tesco quickly concluded that rebuilding and maintaining trust in Tesco had to be at the heart of everything Tesco did in relating to its customers. Thus customer trust in Tesco, which used to be implicit in Tesco's relationship with its customers, now had to be regained and kept by explicit demonstrations of what Tesco would do to protect consumers from potentially harmful events.

In the supply chain a very important consequence quickly emerged – the supply chain had in many cases become too extended and complex in the pursuit of efficiency gains. Tesco would return to simpler and more local supply chains. This would provide a means to ensure product provenance and efficacy, in short to be more effective in supporting the goal of rebuilding and retaining consumer trust.

In Tesco, Philip Clarke became the main voice for the company and appeared on television and in newspaper interviews on numerous occasions during the first half of 2013 explaining what Tesco was doing to address the situation. To his credit he was very open in explaining that Tesco did not know at that time the full extent of the source origins of various ingredients, but as it became clear he would share that knowledge fully with the public together with what Tesco was doing to prevent reoccurrence.

Clearly these events had a major detrimental impact on Tesco and other retailers. It is evident that the most significant impact was not financial – at least in the short term. Thus sales of the products associated with the scandal suffered, but consumers have to eat and so bought substitute products. In the longer term, it was the damage to Tesco's brand reputation that became the real concern. Tesco implemented a series of measures with the aim to regain full knowledge of its supply chain and develop robust control of suppliers and ingredients.

At the National Farmers' Union conference on 27 February 2013 Philip Clarke gave the following commitment: 'Transparency in the supply chain is a key concern, and therefore Tesco will undertake a root and branch review. I am in no doubt that we will find things we don't like... but when we find them, we will change them'.[9]

Tesco understood that there was a major requirement to develop stronger partnerships with its suppliers to make coordinated improvement, and reduce convoluted supply lines, ie take out complexity in order to regain control. This would be based on joint setting and pursuit of goals, with trust at the foundation of the relationship with suppliers.

So in March 2013 Tesco announced changes to make sourcing of its food simpler, shorter and more transparent in order to retain supply chain confidence, to add to existing initiatives. These changes included:

- The local sourcing policy would be extended:
  - Tesco already sourced beef (fresh, frozen and in ready meals) from the UK and Republic of Ireland.
  - From July 2013 Tesco would source all of its fresh chicken from the UK. Over time Tesco would ensure that all chicken in its products – fresh and frozen – was sourced from the UK and Ireland.

- Sustainability farming group committees would introduce:
  - pricing mechanisms to deal with market fluctuations;
  - terms permitting longer supply contracts, with the objective of making it easier for farmers to invest with confidence and plan for the long term.

- The committees would include:
  - Tesco's sustainable dairy group introduced in 2007;
  - beef and pork suppliers, with Tesco in November 2012 investing £25 million in setting up two committees run by farmers.

- Supplier specifications – Tesco provides suppliers with specifications that exactly detail the recipe, the ingredients and where those ingredients are sourced. It added this clear warning: 'Recently, when Tesco discovered that some companies had broken... specifications, Tesco discontinued its commercial relationships with those suppliers and removed their products from shelves.'

- The issue of supply chain complexity was addressed as follows:
  - shortening the supply chain where possible;
  - increasing cooperation between producers, processors and retailers;
  - complexity to be addressed to remove the risk of exploitation by 'rogue elements'.

- A root and branch review to achieve partnership between retailers, processors and farmers. Supply chain transparency would be achieved by:
  - examining all aspects of the supply chain;
  - examining the processes used;
  - achieving total confidence in how products were being sourced.

- Tesco would set up an interactive website to 'offer customers levels of insight into what's in their food never before seen in the UK'.

So, in the wake of the horsemeat events, Tesco had set about repairing its reputation and restoring the public's trust in it in the first half of 2013. This was followed in July 2013 when it announced that it would be appointing, as its new Agriculture Director, Tom Hind. Hind had worked for the National Farmers' Union for 15 years. His appointment fulfilled Philip Clarke's commitment at the NFU conference in early 2013, which followed horsemeat being found in a number of products sold by Tesco, 'to build stronger relationships with farmers and build a more transparent supply chain'. Hind joined Tesco in November 2013 in the new role of Group Agriculture Director. He describes his role on the blog page of the Tesco corporate website as follows: 'I joined Tesco as the first Group Agriculture Director in November 2013 where I'm responsible for our agriculture strategy, building better relationships with farmers and growers and the standards we work to achieve on behalf of our customers with farmers and fishermen'.[10]

Hind's agriculture team includes agriculture experts for each area of farming – proteins, fishing and horticulture. They will develop Tesco's sustainable farming groups covering all agriculture sectors. Hind's role was described as to:

- be the main point of contact between Tesco's commercial teams and farmers across the UK;
- develop innovative ways of working with farmers;
- contribute to building sustainable farms for the future.

It is worth noting that Tesco is British agriculture's biggest customer, and this development gives great credence to meeting the commitments contained in its revised core purpose, values and business model. For example:

- The core purpose: 'We make what matters better, together.'
- The third value: 'We use our scale for good.' This value includes a commitment in the first of the four essentials – 'We trade responsibly.'
- The business model: key enabler number five (of six) – 'operating responsibly'.

The appointment of Hind was received very positively by the NFU. Their Director General Andy Robertson commented: 'Back in February Tesco made a commitment to work more closely with farmers and to source more British food. I see this [new Tesco] role, and Tom's appointment, as a very large step towards delivering on that promise'.[11]

In summary, we conclude that Tesco is questioning extended supply chains that pursue efficiency and lowest-price goals as their primary purpose. Instead, it is now encouraging more local supply chains with the purpose of ensuring product provenance and efficacy. Interestingly, this experience also supports and confirms our premise that 'effectiveness' must always take primacy over 'efficiency'.

Meeting the changing supply channel challenges

In this section we focus on the steps that Tesco has taken and is taking to address the shift in volumes flowing via each supply channel, namely the increase in the convenience, online and discount arenas and the consequent impact this is having on the large store channel.

In addition, it could be argued that Tesco's principal requirement is not actually to re-engineer its supply chain capabilities to meet these challenges. Rather, it is an issue of brand sentiment that needs to be rebuilt, so to conclude our analysis a discussion on this is presented, which goes beyond the issues of rebuilding trust that we examined in depth above.

Supply chain strategy to exploit the growth in the convenience market

Tesco is clearly a pioneer in this area and has generated considerable first-move advantages as a result. It identified the demand for smaller, more local stores in the late 1990s, experimenting with the format through its partnership with Esso, creating petrol forecourt or Tesco Express mini-stores.

With the experience gained here and the insight that convenience provided through smaller, more local stores was a winning formula and matched changing consumer needs, Tesco prioritized growth in this part of its store portfolio from 2002. This campaign was galvanized by its purchase of T&S stores in the second half of 2002, as discussed in Chapter 2. A convenience chain quickly emerged under the Express, One Stop and Metro formats. Tesco's rapid progress in convenience store opening was typical of how, once a decision had been made, it moved very quickly to seize opportunities and implement its adopted strategy. It shows how Tesco can quickly adjust its asset base to reflect a rapidly evolving need for new supply channel structures.

By 2014 this range of stores, just in the UK, had increased to 2,378 (Table 7.4), with 150 new Express stores planned for 2014/15.[12] Tesco has also developed convenience stores in most of its international markets.

Tesco has also learnt a great deal about the unique supply chain challenges that these types of outlets present and how best to cope with them. One problem is that servicing these smaller store formats is more costly than supplying the larger stores such as Tesco Extras, where the economies of scale are obviously larger. So, as more trade diverts from larger to smaller stores, retailers such as Tesco have to be very smart as to how they manage the supply chain process.

TABLE 7.4 Number of UK Tesco convenience stores by format, April 2014

Format	Number of UK stores
Metro	192
Express	1,547
One Stop	639
Total	2,378

SOURCE 'Key Facts', Tesco PLC website, http://www.tescoplc.com/index.asp?pageid=71

They also have to be smart at managing the marketing proposition presented in these types of stores, many of which serve very different needs. For example, Tesco will differentiate some prices, perhaps charging slightly more than in a large Extra store. Another example of the detail of management Tesco is employing, to take the performance of convenience stores to the next level, is to manage the range of products catalogued in each convenience store closely so that they are relevant to the local demographics of the areas they serve. As an example, at Fulham Imperial Wharf, Marylebone High Street and St John's Wood – Express stores in upmarket areas of London – ranges now emphasize local requirements through the addition of:

- a wider Tesco Finest catalogue;
- premium ranges of wine and champagne;
- a strong fresh food presence;
- pushing the boundaries of convenience where space permits, with increased fresh and chilled ranges;
- the Euphorium bakery, offering customers artisan breads and a selection of freshly made premium cakes, sandwiches and salads;
- food to go, offering salad and fruit bars and hot food self-serve counters alongside an extensive range of sandwiches (IGD, 2014).

So it would appear that Tesco still enjoys a significant strategic advantage in this area, in the portfolio of stores, how it manages the supply chain to service them, and the level of sophistication in the marketing proposition that is presented. Tesco, by developing capabilities such as small case sizes and supply chain systems to manage good-quality availability and low waste rates for these types of stores, is arguably well ahead of others in this area, in our view.

Online supply chain strategy

(See the promotional videos at tinyurl.com/oegx8ue, tinyurl.com/qcjxrac and tinyurl.com/lefw9hu)

In this growth area too, Tesco is well advanced and arguably possesses a significant strategic advantage compared to its competitors. For example, it is acknowledged as the largest and most profitable online retailer globally, with sales in 2013 of over £2 billion worldwide (tinyurl.com/mbymd9s).

Tesco, like all progressive retailers, is working to meet the desire for omni-channel retailing access by its customers. Omni-channel retailing is an evolution of multi-channel retailing and concentrates on a seamless approach to the consumer experience through all available shopping channels, such as:

- bricks-and-mortar;
- computers;
- mobile internet devices;
- television and radio;
- direct mail; and
- catalogues.

Thoma (2010) summarizes what is emerging today: 'A new breed of shopper is emerging. Informed, empowered and always connected, this ultra-sophisticated consumer demands real choice when it comes to selecting and purchasing goods. Unlike traditional multi-channel shoppers, this consumer uses all channels – store, catalogue, call centre, web and mobile – simultaneously. Enter the omnichannel shopper.'

Andrew Miles, Tesco's Online Food Marketing Director, said that:

> Clubcard was the 'key thing' for the supermarket's online shopping evolution because it allowed the company to 'understand how customers are shopping through the channels and how customers are evolving'.
>
> He discussed how Tesco had been tracking the shopping behaviour of a real-life couple called Dave and Sue since 2009 to understand how their behaviour was changing.
>
> He described how they are now using online to adapt their shopping dynamically throughout the week as opposed to doing a weekly shop at a Tesco Extra store.
>
> Miles said Clubcard had helped Tesco understand that today, the 'shopper journey is not linear or predictive, it's iterative', as shoppers added and removed products from their online shopping basket throughout the week.
>
> The notion of 'hyper-connectivity' and the 'always-on consumer' is generating new consumer trends around 'immediacy' and 'smart boredom', according to Miles.
>
> He said 'smart boredom' is the theory that downtime is no longer unproductive as people carry out activities such as checking emails on their smartphones as they wait in a queue.
>
> Miles added that the mobile was becoming increasingly important to Tesco and changing the path to purchase. He pointed out that Tesco now received 10% of online orders through mobile, while mobile now accounted for 20% of overall traffic on its site.
>
> tinyurl.com/krmr3ta

In practice, how Tesco grocery customers can now seamlessly move between the conventional physical store solution and the virtual online model is worth exploring. Table 7.5 indicates the range of options that are available.

We can reflect on a few of these developments.

One-hour delivery slots for £1   At the end of April 2014 Tesco announced new home delivery standards that included the availability of one-hour delivery slots that could be booked by customers for

TABLE 7.5 Grocery shopping options at Tesco

Conventional option:
1.   Customers pick their groceries in store.

Online options:
2.   Tesco store staff assemble an online grocery order and the order is delivered by Tesco van to the customer's home in a one-hour time slot selected by the customer.
3.   'Dark stores' – similar to option 2 but from a purpose-built, local grocery home delivery DC rather than a store.
4.   Click & Collect – store staff assemble online grocery orders but instead of opting for a home delivery the customer opts to collect the order from a designated pick-up point. There are options for the collection point:
      – a Tesco store;
      – a more convenient local Tesco Express.
5.   In February 2014 Tesco launched Click Commute Collect:
      – As in 4 above, but instead of collecting from a Tesco store the customer opts to collect from a Tesco home delivery van at one of (currently) six London underground stations.

£1. Tesco claim to have more one-hour delivery slots available than any other retailer in the UK.[13]

Customers could also have the alternative to sign up to have all their groceries delivered from £3 a month so long as each order was a minimum of £25.[14] Tesco claimed that over 200,000 customers were then benefiting from this kind of arrangement. There were alternatives: a mid-week slot, which cost £3 a month, or an anytime plan at £6. Both were available as yearly sign-ups, £30 for mid-week and £60 for anytime. This aligned very closely with Tesco's long-term strategy of providing innovative value propositions, with the aim of building customer loyalty with the company.

Tesco's dark stores As we have already explained in Chapter 5, Tesco moved rapidly to provide a nationwide online delivery service by adopting the 'more effective, less efficient' store-based picking solution rather than purpose-built DCs dedicated to home delivery of online orders.

Then, as individual localities have shown increased demand for the service, Tesco has opened dedicated, purpose-built 'dark stores' to receive, assemble and deliver to the home the online orders placed by consumers. The order routeing is not seen by the consumer, who places online orders as normal: Tesco systems divert orders to the appropriate location. Dark stores are not huge regional DC-type operations but replicate the size of operation seen in a large hypermarket, so enabling the critical order density to be hit earlier in a populous area than for a regional DC. Unlike a store:

- There is no requirement for checkouts etc, as the space is dedicated to order fulfilment.
- All the orders are known (no customers are present), so forecasting is more predictable.
- Fresh food quality is enhanced, with stock rotation observed etc.
- Order accuracy is assisted by picking systems.
- Dark stores can operate 365 days and 24/7; they are not restricted to retail opening hours legislation.
- Efficiency improvement is provided by using automation where appropriate in receive, store, pick and load delivery vehicle stages of the operation.

By the end of 2013, Tesco had six dark stores in the Greater London conurbation – Croydon, Aylesford, Crawley and Erith south of the Thames and Greenford and Enfield north of the river. By the same date Asda had three dark stores (Leeds, Nottingham and Enfield), and Waitrose had one in Acton, west London, underlining Tesco's lead in developing this solution to online grocery picking.

All the forecasts are that online grocery volumes will grow as consumers get more confident about the quality and reliability of the service. The 48-hour lead time remains as a potential block to gaining more users and volume. However, Tesco is trialling next-day delivery in Mansfield, where orders received by 12 midnight will be delivered by 6 pm next day.

Tesco's online Click & Collect service The following benefits are cited by Tesco:

- Convenience.
- Collection is now free (after a free trial to 27 April 2014, Tesco announced it would be free from the end of April 2014 (Vizard, 2014); formerly it started from £2.
- Grocery shopping is picked, packed and safely stored for collection at a time to suit the customer.
- A temperature-controlled collection point is provided; all products are picked on the day of collection and safely stored in the fridge, freezer or cupboard until collection.

The service is offered seven days a week, though the hours available vary according to the store. The customer collecting the order needs proof of ID, order number and the credit card used online to pay for the goods. Tesco also accepts the customer's Clubcard or photo ID. Again, this shows Tesco leading the competition by now offering a free Click & Collect service. Asda offers a free service, but only for baskets of over £25, and Sainsbury's does not offer such a service at all on groceries, only on general merchandise.

Tesco is also quickly expanding extra sites for collection of online picks. IGD forecasts that Tesco and Asda between them had over 500 Click & Collect sites by the end of 2014. It adds that Waitrose is experimenting with collection from lockers.

The Tesco website offers Click & Collect groceries from over 230 locations as at March 2014 and advises that Tesco is continually opening new collection points. When customers use online shopping they will see a prompt for 'Click & Collect' if a location close to them offers Click & Collect groceries when they book a delivery slot. The option is currently free. The convenience of the service seems to be the main benefit that Tesco is seeking to provide, continually striving to make lives easier for customers.

In addition, Tesco is implementing its online offer in Ireland, the Czech Republic, Poland, Budapest, Bangkok and Shanghai. Tesco is also offering customers the opportunity to 'shop in virtual stores'. Thus, commuters in Seoul were able to access digital images of products located in a 'mock store' on underground stations as they returned home from work. Using their smartphones with the appropriate app they placed an order, which was then assembled and delivered to the customers on their arrival at home. This option has subsequently been rolled out to other locations, such as bus stops in university campuses.

Other online developments Tesco has had an online wine service for many years. Added to this, an online multi-channel strategy encompasses other ranges, including clothing and general merchandise, through Tesco Direct, where again customers can use the free Click & Collect service from over 1,700 stores across the UK[15] (ordering by 3 pm will mean their goods are available for collection from 4 pm the next day), and many aspects of Tesco's retail services like Tesco Bank and Tesco Mobile as well, much of which was discussed in earlier chapters.

Tesco's online approach is now all brought together within its digital strategy. Again, we highlighted much of this in earlier chapters, but in summary Tesco now has a well-developed, integrated digital strategy. Tesco understands that a retailer needs to have more than a physical presence backed up by a website. Its virtual presence needs to be just as alluring and able to intermix seamlessly with the physical assets it possesses.

Famously, Philip Clarke is quoted as saying: 'I don't want us simply to be a part of the future: I want us to help to shape the future'.[16]

Developments such as Hudl and Blinkbox underlined Tesco's ambition in this area. The 'T' button on the Hudl facilitated access to services that included:

- movies;
- Tesco current account;
- home shopping;
- 'Find a Tesco store'.

Blinkbox, Tesco's digital entertainment service, now provides access to television, music (12 million songs), books and the recently launched Clubcard TV. Other initiatives include an App Development Centre in Clerkenwell – 40 app development staff co-located with 800 Blinkbox employees.

In summary, Tesco after many years of experience in using online to interconnect with its customers is trying to capitalize on this experience to compete strongly and lead the market. As the need for an omni-channel solution becomes more apparent, as well, Tesco is able to combine its unmatched UK store coverage to add to its competitive proposition. Free Click & Collect services across the whole of the UK, for example, are a key part of what Tesco can do better than anyone else. Coupled with innovations like the Hudl and Blinkbox, Tesco feels it is well placed to be able to exploit future growth in demand for online business in the virtual and physical supply chain offerings it now possesses.

Competing with the discounters and market polarization

The third area of growth highlighted in this chapter, and by IGD in its report, is the growth of the discounters. In addition, there is the growth being enjoyed by the more upmarket retailers, which combined with the discounters' growth is polarizing the market and squeezing the retailers in the middle.

To counter this Tesco has undertaken a number of initiatives.

Major relaunch of the Everyday Value range   Tesco is very aware that, in the UK, Ireland and many of its markets in eastern Europe in particular, market share is being eroded by the rise of the discounters. The sub-brand range Everyday Value is where Tesco competes as strongly as it can for customers who are seeking the very best prices for groceries. The Value range was first launched in 1993. It was refreshed and relaunched with fresh packaging to promote it in 2012 and covers 550 products,[17] not just cupboard staples, but a full range of items that are used day to day, including produce, main meals and desserts.

Pricing strategy – prices that come down stay down   Tesco is well aware, however, that it must compete more strongly on price, as the discounters are redefining what can be achieved in this area, and many customers, as we have discussed, are seeking out these values more and more keenly. Shopping for groceries with discounters is perceived as more acceptable than perhaps it used to be by the average UK customer.

In February 2014 Tesco heralded a new launch in this endeavour with its new campaign to lower the price of many of its products. It coincided with an announcement that it was going to sacrifice some margin to pay for this, however. (Tesco was not being drawn on how much margins would fall from the 5.2 per cent they had been for the previous 18 months, but Deutsche Bank predicted 4.5 per cent for the year ahead in February 2014 as Tesco proposed a £200 million campaign to lower prices permanently from this time (Thesing, 2014).

Up to the time of writing Tesco had announced a series of price-cutting campaigns, focused on popular items that customers regularly purchase:

- four pints of milk down to £1 (tinyurl.com/lyw5o2l);
- very competitive pricing on staples such as 1 kg carrots and salad items like tomatoes, cucumbers, peppers and salad onions;
- from 22 April 2014, very competitive prices on 30 more staple products, such as Tesco bread, bacon, baked beans, broccoli and sugar.[18]

A significant difference to previous strategies was that lower prices would stay down on these kinds of promotions and not bounce back up again after a few weeks, which it was argued was confusing customers and producing customer uncertainty about Tesco's low-price credentials.

It is early days, but combined with offering lower-priced and free services such as for online delivery and Click & Collect, discussed above, Tesco is making a renewed concerted effort to provide a better financial deal for customers to try to turn round year-on-year like-for-like decreases to increases once more.

Clubcard Fuel Save (See the promotional video at tinyurl.com/
pmwaml6)

A further initiative launched in the first half of 2014 was an addition to the benefits Clubcard users could derive from using their
Clubcard with Tesco. After it had been successfully trialled in South
Wales and Norwich at the start of the year, Tesco quickly launched
the idea as a national campaign from March 2014. For every £50
spent across a month, digitally or physically, customers earned 2p a
litre off their fuel the following month. It is a cumulative concept, so
small and large baskets combine, with the potential of saving 20p a
litre in one transaction a month. Tills automatically add Clubcard
fuel points each time customers shop, so it is simple to use and a
bonus for loyal shopping in effect for the 16 million Clubcard holders who shop at Tesco.

So Tesco is increasingly thinking of how to set its stall out to be
more competitive on price, to better compete with the discounters,
but also to incorporate its differentiating points, such as 16 million
Clubcard holders, over 1,700 Click & Collect locations for Tesco
Direct and so on.

Major relaunch of the Tesco Finest ranges (See the promotional videos
at tinyurl.com/mc8j283)

Tesco is also a retailer for everyone and hence has to compete at
the premium end of the spectrum as well. And here too, as has been
noted, Tesco's competitors appear to have been increasing market
share at Tesco's expense, notably Waitrose. As Tesco is the market
leader, many of its rivals have benefited from publicly stating they are
matching Tesco's prices, and this kind of strategy has proven to be very
successful for them. On top of this, Tesco, as we noted, suffered more
than any other retailer over the 'horse meat scandal' early in 2013.

A major initiative that gave Tesco the opportunity to restate its
credentials as a retailer really able to compete at the premium end
of the grocery market came with the relaunch of the Finest range in
autumn 2013. Following on from the Everyday Value relaunch the
previous year the same exhaustive overhaul of the catalogue, packaging, ingredients, marketing and overall presentation of the range was
undertaken in a huge coordinated effort for the group. It underlined

again Tesco's sure-footedness at managing such a promotion, illustrating how the full Tesco team, including buyers, technologists, marketers, logisticians, strategists and so on, could be brought together to focus on the collective delivery of a major company objective.

The relaunch was supported by a very high-profile advertising campaign with the sponsorship in the autumn of one of the most popular TV shows in the UK, *Downton Abbey*.

Refreshing and repurposing the large store

(See the promotional video at tinyurl.com/kxvfozu)

There is an important other side of the coin when it comes to the growth in online, convenience and discount shopping. There is a significant negative impact on 'conventional' stores like hypermarkets and supermarkets. Tesco has experienced this and is suffering from a large reduction in footfall in these bigger store formats.

To correct this it is partway through a major refresh-and-repurpose £1 billion campaign to revitalize these stores. The overriding aim is to make them warmer and more welcoming to shoppers: they had been described as 'cold and functional', as we noted in Chapter 2. Tesco UK Superstores 'were a little bit functional and a little bit efficient and lacked the warmth and friendliness they were looking for,' said Tony Hoggett, Managing Director, Tesco UK Superstores in 2013.[19]Additionally, there is a need from the demand and supply side to reduce the size of these types of stores. From the demand side there is much debate and anecdotal evidence that customers find the Extra format hypermarkets too large. From the supply side too, it makes more sense to supply many of the general products such as large electrical items, furniture and so on through Tesco Direct, to be supplied online and through services like Click & Collect, than incurring the significant cost of running dispersed inventory holdings across the UK for these types of ranges. Customers invariably prefer the lower prices that can be obtained online for many of these products too.

So what should be done to make the Extra type store more attractive as well as repurposing some of the vacant space left by moving some catalogue ranges to Tesco Direct?

In Chapter 2 we looked extensively at what Tesco is doing to refresh these larger stores, and on top of this many more trials are under way to make these so-called 'destination' shops, by adding, for instance, food service outlets to these locations.

An example of these ideas pulled together can be seen at Tesco's new 'destination format' Extra store in Watford, which was reopened in 2013 as part of the 'build a better Tesco' ambition in the UK. A group from IGD visited in August 2013 and, in summary, found the following:

- The biggest change is Tesco's 'food first' policy. All the food has been brought to the front of the store, with fresh produce taking up more space. Also located here are 'food to go' and 'food for later' offers.
- The Euphorium bakery, with artisan breads, bakery classics and products of the month or day.
- The Giraffe restaurant occupies its own area at the front of the store.
- A Harris + Hoole coffee shop.
- General merchandise, clothing, and health and beauty are positioned along the back of the store:
  - F&F (Florence and Fred) located in the back corner of the store has a high street fashion look and feel.
  - General merchandise is displayed on multiple fixtures and fittings, allowing greater dwell time and more of a department store ambience.
  - Health and beauty is a separate area.

These changes aim to deliver stronger 'leisure destination' impacts, with improved in-store ambience, more relevant ranges and greater personality. The IGD report suggested that this resulted in a store no longer 'overly oriented around being operationally effective, but one that creates more excitement for the shopper. Throughout something that stands out is that cross merchandising is maximised for shopper ease.'

So, in short, amid falling sales in its larger stores, Tesco is trying to fill some of the excess space with restaurants and other services, to make its outlets 'warmer and less clinical' and more attractive as shopping destinations, and is significantly investing in these types of stores to achieve this across its entire estate in only a few years.

Rebuilding the Tesco brand

At the beginning of the book we defined what we meant by the supply chain. We took Michael Porter's (1985) view that all aspects of marketing and service that customers value should be incorporated as part of the mix in managing the chain of supply.

Taking this perspective to define the domain of what should be explored when examining the supply of value for customers has hence been a feature throughout the book. We very much see, as Leahy, Clarke and Lewis do, that the marketing and supply chain management worlds need to be completely integrated if companies like Tesco are to compete successfully.

Reflecting on this view, some commentators argue that currently the biggest challenge Tesco has in providing value as perceived by customers so that it can grow the Tesco business year on year is not so much a problem of the physical supply chain, although we have highlighted in this chapter some of the challenges it is facing in this regard, but instead it is an issue of brand identity.

Indeed, in an interview with Graham Ruddick of the *Daily Telegraph* on 24 February 2014, Philip Clarke himself admitted that the Tesco brand was 'carrying baggage' and would need to be 'overhauled' as Tesco redoubled its efforts to become a profit growth business once more.[20]

We have in this chapter tried to analyse the manifold reasons why Tesco is struggling to get back to being a growing business again. It has certainly been hit by the shift in channels, the depressed economic backdrop lasting longer than anticipated, the rise of the discounters and the polarizing of the market and of course the loss of trust resulting from the horsemeat scandal. And, as pressure comes on, marketing budgets are trimmed, money available for future investment is harder to come by and there is a danger that this will restrict future performance. A vicious rather than a virtual circle could define the Tesco business model.

But Tesco also has many unique strengths, as has been discussed, and the key would seem to be to bring these together to differentiate Tesco in the eyes of its many customers. Tesco certainly sees the criticality of going back to what it traditionally did really well and orientating itself around the customer in everything it does and develops. And there is clear evidence, as highlighted in this chapter, that this is beginning to happen, with more initiatives no doubt to come in the future in this regard. The ethos of 'Better, simpler, cheaper' once again is what should underpin Tesco's branding message. It is what Tesco does – in short, constantly trying to make the lives of all its customers, each with different needs, which invariably change constantly, of course, progressively easier.

There was a temptation perhaps in the early days when the going became tougher at the outset of Clarke's CEO tenure for the company to become too focused on efficiency and to forget that effectiveness must come first as Lean philosophy strongly advocates. The grocery market is as competitive as it has ever been in the UK, with deals and price campaigns seemingly almost continuously evident. But, if Tesco can get back to providing unbeatable effectiveness for customers first and only then chase efficiencies in the way it manages its processes, including the supply chain process, it should be able to pull itself out of this doldrums period, in our view.

It is going to be tough, especially to compete better with the discounters. But the UK economy at last is looking to show signs of stronger growth, with average wages about to grow faster than inflation once more. Perhaps Tesco's operational excellence, supply chain prowess and strong foundations will allow it to capitalize again as it did for the 20 years or so after the last recessionary period in the early 1990s.

Conclusion

This chapter has examined the major challenges Tesco faces in protecting its market share in the UK and trying to grow its business. Tesco demonstrates that it is not complacent about these challenges. It is developing strategies to show that it remains relevant to the changing needs of its customers – not just by responding to these changes, but by helping to shape them.

Aligning the business around the new needs and values of today's customer, often through fresh supply channels, is critically important if Tesco is going to remain relevant and wanted. Managing the end-to-end, the multi-channel, and the digital and physical chains of supply brings the whole business together, however. Tesco as a team works tirelessly to improve its supply chain capabilities to better support the ambitions of the company, as we have explored throughout this book. By developing unmatched capabilities in managing what perhaps is better termed 'the value chain', which includes all the marketing and supply chain aspects in combination, Tesco is world renowned as being a leader.

How ironic then that it was in the supply chain that it encountered the huge problems that flowed from the horsemeat scandal in early 2013. A major strength of the business became its Achilles heel, it could be argued.

But perhaps more can be learnt about how to improve still further from problems that occurred than from successes and, by really analysing what went wrong and appreciating afresh how important it is for a business like Tesco that it has the trust of its customers, a stronger and more capable supply chain and company overall will emerge.

The chapter has highlighted that, as well as many challenges, there are many opportunities for Tesco, especially in the anticipated growth areas of convenience, online and discount. Despite the tough times that it is going through, a belief in what the company stands for and how it should approach and do things is clearly strongly present. Whether it will be enough is a theme of Chapter 8.

Key chapter summary points

1 The supply chain can be viewed as a system that holistically delivers and responds to system purpose, eg customer needs.

2 The system needs to be dynamic, because purpose evolves too.

3 The trick is aligning the system to ensure it is continually providing value that meets customer needs.

4 Evolutionary change should be relatively easy to accommodate in terms of adjusting the supply chain system to keep it optimized with incremental value need changes.

5 Revolutionary changes in customer needs are a threat if the system is unable to be flexible or adaptable enough to be able to respond in a timely fashion. This is why complacency is perhaps the biggest danger facing any organization!

6 The chapter provides a case study illustration of this, as the movement of supply channel flows brought about principally by macro external environmental changes (economic, technological and sociological) is rapidly altering the grocery market landscape. In some ways Tesco is forward-thinking enough to cope, but in other ways the changes are providing a profound challenge for it.

Notes

1 Companies will only survive if they adapt quickly and stay in tune with their customers' changing habits, *Daily Telegraph*, 22 September 2013

2 files.the-group.net/library/tesco/files/pdf_316.pdf

3 *ibid.*

4 S Butler, Farmfoods shocks industry to become fastest growing grocer, *Guardian*, 17 February 2014

5 files.the-group.net/library/tesco/files/pdf_316.pdf

6 Highlighted in Young people lose a whole day a week to surfing web, *Metro*, 30 April 2014, p 11

7 files.the-group.net/library/tesco/files/pdf_316.pdf

8 Tesco wins top award for cutting carbon emissions, www.tescoplc.com/index.asp?pageid=17&newsid=960, 1 May 2014,

9 tinyurl.com/co6ergo

10 tinyurl.com/omz4tnz

11 tinyurl.com/oh7njvh

12 Tesco preliminary results 2013/14, tinyurl.com/pvnsbc8

13 tinyurl.com/m76twdt

14 tinyurl.com/mnbb33y

15 tinyurl.com/ob62e4d

16 files.the-group.net/library/tesco/files/pdf_316.pdf

17 tinyurl.com/k37vre4

18 tinyurl.com/m76twdt

19 Better Stores, Better Service, Tescoplc Video Library, tinyurl.com/kxvfozu accessed 30/01/2014

20 Tesco brand has 'baggage', admits Chief Executive Philip Clarke, tinyurl.com/lpeahwl)

Conclusions

This chapter focuses on the key points from the book. Here are the summary points from each chapter, set out and linked together.

In Chapter 1 we set out the context for the book and identified Tesco's recognition that a core ingredient of its success over the last 20 years has been to do with the way it manages its supply chain. However, we noted that competing through the supply chain may be easy to explain – but it is very hard to achieve.

We asserted that Tesco, as a business that manufactures nothing, envisages that a key source for creating competitive advantage is through continually improving the capability of its supply chain operations, from plough to plate. Given Tesco's success in fulfilling this ambition, especially over the two decades to 2013, it presents an exemplary case study for others to learn from.

Our starting point was to envisage the supply chain as a simple system: inputs and outputs to meet a declared purpose, with a live feedback loop to check on progress against purpose. The model was used throughout the book to illustrate that Tesco's supply chain, although complex to the unintuitive observer, can essentially be reduced to a simple level. A key point to understand is that any organization that seeks to compete through its supply chain needs to start with real clarity about its core purpose from the perspective of its customers.

In Chapter 2 we presented a background summary of Tesco's history, tracing its origins and growth up to the current day in four eras, largely defined by the principal leaders of the organization. A remarkable point is that until Clarke resigned in July 2014 there had really been only four in Tesco's 95-year history. A key aspect of its culture that has been acquired through its development is that it focuses on the customer rather than focusing on its competitors!

In Chapter 3 we started to break down how Tesco has gone about the supply chain optimization process. What was emphasized is how important a holistic approach is in achieving sustained progress. In addition, the criticality of ensuring alignment with overall corporate strategy was underlined. What has given Tesco real strength is the consistency of strategy, which has allowed the journey of supply chain development to take place step by step in a sure-footed manner: gains building on gains, building on gains. Tesco's plans, execution and continuous improvement are delivered by a team of people clear about the direction in which they are heading and their individual roles in delivering on this journey.

In Chapter 4 the root of a supply chain orientation, an obsessive understanding of how customers perceive value, was explored. Conventionally, this may have been seen as the domain of the marketing team in many organizations, but in reality marketing and supply chain management are completely intertwined in this common endeavour of meeting customer needs. Tesco understands this and uses a completely integrated team approach to sense and react to customer values.

An important point here, which really differentiates Tesco from many of its competitors in the way it uses its supply chain to provide value, is that Tesco does not restrict value creation by stopping at the supermarket shelf: it defines it as aiming to make the life of the Tesco shopper easier in the whole search, acquisition and consumption process and to create loyalty so customers feel motivated to return again and again.

Finally in this chapter it was emphasized that, while listening to customers is important, taking action to do something about the insight gleaned is what in the end makes the difference.

This led into Chapter 5, which was all about how Tesco acts on this insight in managing its supply chain. It described the journey that Tesco has been on in developing the capability to create a supply chain that provides absolute effectiveness. Tesco's supply chain has been described as world-class and this chapter set out how Tesco has gone about earning this accolade. A key point is that organizations cannot move to a world-class supply chain overnight and require an agreed framework to follow as a 'road map'. For Tesco the principles and framework provided by Lean philosophy proved extremely valuable in helping the group navigate its way on this journey. Following Ackoff's (2010) advice to focus on effectiveness rather than efficiency was an important guiding principle.

In Chapter 6, a more reflective stance was taken to examine how Tesco's approach makes it different to many other organizations and leads it to take what on the face of it may seem to be quite counterintuitive, unconventional decisions, which invariably in fact further distance it from its competitors. A key aspect of this is that in a complex world the pursuit of simplicity is critical to growing organizational capability providing an enduring strength. 'Simple' must not be confused with 'easy'.

Overall, what was concluded was that Tesco has acquired the capability to be a 'smart' organization, for the most part being able continually to stay ahead of the chasing pack from the early 1990s until recent years. There is thus good historical evidence that Tesco has the capability to emerge from its current challenges and return to the path of being a growing business once again in the near future.

Finally, in Chapter 7 the current period of challenge up to mid-2014 was examined. Again the suggestion was made that the supply chain can be viewed as a system that holistically delivers and responds to the system purpose, eg customer needs. What appears to be occurring is that the macro environmental changes currently evident are reshaping the retail marketplace in a profound way and over a relatively short time period. The degree of adaptation required and the time period that retailers have to achieve alignment to this are very challenging and perhaps the core reason why some of the larger players, including Tesco, are struggling in their performance at present.

However, Tesco is seizing many of the opportunities presented by this era of change as well and, by returning to its core roots of sensing and responding to customer needs, and by combining its strengths with this understanding, is intending to come back to growth through its mastery of the supply chain.

Tesco's current position is summed up well by a quote of 9 May 2014 from Kevin O'Marah, Chief Content Officer for SCM World. Writing about Tesco's plans for a Hudl smartphone he said:

'Unlike Apple or Google, Tesco's core business is under siege from low-budget competitors.' And there had been criticism of Tesco, he said, 'for failing to respond with even lower prices. I think this is short-sighted and fails to credit Tesco for attacking omnichannel retail with aggressive e-commerce capabilities designed to enhance total demand capture'. [1]

In summary, Tesco recognizes that in its supply chain it has a differentiating source of competitive advantage, and this book has aimed to explain this and explore how it has been achieved. The 'Better, simpler, cheaper' approach is key to this endeavour. This book has demonstrated:

• what Tesco aims to do;
• why it is doing it; and importantly
• how.

A final point is that *how* critically depends on engaged and motivated colleagues. Tesco employs over 500,000 staff across the world, and each and every one of them plays a crucial role in repeatedly and consistently delivering value for customers. 'Every little helps'!

Note

1 tinyurl.com/kstetf3

APPENDIX 1
World of Retail retailer data –
store sales and profits for
retailers that operate UK
food stores

Retailer	UK			Period	Global Deloitte 2015 Report (data up to June 2014)	
	Turnover	Profit			Group revenue	Net income
		Operating	Pre-tax			
Tesco	£43,570m	£2,190m	Not given	Year to 22 February 2014	$100,213m	$1,529m
Aldi	£5,277m	£271m	£260.9m	Year to 31 December 2013	$81,090m[e]	n/a
Booker	£4,681m	£124m	£122m	Year to 28 March 2014	Not in top 250	
Co-op	£10,534m	(£148m)	(£277m)	Year to 4 January 2014	$12,652m	($3,601m)
Costco	No figures available				$105,156m	$2,061m
Costcutter	£646m	£8m	£10m	Year to 29 December 2012	Not in top 250	
Farmfoods	£721m	Not given	£15m	Year to 28 December 2013	Not in top 250	
Iceland	£2,669m	£161m	£162m	Year to 28 March 2014	$4,309m*	n/a
John Lewis	£9,028m	£424m	£329m	Year to 25 January 2014	$14,164m*	$159m
Lidl (Schwarz)	Lidl does not provide details – no figures available				$98,662m[e]	n/a

Marks & Spencer	Food £5,063m Clothes £3,674m Home £419m —————— Total £9,156m	£619m	Not given	Year to 29 March 2014	$16,391m	$804m
Morrisons	£17,680m	(£95m)	(£176m)	Year to 2 February 2014	$27,739m	($373m)
Musgrave	No figures available				€4,833m**	€68m**
Sainsbury's	£23,949m	£1,009m	£898m	Year to 15 March 2014	$38,076m	$1,133m
Walmart/Asda	£25,352m	£994m	£914m	Year to 31st December 2013	$476,294m	$16,635m
Whole Foods Market	No figures available				$12,917m	$551m

NOTES:

^{e} = Estimate.

* = Wholesale plus retail.

** = From Kamcity.com (not in Deloitte top 250).

SOURCE KamCity.com (www.kamcity.com/wor).

APPENDIX 2
World of Retail retailer data – store numbers summary for food retailers that operate UK stores

Retailer	Date for store numbers	Total UK stores	Total global stores including UK	Notes
Tesco	22 February 2014	3,378	UK 3,378 EU 1,810 Asia 2,861 ———— Total 8,049	UK – Extra, Homeplus, Superstores, Metro, Express, 'dark stores' (dotcom only), Dobbies Garden Centres, One Stop. Europe – Eire, Czech Republic, Hungary, Poland, Slovakia, Turkey. Asia – China, Malaysia, South Korea, Thailand.
Aldi	Not given	625+	9,285+	Aldi does not disclose exact store numbers. UK figure includes Ireland. Europe 7,010, Asia 0, USA 1,300 and Australia 350.

(Continued)

Retailer	Date for store numbers	Total UK stores	Total global stores including UK	Notes
Booker	September 2014	202	208	UK = 172 Booker Cash & Carry + 30 Makro. India – 6 stores. The group also operates delivered wholesale businesses, consisting of Booker Direct, Ritter Courivaud, Classic Drinks, and Chef Direct. Booker also operates Premier, one of the largest symbol groups in the UK, with over 3,000 stores independently owned by retailers.
Co-op	January 2014	2,800+	Nil	Includes 2,300 convenience stores.
Costco	January 2015	26	671	
Costcutter	December 2012	1,700+		UK and Ireland –1700+, including Kwiksave, Costcutter and myCostcutter banners. A further 800 Mace, Your Store and Supershop from P&H.
Farmfoods	February 2015	300+	Nil	Farmfoods policy is not to provide exact store numbers.
Iceland	March 2014	833	844	11 stores in Ireland, Czech Republic, Portugal and Spain.

Retailer	Date for store numbers	Total UK stores	Total global stores including UK	Notes
John Lewis	April 2014	358	Nil	317 Waitrose, 31 John Lewis department stores and 10 John Lewis at home.
Lidl (Schwarz)	Not given	600	10,300+	Lidl does not disclose exact store numbers.
Marks & Spencer	March 2014	798	1,253	UK – 293 traditional, 447 Simply Food and 48 outlets. Global – no breakdown by type.
Morrisons	March 2014	606	Nil	
Musgrave	31 December 2013	2,544	3,573	UK – Budgens, Centra, Londis, Mace, Marketplace and SuperValu. Ireland – Centra, Daybreak, Day Today, Marketplace and SuperValu. Spain – Diaisur.
Sainsbury's	7 June 2014	1,230	Nil	592 supermarkets and 638 superstores.
Walmart/ Asda	30 April 2014	592	10,994	UK – 592 Asda stores. North America, South America, Asia and Africa.
Whole Foods Market	9 January 2014	8	373	UK, USA and Canada.

SOURCE KamCity.com (www.kamcity.com/wor).

APPENDIX 3
Number of stores by territory for food retailers that operate UK food stores

Number of stores

Retailer	UK	Europe	Scandinavia	Russia	North America	South America	Asia	Australasia	Africa	Middle East	Totals
Tesco	3,378	1,810					2,861				8,049
Aldi	625+	7,010+			1,300+			350+			9,285+
Booker	202						6				208
Co-op	2,800										2,800
Costco	26	1			596		41	7			671
Costcutter	1,700+										1,700+
Farmfoods	300+										300+
Iceland	833	11									844
John Lewis	358										358
Lidl	600+	9,322+	380+								10,302+
Marks & Spencer	798	158						144		153	1,253

Morrisons	606					606
Musgrave	2,544	1,029				3,573
Sainsbury's	1,230					1,230
Walmart/ Asda	592		5,258	3,922	861	380	11,013
Whole Foods Market	8		365				373

SOURCE KamCity.com (www.kamcity.com/wor).

APPENDIX 4
Tesco innovations as it moves
into international territories

Europe	Conventional stores							Online orders					Tesco Finance			Tesco Mobile	Hudl tablet	Florence and Fred clothing brands
Innovations	Hypermarket	Superstore	Metro	Convenience	One Stop convenience	Garden centres	Virtual stores	Home delivery	Click & Collect: From store	Click & Collect: From van, eg at tube station	'Dark stores' picking	Clubcard	Credit card	Loans etc	Bank			
UK	✓	✓	✓	✓	✓	Dobbies		✓	✓	✓	✓	✓	✓	✓	✓	✓	✓	F&F
Eire	✓	✓	✓	✓				✓	✓	✓✓✓		✓	✓	✓		✓	✓	F&F
Czech Republic	✓	✓	✓	✓				✓				✓	✓	✓		✓	✓	F&F
Slovakia	✓	✓	✓	✓				✓	✓			✓	✓	✓		✓	✓	F&F
Poland	✓	✓	✓	✓				✓	✓			✓	✓	✓		✓	✓	F&F
Hungary	✓	✓	✓	✓				✓				✓	✓	✓		✓	✓	F&F

Middle East	Turkey	✓		✓			✓	F&F
Asia	Malaysia	Malls	✓	✓			✓	F&F
	Thailand	✓	✓	✓	✓	✓	✓	F&F
	South Korea	Malls	✓	✓		✓	✓	F&F
	China	Malls	✓	✓			✓	F&F

NOTES:

✓ Innovation found here

✓✓ Located at tube stations and bus stops. Travellers scan codes under pictures of products and place order using their mobile phone. Order is subsequently delivered to the customer's home

✓✓✓ Located at two Luas tram stops in Dublin

APPENDIX 5
Tesco CSR reporting –
standstill summary of
2013/14 performance:
three ambitions and four
essentials

Three ambitions

Tesco's 'three ambitions' are:

1. creating opportunities;
2. improving health;
3. reducing food waste.

Ambitions	Measures	Achieved	Commentary
Creating opportunities	Number of opportunities for young people created across the Tesco Group	158,000 in total: – at Tesco 76,500; – hard-to-reach groups 1,500; – preparing for work 80,000.	This measure consolidates the number of opportunities for young people (under 25) created across all Tesco's operating markets. The initiatives are run in the different operating markets to help young people get started in a career and are tailored to local needs. To qualify as an opportunity the activity must: – involve active participation, eg through career taster days, schools' outreach programmes or mentoring; – provide support that will help improve the young person's future career prospects, eg through scholarships or training; – be an opportunity that would not have existed without Tesco's involvement, eg learning through its core skills training that has been developed by Tesco training experts.

health …comparison of most and least healthy *customer shops by product category (UK)*

Category	Most healthy 5%	Least healthy 5%
Produce, eg fruit and vegetables	46.7%	7.7%
Grocery 2., eg rice and tinned vegetables	11.3%	9.1%
Meat, fish and poultry	6.0%	5.3%
Frozen	3.8%	5.6%
Convenience, eg ready meals	4.4%	10.6%
Bakery	5.0%	9.6%
Dairy	10.1%	13.3%
Grocery 1, eg cereals and hot drinks	4.8%	7.1%
Impulse, eg snacks and soft drinks	6.6%	30.5%

Tesco used Clubcard data to establish the nutritional profile of typical Tesco shopping baskets in the UK. The information in the 'Achieved' column shows how the most healthy and least healthy baskets differ at a product level. The healthiest baskets have a much higher proportion of fruit and vegetables, and the least healthy baskets have a higher proportion of snacks and soft drinks. This analysis is important in helping Tesco to focus work where it can make the biggest difference to the health of its customers. Current analysis is based on two-thirds of the items going through Tesco tills in the UK. Achieving 100% coverage is a priority for the future. It is based on a sample of 2.15 million real customer baskets (year ending July 2013). It excludes baskets with fewer than 15 distinct products. Tesco will also start to carry out this analysis for its international markets.

(continued)

Ambitions	Measures	Achieved	Commentary
Reducing food waste	Reducing food waste in Tesco's UK operations. This will be rolled out to Tesco's international operations in future years.	56,580 tonnes (within the scope of KPMG LLP's limited assurance opinion). This figure represents food that was wasted in Tesco stores and distribution centres in 2013/14, which is equivalent to 0.9% of the number of food products sold in Tesco's stores over the same period.	Tesco UK food waste by category (percentage breakdown of total tonnage value): Bakery 41% Grocery 4% Produce 21% Counters 2% Convenience 8% Frozen 2% Dairy 8% Beers and spirits 2% Impulse 6% World foods 1% Meat, fish and poultry 5% Hotspot analysis (UK) – Tesco has identified food waste hotspots across the value chain for 25 of the most frequently purchased products in the UK. WRAP, Tesco suppliers and an independent consultancy, Best Foot Forward, have worked with Tesco to calculate and validate this information.

Underpinning Tesco's three 'big ambitions' are its four 'essentials', which are:

1. trading responsibly;
2. reducing Tesco's impact on the environment;
3. being a great employer;
4. supporting local communities.

Essentials	Performance KPIs	Feedback/accreditation	Measure	2013/14 actual performance
Trading responsibly	Putting Tesco customers first	Based on *customer* feedback	'Tesco is a company I can trust.'	60%
			'Tesco treats its suppliers fairly.'	33.5% (customer view)
			Percentage of new own-brand products Tesco's customers approve before launch.	98%
	Building strong partnerships with Tesco's suppliers to provide high-quality products	Based on *supplier* feedback	Supplier response rate (questionnaire to over 15,000 suppliers in 45 different countries).	39%
			Percentage of positive responses to the question 'I am treated with respect?'	67%

(continued)

Essentials	Performance KPIs	Feedback/accreditation	Measure	2013/14 actual performance
Reducing Tesco's impact on the environment	Aiming to be a zero-carbon business by 2050 and using scarce resources responsibly	Calculated according to the WRI/WBCSD Greenhouse Gas (GHG) Protocol	Reduction in CO_2e emissions per square foot of Tesco stores and distribution centres across the group against a 2006/07 baseline.	34.7%
			Reduction in CO_2e emissions per case of goods delivered across the group against a 2011/12 baseline.	7.8%
			Water consumption across the group in Tesco's direct operations (average water intensity across the whole business was $0.21m^3$/sq ft).	$32.9mm^3$
			Percentage of waste Tesco produces that is recycled, reused or converted to energy across the group. (This excludes Tesco, Thailand and Kipa, Turkey, where this information is unavailable.)	86%

Being a great employer	Creating opportunities that make Tesco colleagues happy and proud of what they do	Pride in working at Tesco.	63%
		Percentage of colleagues on development programme.	6.2%
		Diversity in Tesco's workforce – percentage of colleagues who are female.	Board 27% Senior managers – directors 22% Senior managers – all 30% All employees – 57%
Supporting local communities	Citizenship – being a good neighbour and running the business to the highest standards	Colleague and customer fundraising.	£22.7m
		Percentage of pre-tax profits donated to charities and good causes.	2.3% (almost £53m)
		The average percentage of votes cast in favour of AGM resolutions.	97.8%

SOURCE Data obtained from Tesco (2014)

APPENDIX 6
Evolution of Tesco corporate social responsibility (CSR) reporting 1999–2014

1999–2006

1999 – Tesco annual report includes a page on 'support for communities and the environment'.

2000 – Tesco and Sainsbury's cited as the only two UK food retailers taking a proactive approach to CSR. Safeway (now part of Morrisons) and M&S were cited as being reactive. Remaining food retailers were cited as being non-active. (See Piacentini, MacFadyen and Eadie. 2000.)

2002 – Tesco issues its CSR review as a separate document for the first time

2006 – Tesco adds a new, fifth segment to its Steering Wheel. 'Community' joins 'customer', 'finance', 'operations' and 'people', emphasizing the importance Tesco places on putting community, corporate responsibility and sustainability at the centre of its business plan. The 'community' segment sets out two core objectives:
1. Be a good neighbour.
2. Be responsible, fair and honest.

2008–12

2008 – The 'community' segment of the Tesco Steering Wheel is extended to consist of five core objectives:
1. Actively supporting local communities.
2. Buying and selling our products responsibly.
3. Caring for the environment.
4. Giving customers healthy choices.
5. Creating good jobs and careers.

2012 – Tesco modifies the wording of four of its five core objectives as follows:

• Actively supporting local communities – no change

• Buying and selling our products responsibly has added:
  a. Working with our suppliers
  b. Providing good-quality, safe and affordable food

• Caring for the environment has added: Our journey to zero carbon

• Giving customers healthy choices has added: Helping our customers make healthier and greener choices

• Creating good jobs and careers has added: Building our team

2013–

2013 – Tesco added a third 'value': 'We use our scale for good.' Tesco plans to use this third value to achieve three 'ambitions':

Ambition 1 – To create new opportunities for millions of young people around the world – by inspiring, equipping and enabling millions of young people to succeed in the world of work.

Ambition 2 – To improve health and through this help to tackle the global obesity crisis – by helping and encouraging 500,000 Tesco colleagues and 50 million customers to live healthier lives.

Ambition 3 – To lead in reducing food waste globally – by working with Tesco's producers and suppliers and helping the customers Tesco serves to find ways to reduce food waste.

Tesco outlines four 'essentials' to deliver these 'ambitions':

1. *We trade responsibly* – putting customers first and working with suppliers to innovate and provide high-quality products.

2. *We are reducing our impact on the environment* – aiming to be a zero-carbon business by 2050 and to use scarce resources responsibly, including in the supply chain.

3. *We are a great employer* – creating inspiring work that makes Tesco colleagues happy and proud of what they do.

4. *We support our local communities* – being a good neighbour and running the Tesco business to the highest standards.

APPENDIX 7
Tesco key events timeline

Decade	Year	CEO	UK events	International events
1910s	1919	Jack Cohen	Jack Cohen starts trading from a market stall in the East End of London.	
1920s	1929		Tesco brand name established at a London shop.	
1930s	1932		Tesco Stores Limited becomes a private limited company.	
	1934		Tesco operating just under 50 stores.	
	1939		Tesco now has 100 stores.	
1940s	1947		Tesco Stores (Holdings) Ltd floated on the Stock Exchange.	
	1948		First self-service Tesco store opens in St Albans, Hertfordshire.	
1950s	1950		Tesco has 20 self-service stores.	
	1955		Burnards chain of 19 stores acquired.	
	1956		First Tesco supermarket opens, in a converted cinema in Malden, Essex.	
	1957		70 Williamson's stores taken over, bringing the total Tesco stores to 180.	
	1959		Purchase of Harrow Stores, with 200 branches.	

(Continued)

1960s		
	1960	Largest Tesco supermarket, 4,200 sq ft, opens at Cheltenham.
	1960	Purchase of Irwin's, a chain of 212 branches in the north of England.
	1961	New Tesco store in Leicester, 16,500 sq ft, features in the *Guinness Book of Records* as the largest store in Europe.
	1963	Green Shield stamps introduced into Tesco stores.
	1964	Resale price maintenance abolished after pressure from Tesco and Sainsbury's. This gave retailers the freedom to set prices.
	1964	Purchase of Charles Phillips, adding 97 self-service stores.
	1965	Cadena Cafes, a chain of 49 cake shops and restaurants, taken over.
	1965	Adsega, a chain of 47 supermarkets, taken over.
	1968	Victor Value chain of stores bought.
	1969	Jack Cohen knighted in the New Year's Honours List, for his services to retailing. He becomes first Life President of the company.

Decade	Year	CEO	UK events	International events
1970s	1971	Ian MacLaurin appointed to Tesco board in 1971 and becomes sole Managing Director in 1975 following the death of Laurie Leigh	Ian MacLaurin appointed to Tesco Board in 1971.	
	1973		New Tesco House, the new head office, built at Cheshunt.	
	1973		Leslie Porter appointed Chairman.	
	1977		Green Shield stamps replaced by a price-cutting campaign under the banner 'Checkout at Tesco'.	
	1978		First steps in takeover of the 3 Guys chain of stores in Ireland.	
	1979		Jack Cohen dies.	
	1979		Tesco sales exceed £1 billion.	
	1979		Terry Leahy joins Tesco in a marketing role.	

1980s		
1980	Acquisition of Cartier, a Kent-based retailer.	
1982	Computerized checkouts introduced into the first Tesco stores.	
1982	Tesco sales exceed £2 billion.	
1982	Victor Value limited-range discount stores launched.	
1983	Tesco Stores (Holdings) Ltd becomes Tesco PLC.	
1985	100th superstore opens at Brent Park, Neasden.	
1985	Sir Leslie Porter retires as Tesco Chairman, succeeded by Ian MacLaurin.	
1985	Tesco sponsors first Viewdata home shopping scheme in Gateshead pensioners' homes.	
1986	Victor Value division of 45 stores sold to Bejam Group plc.	Tesco Stores Ireland Ltd (formerly 3 Guys) sold to H Williams, a Dublin-based supermarket group.
1987	Acquisition of Hillards, a supermarket chain with 40 stores in Yorkshire.	
1987	Announcement of six new composite distribution warehouses, cost £70m.	
1987	Launch of Customer First customer service campaign.	

(Continued)

Decade	Year	CEO	UK events	International events
	1989		Ian MacLaurin knighted in the New Year's Honours List.	
	1989		First 'composite' multi-temperature distribution centre, in Doncaster, begins operation.	
1990s	1991		Tesco becomes Britain's biggest independent petrol retailer.	
	1992		Terry Leahy appointed to Tesco board as Marketing Director.	
	1992		First Tesco Metro store opens at Covent Garden, London.	
	1993		Value lines range of low-priced basic products launched.	Acquisition of Catteau, a chain of 92 food stores in northern France.
	1994		Launch of 'One in Front' scheme to cut checkout queues.	Acquisition of 51% share in Global, with 43 stores in north-west Hungary.
	1994		Purchase of Wm Low, with 57 stores in Scotland and the north of England.	
	1995		Completion of new 505,000 square feet depot at Magor, South Wales – the UK's largest dry grocery warehouse.	Opening of Tesco Vin Plus wine supermarket, near Calais.
	1995		Launch of Tesco Clubcard customer loyalty scheme.	£8m investment in Polish retailer Savia, with 36 stores in southern Poland.

(Continued)

1995	Tesco joins CompuServe shopping-by-computer scheme.	
1995	Tesco has largest UK dry grocery market share in the food retail industry.	
1995	Would I Buy It staff initiative launched, focusing on product quality.	
1995	Official opening of the first of nine recycling service units, to recycle 100% of transit packaging.	
1996	Tesco voted Retailer of the Year in the inaugural Retail Week Awards.	£77m purchase of 13 Kmart stores in the Czech Republic and Slovakia.
1996	Chairman Sir Ian MacLaurin becomes Lord MacLaurin of Knebworth.	The Polus store, first Tesco hypermarket in Central Europe, opens in Budapest.
1996	Tesco opens Customer Service Centre call centre in Dundee.	
1996	New internet superstore launched, enabling customers in west London to buy any of the 20,000 products available at Tesco Osterley.	
	Belfast Metro opens – the first Tesco store in Northern Ireland.	

Decade	Year	CEO	UK events	International events
	1997	Terry Leahy 1997–2011	Tesco buys food retail operation ABF in Northern Ireland and the ROI for £630m.	The purchase of 75 ABF stores in the Republic of Ireland and 34 stores in Northern Ireland.
	1997		Chairman Lord MacLaurin voted Businessman of the Year.	First Tesco superstore in France opens in Villepinte, a suburb of Paris.
	1997		Tesco forms Tesco Personal Finance (TPF) with the Royal Bank of Scotland.	Fogarasi store, the second Tesco hypermarket in Hungary, opens.
	1997		Four Tesco stores open on a 24-hour basis, one day a week.	Sale of Catteau, the Tesco French subsidiary, is announced.
	1997		First Tesco Extra store opens in Pitsea, Essex.	
	1997		Tesco comes top in first Retail Industry Awards.	
	1998		Tesco awarded Multiple Retailer of the Year for the second year running, in the Retail Industry Awards.	Tesco moves into the Far East, taking a controlling interest in Lotus Thailand, a chain of 13 hypermarkets, for £200m.
	1999		In a *Management Today* survey of board directors, Tesco is named Britain's Most Admired Company.	In a joint venture with Samsung Corporation, Tesco moves into South Korea, buying two Homeplus hypermarkets and three development sites.

1999	Tesco publishes supermarket price comparisons on the internet, to help shoppers get the best deals.
1999	Tesco voted Britain's Most Admired Company for the third time.
2000s	
2000	Tesco.com is launched.
2001	Prime Minister Tony Blair launches the 10th Tesco Computers for Schools scheme.	Tesco opens its first store in Taiwan.
2001	Florence and Fred, a new Tesco clothing range, is launched.	Tesco forms a joint venture to develop hypermarkets in Malaysia and opens its first store in 2002.
2001	Tesco launches a new corporate social responsibility website at www.tesco.com/everylittlehelps.	A Tesco team in Japan investigates the opportunities of building stores there, operating in convenience store format. The first store opened in 2003.
2002	Terry Leahy is knighted for his services to food retailing.	Tesco announces a new strategic relationship with US supermarket Safeway Inc to take the Tesco.com home shopping model to the United States.
2003	Acquisition of 870 T&S (One Stop) stores in the UK, 450 of which are converted to Tesco Express in the following three to four years.	Tesco entered Turkey in 2003 under the banner of Tesco Kipa stores.

(Continued)

Decade	Year	CEO	UK events	International events
	2004			Tesco acquired a 50% stake in the Hymall chain in China and raised this to 90% in December 2006. Most stores were in the Shanghai area.
	2005		Tesco.com weekly grocery orders reach 150,000.	
	2006		The number of Clubcard members reaches 13 million .	
	2007		Leahy announces Tesco's 'green' targets on CO_2 etc in a speech, 'Carbon and the Consumer', at a forum in Central London.	Following an investigation into potential stores in the United States, Tesco sets up a business based in California to operate convenience stores. It opened the first Fresh & Easy store in November 2007. By the end of 2012 Tesco had over 200 Fresh & Easy stores in Arizona, California and Nevada.
	2007		Tesco commits £25 million to create a new Sustainable Consumption Institute (SCI) at the University of Manchester, a multidisciplinary centre of global excellence, researching major issues associated with sustainability and encouraging customers to adopt more sustainable lifestyles.	

(Continued)

	2008	Tesco Personal Finance: Tesco acquires RBS's 50% stake of the joint venture.
	2008	Tesco named Retailer of the Year and E-tailer of the Year at the World Retail Awards in Barcelona, global retailing's most prestigious awards ceremony.
	2008	Tesco acquired 36 hypermarkets in South Korea from Homever.
	2009	TPF renamed Tesco Bank, with plans for it to become a full retail bank.
2010s	2011	Tesco opens the world's first zero-carbon supermarket in Ramsey, Cambridgeshire.
Philip Clarke 2011–14	2011	Tesco launches the country's first ever drive-through supermarket at Baldock Extra Store to help busy customers who want their shop picked and packed but who don't have the time to wait at home for delivery: a forerunner of the Click & Collect service.
	2011	Tesco is named the best UK company for its efforts in tackling climate change, by industry-renowned FTSE 350 Carbon Disclosure Project.
	2011	Tesco launches two new rail services, which together will save 10,000 tonnes of CO_2 and remove 40,000 lorries from the road annually (Daventry to Thurrock and Daventry to Magor, South Wales).
	2011	In August 2011 Tesco announced it would be selling its Japanese stores.

Decade	Year	CEO	UK events	International events
	2011		Tesco joins the Sustainability Consortium, an independent group of global businesses, academics, governments and non-governmental organizations that work collaboratively to drive innovation in consumer product sustainability. The Tesco-funded SCI at the University of Manchester also becomes an academic member of the Consortium.	
	2012		Tesco takes a 49% minority stake in Harris + Hoole, which operates coffee shops. Some are stand-alone and some located in a Tesco store.	Tesco launches its first online grocery shopping service in Central Europe in Prague, Czech Republic. The service brought a wide range of fresh and frozen food to customers as well as a number of non-food items. In October 2012 the online service was also launched in Slovakia.
	2012		Tesco wins the Green Retailer of the Year Award at the annual Grocer Gold Awards.	Tesco Homeplus expands the trial of its virtual stores to more than 20 bus stops in South Korea, giving busy commuters the opportunity to do their grocery shopping 'on the go'. The new stores follow the launch of the world's first virtual store, opened by Tesco in a Seoul underground station in 2011.

2012	Tesco's first all-LED store opens in Loughborough (part of Tesco's drive to reduce carbon emissions from its stores).	
2012	Tesco named top UK retailer for tackling climate change.	
2013	Tesco.com: for the fourth year running, *Good Housekeeping* readers voted for Tesco as their grocery home delivery service of choice.	In September Tesco sold 150 Fresh & Easy stores in the United States to Yucaipa Companies. Tesco filed for Chapter 11 bankruptcy in October 2013 for the remaining business.
2013	Apprentices: Tesco (the UK's biggest private sector employer) awarded the highest accolade in the City & Guilds Lion Awards for 2013 and named Employer of the Year.	Tesco announces a joint venture to develop shopping malls in China. The partner is China Resources Enterprise, Limited, with definitive agreements to combine Chinese retail operations to form the leading multi-format retailer in China. Tesco will have a 20% stake in the joint venture.
2013	Tesco launches Hudl, a 7-inch HD tablet that aims to open up a world of entertainment and connectivity to all. It was designed by Tesco for its 20 million customers, focusing on accessibility and convenience.	

(Continued)

Decade	Year	CEO	UK events	International events
	2013		In BBC TV's *Christmas Supermarket Secrets*, Dan Jago, Tesco's Head of Wine, revealed that: a. Tesco accounts for one in every four bottles of wine sold in the UK (including wine sold through restaurants and hotels); b. 84% of all wine sold in the UK is via supermarkets; c. Tesco is the largest wine buyer globally.	
	2013		Tesco buys the restaurant chain Giraffe for £48.6m.	Tesco enters into an agreement with Trent Limited, part of the Tata Group, to form a 50:50 joint venture in Trent Hypermarket Limited (THL), which operates the Star Bazaar retail business in India. Tesco's investment will be around £85 million.
	2014		Online grocery shopping continues to rise in popularity, with the growth of smartphones rapidly accelerating the trend. Over Christmas 2013, Tesco said customers placed over 3 million online grocery orders, up 11%, with one-third placed on a mobile device.	
	2014		Tesco launches the first Tesco smartphone and Hudl 2. (Since launch to May 2014 over half a million Hudls – Tesco's tablet – were sold.)	Tesco announces that F&F, which launched in the UK and Ireland in 2001, will be opening seven stores on the east coast of America in 2014 in partnership with the Retail Group of America. (F&F currently has 43 franchise

2014		stores in 10 countries – Saudi Arabia, Georgia, Kazakhstan, Switzerland, Gibraltar, the UAE, Bahrain, Jordan, the Philippines and Armenia.)
2014		Tesco announces that Philip Clarke will step down as CEO, to be replaced by Dave Lewis from Unilever – with a six-month handover period.
2014	Dave Lewis 2014–	Tesco profits overstated by £265m connected to the timing of supplier payments, linked to events prior to Dave Lewis's arrival. Philip Clarke leaves and Tesco announces nine senior staff suspensions – subsequently four of these have left Tesco. Financial Conduct Authority announces it will be investigating these overstatements and their implications.

REFERENCES

Ackoff, Russell (2010) *Differences That Make a Difference*, Triarchy Press, Axminster

Argyris, Chris (1997) Double loop learning, *Harvard Business Review*, September

Bowersox, D J, Closs, D J and Stank, T P (2000) Ten meg-trends that will revolutionise supply chain logistics, *Journal of Business Logistics*, 21 (2), pp 1–16

Brennan, R and Henneberg, S C (2008) Does political marketing need the concept of customer value?, *Market Intelligence and Planning*, 26 (6), pp 559–72

Butz, H E and Goodstein, L D (1996) Measuring customer value: gaining the strategic advantage, *Organizational Dynamics*, 24 (3), pp 63–77

Carter, C R *et al* (2009) Affiliation of authors in transportation and logistics academic journals: a re-evaluation, *Transportation Journal*, Winter

Christopher, M (1992) *Logistics and Supply Chain Management*, Financial Times Pitman, London

Collis, David and Rukstad, Michael (2008) Can you say what your strategy is?, *Harvard Business Review*, 86 (4), April, pp 82–90

de Bono, Edward (1998) *Simplicity*, Viking, New York

Deloitte (2013) *Global Powers of Retailing 2013: Retail Beyond*, Deloitte, London

Deloitte (2014) *Global Powers of Retailing 2014: Retail Beyond Begins*, Deloitte, London

Drucker, Peter F (1954) *The Practice of Management*, Harper & Collins, New York

Evans, B and Mason, R (2011a) Exploring how to sustain business process improvement gains in complex operations, Proceedings of 18th International Symposium on Logistics, Berlin, July

Evans, B and Mason, R (2011b) What does success look like?, *Lean Management Journal*, 1 (11), July/August, pp 7–13

Evans, B and Mason, R (2012) Tesco: a critical and relentless pursuit of excellence, *Lean Management Journal*, 2 (2), March, pp 11–15

Evans, B and Simons, D (2000) Lean delivery road map: how to make it happen, *Logistics and Transport Focus*, 2 (9), pp 2–8

Gallarza, M G, Gil-Saura, I and Holbrook, M B (2011) The value of value: further excursions on the meaning and role of customer value, *Journal of Consumer Behaviour*, **10** (4), pp 179–91

Gladding, N (2014) The next five years: how the UK grocery market will evolve, IGD report, 30 June, http://www.igd.com/our-expertise/Retail/retail-outlook/21115/The-next-five-years-How-the-UK-grocery-market-will-evolve/?a=1&ecid=10678&uid=evansb13@cardiff.ac.uk

Hines, P *et al* (2000) *Value Stream Management: Strategy and excellence in the supply chain*, Prentice Hall, London

Hoffman, Andrew (2014) The tide is receding, 24 February, http://blog.milesfranklin.com/the-tide-is-receding

Humby, Clive, Hunt, Terry and Phillips, Tim (2003) *Scoring Points: How Tesco is winning customer loyalty*, Kogan Page, London

IGD (2014) How Tesco is pushing the boundaries of convenience, IGD report, http://www.igd.com/our-expertise/Retail/Convenience/15692/How-Tesco-is-pushing-the-boundaries-of-convenience/

Jobber, D (1998) *Principles and Practice of Marketing*, 2nd edn, McGraw-Hill, London

Johansson, H J *et al* (1993) *Business Process Reengineering: Breakpoint strategies for market dominance*, John Wiley & Sons, Chichester

Kaplan, R S and Norton, D P (1996) Using the balanced scorecard as a strategic management system, *Harvard Business Review*, **74** (1), January/February, pp 75–85

Kaplan, R S and Norton, D P (2008) *The Execution Premium: Linking strategy to operations*, Harvard Business School Press. Boston, MA

Kiff, J and Simons, D (2002) *After-Sales and Parts Supply Systems*, ICDP Research Report 07/02, ICDP, Solihull

Kotler, P *et al* (2001) *Principles of Marketing*, Pearson Education, London

Leahy, T (2012) *Management in 10 Words*, Random House Business Books, London

Levitt, Theodore (1960) Marketing myopia, *Harvard Business Review*, **38**, July/August, pp 24–47

Levitt, Theodore (1968) What business are you in?, *Harvard Business Review*, March–April

Meyer, C and Schwager, A (2007) Understanding customer experience, *Harvard Business Review*, February, pp 117–26

Piacentini, M, MacFadyen, L and Eadie, D (2000) Corporate social responsibility in food retailing, *International Journal of Retail and Distribution Management*, **28** (11), pp 459–69

Piercy, N (2000) *Market-Led Strategic Change*, Butterworth and Heinemann, Oxford

Porter, Michael (1980) *Competitive Strategy: Techniques for analyzing industries and competitors*, Free Press, New York

Porter, Michael (1985) *Competitive Advantage: Creating and sustaining superior performance*, Simon & Schuster, New York

Potter, A and Disney, S (2010) Removing bullwhip from the Tesco supply chain, POMS 21st Annual Conference, Vancouver, Canada, 7–10 May

Potter, A, Mason, R and Lalwani, C (2007) Analysis of factory gate pricing in the UK grocery supply chain, *International Journal of Retailing and Distribution Management*, 35 (10), pp 821–34

Powell, D (1991) *Counter Revolution: The Tesco story*, Grafton Books, London

Reichheld, Frederick F (1996) *The Loyalty Effect: The hidden force behind growth, profits, and lasting value*, Harvard Business School Press, Boston, MA

Ryle, Sarah (2013) *The Making of Tesco*, Bantam Press, London

Simons, D (2000) Managing distribution within the value stream, in *Value Stream Management: Strategy and excellence in the supply chain*, ed P Hines *et al*, Prentice Hall, London

Smith, D and Sparks, L (2004) Logistics in Tesco, in *Logistics and Retail Management*, ed J Fernie and L Sparks, Kogan Page, London

Spear, S and Bowen, H K (1999) Decoding the DNA of the Toyota production system, *Harvard Business Review*, September–October, pp 96–106

Spear, Steven (2009) *Chasing the Rabbit*, McGraw-Hill, New York

Tesco (1999) *Annual Review and Summary Financial Statement 1999*, Tesco, Cheshunt

Tesco (2000) *Annual Review and Summary Financial Statement 2000*, Tesco, Cheshunt

Tesco (2001) *Annual Review and Summary Financial Statement 2001*, Tesco, Cheshunt

Tesco (2003) *Annual Review and Summary Financial Statement 2003*, Tesco, Cheshunt

Tesco (2004) *Annual Review and Summary Financial Statement 2004*, Tesco, Cheshunt

Tesco (2005) *Annual Review and Summary Financial Statement 2005*, Tesco, Cheshunt

Tesco (2006) *Annual Review and Summary Financial Statement 2006*, Tesco, Cheshunt

Tesco (2007) *Annual Review and Summary Financial Statement 2007*, Tesco, Cheshunt

Tesco (2008) *Annual Review and Summary Financial Statement 2008*, Tesco, Cheshunt

Tesco (2010) *Annual Review and Summary Financial Statement 2010*, Tesco, Cheshunt

Tesco (2011) *Annual Review and Summary Financial Statement 2011,* Tesco, Cheshunt

Tesco (2012) *Annual Review and Summary Financial Statement 2012,* Tesco, Cheshunt

Tesco (2013a) *Tesco and Society Report 2013: What Matters Now: Using Our Scale for Good,* Tesco, Cheshunt

Tesco (2013b) *Tesco PLC Annual Report and Financial Statements 2013,* Tesco, Cheshunt

Tesco (2014) Tesco and Society Report 2014, Tesco, Cheshunt

van Hoek, R, Ellinger, A E and Johnson, M (2008) Great divides: internal alignment between logistics and peer functions, *International Journal of Logistics Management,* **19** (2), pp 110–29

Womack, J P and Jones, D T (1996, 2003) *Lean Thinking: Banish waste and create wealth in your corporation,* Simon & Schuster, New York

Womack, J P, Jones, D T and Roos, D (1990) *The Machine That Changed the World,* Rawson Associates and Macmillan Publishing, New York

Zokaei, K and Hines, P (2007) Achieving consumer focus in supply chains, *International Journal of Physical Distribution and Logistics Management,* **37** (3), pp 223–47

INDEX

CPSIA information can be obtained at www.ICGtesting.com
Printed in the USA
LVOW03s1704211015

459179LV00028B/154/P